BREAKING SEAS

Glenn Damato

NINTH
CIRCLE
PRESS

BREAKING SEAS

An overweight, middle-aged computer nerd buys
his first boat, quits his job, and sails off to adventure

Published by
Ninth Circle Press
13428 Maxella Avenue suite 339
Los Angeles, CA 90292

ISBN 13: 978-0-9858162-0-9

ISBN 10: 09858116201

DEDICATION

*For everyone who ever bit off more
than they could chew. On purpose.*

Table of Contents

Prologue

Part I Breaking Rules

Off *Isla de Cedros*   1

The Hand We Are Dealt   9

It's a Blunderful Life   22

How Hard Could This Be?   39

Theory Versus Practice   53

Dust Monkey   74

Orphans Preferred   93

Part II Breaking Out

State of Grace   115

Shakedown   139

Force of Evil   154

Geographic Flexibility   184

Mutiny Postponed   200

Never Make a Night Entry   209

Scavenger Hunt   222

(continued)

Part III Breaking Free

Churn Churn Churn   245

A Modicum of Shame   256

It's Not You, It's Me   267

Tourist Attraction   297

Karma Houdini   316

Apotheosis   332

Being is Becoming   337

Epilogue

Acknowledgments

Prologue

If you are an aficionado of popular sailing stories, I should warn you about this book.

Breaking Seas is not a memoir about a confident mariner underway with his resourceful family. Nor is it an account of a photogenic teenager whose wealthy dad taught her to sail when she was seven and later bought her a sixty–foot racer to undertake a record–breaking circumnavigation. It's not even one of those books about a crusty old sea dog willing to share his seventy-three years of blue water wisdom.

Breaking Seas is *my* story, the story of a fat, pasty-faced, out-of-shape software dweeb who, without any prior boating experience, bought his first vessel at age forty-one, a broken-down forty-four-foot cutter named *Serenity*, repaired her, outfitted her, and sailed into the jaws of a pitiless sea.

Yes, there really is a man that crazy.

I respect the sailors who have lived those other tales and took the time to recount their adventures. Those seafarers *deserve* to be out there with the wind, the waves, and the whales. They have paid their dues. Sailing is in their blood—likely passed down as a family tradition. If you'd prefer to read one of their sailing stories, you have a vast selection from which to choose. Another such book is published practically every day. But if you are ready for a different kind of sea epic, I hope you enjoy *Breaking Seas*.

When I first contemplated buying a boat, I decided that if I was going to do something I always wanted to do, I might as well go all the way.

All. The. Way.

Buy a *big* boat. *Totally* fix her up. Quit my job. Inform my friends, relatives, and colleagues I am sailing around the world.

Nothing less would do.

You might ask, "Glenn, for the love of God, why didn't you use some brains and start out gradually? Why not learn the ropes on a modest-sized daysailer, gain some hands-on experience, and then begin making local passages over the weekend?" Yes yes yes, all of that makes perfect sense. For other people. Not for me. I believe that anything worth doing is worth overdoing.

Like countless other mariners throughout history, I imagined the sea offered respite from my personal demons as well as a path toward transformation. All that would require sailing extreme distances.

I was unmarried. My crew was a collection of strangers, hardy souls who responded to an ad I placed in the San Francisco area sailing magazines. I chose them for their self-described sailing ability. They chose *Serenity* for reasons I will never understand. At one point I had an all-girl crew—just three women and me. Fellas, it ain't as much fun as it sounds.

The crew was temporary. Eventually I would be alone with the sea and my vessel. Single-handing on the ocean was a prospect so terrifying that it became irresistible. I had to do it, danger and my lack of experience be damned.

As you can tell by this point, I probably wouldn't even be a runner–up in the World's Most Sensible Man contest.

This is not to say I didn't give this ocean sailing thing a lot of prior thought and study. I've always had a knack for learning complex subjects straight out of books. I had snagged my first computer job by getting hired in the administration department and then studying up on the company's software until I could finagle a technical position on practical skill alone. Also, I earned an airplane pilot's license without attending "ground school"— perfectly legal according to the Federal Aviation Administration, as long as you can pass the written exams and flight tests.

I figured I could learn what I needed to know about ocean voyaging from books and from working on the boat, and occasionally doing a bit of daysailing around San Francisco Bay. By the time *Serenity* was outfitted, I'd be ready.

Once I knew the difference between a sheet and a shackle, I was convinced not only that sailing was simple, but that I could personally improve upon much of the conventional knowledge in sailing books. I mean, why not? The usual sailing techniques and equipment had been around for centuries, and therefore must be outdated and overdue for a makeover. I dreamt up this strategy without ever having sailed a mile on the ocean, in my boat or any other sailboat, and without ever having spent a night or fixed a meal on board, underway or tied to the dock.

It did not work out quite as I planned.

I submit that reading about my adventures aboard *Serenity* is more interesting than stories about the typical cruise taken by experienced mariners. I'll bet those know–

it–alls go months—even years—without smashing up other vessels in the marina or spilling eight gallons of raw sewage all throughout their cabin and cleaning it up while being tossed around by state six seas. I almost feel sorry for them. Using standard equipment and doing things by the book: How boring is that?

Before we begin *Breaking Seas*, I'd like to thank all my shipmates who sailed aboard *Serenity*. To my crew: none of these adventures could have happened without your trust and skill—which you can go right ahead and interpret as meaning, "Not all of this was my fault." And by the way, I slept with a weapon clutched in my right hand. Don't take it personally.

I'd also like to give thanks to my guardian angel (or Whomever) for protecting my crew and myself and keeping us safe until *Serenity* returned to the United States. I consider this the single–most surprising fact of our voyaging: Through it all, no one who stepped aboard *Serenity* while I was skipper suffered any injury—neither a scratch nor a burn, nor even so much as a sprained finger —a fact for which I am humbly grateful. And baffled.

It must be true what they say: God watches over drunks, children, and sailors.

GLENN DAMATO

Marina del Rey, California

October 2012

Part I

BREAKING RULES

Off *Isla de Cedros*

I had a plan, a simple plan, and I believed it would work.

It *had* to work.

My current predicament came about as the result of trying to play it safe; but irony wasn't what I needed to get out of this mess. I needed *power,* engine power, because I was trapped off the lee shore of Cedros, and twelve-foot swells rolling in from the west were blocking my escape. A joint effort between those swells and the howling wind were pushing *Serenity* toward a wall of rock.

My engine was dead. I was alone. Darkness would fall soon. There were no soft sandy beaches here, no people in sight, no other boats—just gorgeous caramel–colored cliffs glistening in the low sunlight. The surf burst against the rocks with detonations and streamers of foam that reminded me of Fourth of July fireworks.

I could call for help on my radio, either the VHF or the single sideband, or even activate my Emergency Position Indicating Radio Beacon. But it wouldn't do any good. Well before anyone could get here, I'd be against the rocks with my boat and we'd be smashed to pieces.

An hour earlier I had been enjoying a pleasant afternoon off the mountainous and sparsely populated west coast of the Baja Mexico peninsula. This was "real" Baja, barren and remote, hundreds of miles from the tourist hotspots. I hadn't seen any signs of human life all day except, hours ago, a couple of tiny fishing craft and a sleek white cruise ship racing south.

Cedros lies off the coast of Baja, so I had to decide whether to pass to the east or the west of it. If I were going to pass it at night (I was) and I were sailing during autumn or winter (it was November), I faced a decent chance of dangerous Santa Ana winds coming off from the main coast and blowing across Bahia Vizcaino, the fifty miles of sea that separated Cedros from Baja. Sure, those winds were generally less of a threat in Baja than in Southern California, but the mountains around Vizcaino and Cedros sometimes funneled and amplified the wind, creating hazardous conditions.

I decided to take the safer westward passage, where the wind would be steady and lighter, but strong enough to allow me to sail until midnight, when calm conditions might require starting the diesel engine.

For a while everything was sunshine and lollipops. I was ten miles offshore on a comfortable beam reach and making excellent progress. I underestimated the amount of leeway I was picking up, and found myself blown several miles closer to shore. No big deal—I adjusted the autopilot to round up about ten degrees and then trimmed the unreefed mainsail and the 150-percent genoa. Yeah, that's a lot of canvas, but I needed the extra push to fight through the swells that had plagued me all day. Every time I had adjusted course, those swells seemed to change direction. *Serenity* was a heavy-displacement, full-keel vessel and not the most efficient craft to windward, but her weight gave her stability.

A half an hour and another course adjustment later, the wind was slowly but steadily changing direction. I should have been farther offshore but I wanted to top off my diesel tanks at Bahia Tortugas, one of the few spots for private vessels to buy fuel in the seven hundred miles between San Diego and Baja's southern cape.

The wind continued to clock, and it grew stronger. The shoreline snuck up on me, and for the first time I could see the individual specks of foam bursting from the rocks.

Two things needed to be done, preferably at the same time: change course, and adjust the sails—including the position of the main boom, a twenty-foot aluminum cylinder pulling down the foot of the fifty-foot mainsail. This requires two people. Being alone, I worked out a technique where I would dial a new course into the autopilot, and as the boat turned, *quickly* reposition the sails. The latter part was crucial because if I lost the wind, I would lose headway through the water, and since the water moving past the rudder is the only way to steer a boat, *Serenity* would be out of control.

Winch handle ready, I set the new course maybe sixty degrees off the wind and then yanked the main sheet out of the cleat and hauled the main boom close to the boat's centerline. I threw myself across the deck onto the starboard winch and cranked it like mad to bring the clew of the massive, oversized genny back as far as I could. As expected, *Serenity* listed away from the wind until the deck was so tilted I couldn't stand upright. On a monohull vessel there is no other way to sail so close to the wind.

I saw the autopilot "hunting"—jerking the wheel left and right—and I knew what was happening. With these big swells coming almost directly at me, the wind alone could not maintain sufficient headway, and as the sails generated forward thrust, the swells took it away. Fortunately, I had a solution: engine power, good ol' "iron wind."

I reached down into the footwell and turned the switch to start *Serenity's* diesel. There was a *growl* from below and then sweet, sweet vibration coming up through the deck. A year earlier I had spent $12,000 of my hard-earned money on a new, top-of-the-line engine to replace the twenty-five-year-old dinosaur that came with the boat. *Serenity* regained headway and assumed a close-hauled tack. The caprails let some water wash across the deck—I should have expected that—and my sweats, dry for the past two days, got soaked.

But I hardly noticed, because the boat wasn't holding the new course.

Part of the problem was that enormous genny throwing *Serenity* off balance, producing strong lee helm— a tendency for the boat to fall off the wind, requiring constant pressure from the rudder to hold course. But *Serenity's* hydraulic autopilot had done an admirable job keeping the rudder where it should be—up until this moment. Now I watched the bow fall off, and the wheel didn't move. The autopilot wasn't steering.

No no no no no! This cannot be happening!

Serenity was twisting broadside, listing farther until the entire starboard side of the hull was awash in swells. I scrambled to the wheel and yanked out the knob to disconnect the autopilot . . . pulled the wheel to the left . . . but it would not budge.

Stuck!

There was no way to control the direction of the boat.

The wind was pushing it over. Real panic knotted my gut. In a few seconds the vessel would be on her side, and I had foolishly left the companionway hatch wide open. The sea would pour in and sink the boat in seconds.

I was stunned for a moment, trying to come up with a plan, when I heard a long electronic shriek coming from my engine control panel.

Red light. *Beeeeeeep* . . . The engine was overheating.

I knew what the instruction manual said about this: *You must turn the engine off immediately, otherwise seizure and permanent damage will occur.* That buzzer wouldn't be going off for nothing—I must trust it and avoid destroying the engine.

I hit the kill switch. The reassuring vibration in the hull ceased. I now had no choice—the sails had to come down. I tightened the main boom topping lift and released both the main halyard and the sheet for the genoa. The genny instantly flew across the water—force gone, the bow jerked to port and the starboard caprail came out of the water. There was still the main; it luffed, but the wind pressure wouldn't let it drop. I climbed atop the cabin and hauled it down as fast as I could until most of my topsides were covered in off-white Dacron shimmering in the late afternoon sun.

The boat was now at the mercy of the wind and swells. The rocky coast was too damn close. My mind raced. Dropping an anchor was not an option. The water was over two hundred feet deep, and even though I had a long enough rode to reach bottom, there would be no scope— anchors dig in sideways, so like most cruisers, I could anchor against strong winds only in shallow water.

No . . . I had to get back both my power and my

5

steering. With steering alone, there was a chance, a slim chance, that I could claw off the lee shore without the engine.

Fighting the crazy, disorienting pitching of the deck, I pulled open the lazarette and examined the autopilot mechanism. No leakage . . . the accumulator was full . . . the arm linking the cylinder to the quadrant was in place and had the right amount of play . . . so I tried to pull the quadrant by hand, and it wouldn't budge. I stuck my head down lower, and I saw the trouble.

Dock lines!

They had shifted, wedged under and around the quadrant, preventing it from moving properly. Overloaded, the autopilot—my trusty hand-crafted hydraulic robot steering system—shut down but the thick coils of rope would not let the wheel turn the quadrant. Furious, I pulled the lines out and threw them down the companionway. Once the autopilot was reset, I had my steering back.

I dialed a course parallel to the shore, hoping I could buy some time. I hauled the mainsail back up, winched the genoa aft, and hoped.

It was no good. The autopilot was hunting again because the boat could not achieve headway through those swells. No relative motion with the water, no steering.

I needed my engine back. I climbed below and as soon as I disconnected my harness and sat down out of the wind, I was overcome with an impulse to just close my eyes . . . and *sleep*. Take a nap. Escape. Or even read a book —anything to make the nightmare vanish.

The mad rocking brought me to my senses. I grabbed the companionway ladder and pulled it away to reveal the engine, a Yanmar still shiny from its factory coat of gray paint.

Okay. One step at a time. Overheating. No cooling water?

The sea strainer was full of water, no debris visible.

I pressed the back of my hand against the raw water pump. It was hot.

Hot, as in burned out. This was the pump that shot cool seawater through a freshwater heat exchanger that cooled the engine. I grabbed a flathead (always have tools handy) and took off the pump housing cover. Inside I found the black rubber impeller, sort of a soft "paddlewheel" designed to pump seawater from the strainer to the heat exchanger. Every make and model of diesel engine requires a specific type of seawater impeller, and mine came with five "blades," making it look like a five-studded star.

Except now it had two blades.

Two blades weren't enough. The other three blades? Burned off. Something had cut off the seawater, and these impellers require water as lubrication. Without a constant flow, the friction between the housing and the rubber destroys the impeller.

I had a pretty good idea why the water supply was cut off. The sea water intakes were low on the starboard side —but not low enough. The *extreme* degree of tack coupled with the swells had resulted in air pockets coming through the water system, enough to cause the burnout.

This I could fix. These impeller burnouts do happen. That's why I carried no fewer than six spares. Six! And I knew exactly where they were.

Elated over having found the problem and that it was

fixable, I pulled the replacement impeller out of the box and crouched down to install it into the housing.

It would not fit. It was the wrong size. It was the wrong impeller type.

I grabbed at the other boxes, tearing them open, flinging impellers all over the deck. They were all the same. All wrong. None of them would fit. The center hub would not even go on the spindle.

This was impossible. Before I left San Diego I checked the parts manual and looked up the part number for that impeller. I called four marine shops before I found one that stocked the exact type I needed. Drove thirty miles to the shop. Waited while the clerk located the impellers in the stockroom. They were pricy, but I bought six of them —why not? Better get them now, here in the States, because they'd be a real bear to get in Polynesia. Wise decision.

I had done everything right.

Except test fit one of the new impellers.

That I hadn't done.

Now I was paying the price: no engine, unable to claw off a lee shore in a heavy-displacement full-keel boat against twelve-foot swells, unable to anchor, unable to reach anyone via radio who could pull me off the boat before I hit the rocks.

The urge to sit down and burst into tears of rage and frustration was becoming stronger by the second. *How could I possibly deal with this? I was out of my league. I'd broken too many rules, made too many mistakes. I never should have tried to make myself into something I was not.*

But I didn't sit down and I didn't cry. Instead, I came up with a plan.

The Hand We Are Dealt

Three years earlier—

Another Friday night, another fourteen hours spent flying home to California. It was just past 1:00 am local time when I finally slipped my key into my apartment door. My flight had been two hours late. Dinner was a burnt cheeseburger and soggy fries at Newark Airport. Head spinning in a haze of sleep deprivation and dehydration, I dragged my luggage inside and barely made it to the bed before collapsing into a sweaty heap.

Five hours later I was awake and pouring as much caffeine down my throat as I could take. Jet lag would have to take a back seat because today was a special day for me. I was embarking on the first tentative but concrete steps of a major journey. It had been a life-altering decision, requiring irreversible sacrifices.

No, I wasn't getting married. I had decided to sail around the world.

I drove my Camry up the 101 freeway toward Redwood City, the southernmost seaport on the San Francisco Bay. It was shaping up to be one of those familiar Bay Area mornings when the sun struggled to burn off the skim milk fog, but was losing the battle. I turned off the highway and followed the GPS directions to a baby blue building set directly on the waterfront:

Spinnaker Sailing School. My first sailing class was scheduled to start in ten minutes, and I wondered what the other students would be like. Given that the school was not too far from the heart of Silicon Valley, I expected most of the students would be just like me: tech company employees, landlubberly and blubbery, who had never before come within ten fathoms of a sailboat.

This around-the-world journey didn't really begin with Spinnaker Sailing. It began with a drive-by rejection. It took a drive-by rejection to force me to accept, at age forty-one, the realization I would never become a family man, and kick-start another path through life. I didn't know what's wrong with me. Having a family of my own was the one thing I most wanted, and it wasn't going to happen. This understanding had taken on a firmer shape year by year, and now I was ready to choose, sooner rather than later, what I could become instead.

Having just a job wasn't enough. My job was as an instructor at InfoData, a medium-sized Silicon Valley software company, and I was good at it. But it was just a job—and let's face it, an entry-level job at that, the sort twenty-somethings landed just out of college.

Become what, then? An airline pilot? A Hollywood screenwriter? Over the past couple of years, between occasional dates, I obtained a pilot's license and over two hundred hours in the air, and completed a feature-length screenplay. But the airlines were laying pilots off and the screenplay... Well, let's just say I don't have to concern myself with what to wear to the Oscars.

I had another dream in my side pocket: sail around the world. In my own boat. Maybe alone. Probably alone. That's what I could become: An international sailboat skipper.

As a techie my natural first step was to scour the Web for everything about sailing, buying a boat, and circumnavigating. I Amazon-ed myself some books on these topics and then I searched online yacht sale listings. Like the ace nerd I was, I managed to learn a lot about the subject and even the local sailing scene without ever taking my eyes off the computer screen.

Then one Friday afternoon I gathered the guts to call a broker about a specific listing for a cruising cutter in the forty-foot range. The guy invited me to visit, and we'd take the vessel out on the Bay for a test sail. That, I didn't see coming. That, I couldn't let happen. Me, sail a boat? Despite all the books, I didn't have the vaguest idea what I was doing. I could imagine the man's incredulous questions:

"Glenn, have you ever... Well, what sort of boats have you owned before?"

"This will be the first boat, you know, that I've actually owned."

"That right? Congratulations! What sort of boats have you sailed before?"

"Ah, none I guess."

Silence.

"Have you considered starting with something... a bit smaller?"

I did not want to hear that question. I had no answer for it.

Maybe a broker would never say those things— probably he'd just want to sell me the boat and take my money. But I didn't want to look like an idiot. I told the broker I had to check my schedule and hung up. I needed some *hands-on* sailboat training before this becoming-a-skipper thing went any further.

Besides, maybe I'd despise it.

I crossed the threshold into Spinnaker Sailing's lobby and was greeted by the friendly smile of Bob Diamond, whom I would later learn was the school's chief instructor. Like a lot of men from California, he was lean and tall, and had the well-preserved physique of a former college athlete.

Bob showed me into the classroom. A dozen people sat around a massive conference table. I pretended to look through my *Basic Keelboat* manual while sneaking glances at my fellow students. There were six women and six men, including me. None was a techie, I could tell. None was pudgy, nor did anyone display that little nervous-techie frown thing I was probably doing myself as Bob began the class. Like Bob, they were all fit and tanned and... happy.

Where the hell did these people work?

Bob was talking to us. "First, let's go around the table and give everyone a chance to introduce themselves and tell a little bit about their sailing experience."

What? This is supposed to be the *Basic Keelboat* course, the first course, the one for absolute beginners.

Eight of my fellow students had come as couples. Sailing couples.

Brian and Elsa: "My parents had a Cal twenty-two ..."

Larry and Tess: "My dad, he had a Pearson thirty-four... When I was seven..."

Bob and Marybeth: "My parents had a Hunter thirty-two..."

Tyler and Katherine: "My parents had a... My dad had

a... When I was six..."

Everyone had been inducted into sailing by their families, at an early age, and some had apparently been taught to helm a boat before they could write their names. None of this was surprising, in retrospect, because we lived in the San Francisco Bay Area, one of the wealthiest and most sailing-intensive spots on the planet. Still, I stupefied because this course was supposed to be basic.

There were two uncoupled women in the class, both fit and attractive and in their thirties. Cynthia went first. "My dad had a Hobie Cat and then an Ericson twenty-seven when we were growing up in Santa Barbara ."

Then followed Kirsten. "I'm from San Diego and our family had a..."

They were both cute. Maybe mom was right after all. Maybe I would meet my, ah, "special someone" when I least expected it, when we were doing something we mutually enjoyed.

Next to last, just before me, was Alek, a Greek man about my age who bore a striking resemblance to Telly Savalis (picture Kojack, *sans* lollipop) with a compact, powerful build. Not surprisingly, Alek had a commercial fishing and diving background back home in the Greek Isles. He had done sailing and diving in Sardinia, Hawaii, and California, and had even worked as a stuntman in several movies involving boating and diving.

My turn. Alek would be a hard act to follow. My stomach fluttered. No problemo. I'd play up my inexperience as a positive thing, and maybe even mention my long term plans. I visualized their smiles of support.

"Hi, I'm Glenn Damato, and I have never set foot aboard a sailboat in my life. Ever!"

I paused to let everyone laugh, but that's not what they did. They stared.

After an uncomfortable moment, Bob and Alek grinned, chuckled and nodded. Everyone else, the four couples, the people from sailing families, regarded at me as if I were an extraterrestrial who just stepped out of my spacecraft.

"Yeah, today's the big day. First time sailing. I'm hoping to learn a lot because my dream is to buy a boat and sail around the world."

"Wow!" from Bob.

"Cool, very cool," from Alek.

From the rest, scowls all around. *Who is this guy?*

"I think I saw a magazine article when I was about thirteen, an article showing tiny boats with ropes and stuff, and pictures of ordinary people who sailed these boats all over the world. I thought to myself, people actually do that? So that's been my dream for almost thirty years. To be out there with the whales and the dolphins. Just never got a chance to learn how to sail, which is why I'm really looking forward to this class."

To my surprise, a few of the scowls turned into what looked like *snarls*. Snarls of disgust. What, pray, were these folks disgusted about? Were they really that upset that this portly little squirt was intruding on their sacred turf?

There may be some truth to the suspicion that, after more than two hundred years, there is a gradual but noticeable class system emerging in America. And maybe the "upper" classes considered sailing their property, like the US version of polo or cricket. But not all of us can come from affluent California or Seattle families, where Dad was an attorney or a pediatrician or an engineer or

the owner of a restaurant equipment supply company—
and made enough money to pay for a terrific family hobby.

Some folks take this stuff for granted, because even in
the US many people rarely, if ever, spend time with others
who have experienced a markedly different sort of life
than themselves. My brother and I could not have been
introduced to sailing by our father, because our father was
a tenth-grade dropout and his sole "hobby" was watching
sports on television. Our family was working-class Italian,
from northern New Jersey, and if we went to the beach
once a year we considered ourselves lucky. No boats were
ever involved.

I witnessed this same phenomenon at the Palo Alto
Flying Club while working toward my pilot's license. Most
recreational pilots were introduced to aviation by their
fathers. My flight instructors concurred with this
observation, and expressed frustration with it. People who
had never flown in small aircraft would show up for a few
introductory flights, and give up after two or three
lessons. Practically every time, the student pilots who
completed the program were born into flying—they
inherited it paternally.

"My father had a... "

Well, my father didn't have anything except his remote
and a can of Budweiser. As for my brother, he doesn't do
anything outside of work except watch sports on
television, and I think I understand why: Every significant
activity except his work is strange to him, a new world full
of errors and pitfalls where *he* is the rookie and must learn
from someone years younger. We both had slow financial
starts. By the time we could afford pricey hobbies, we were
set in our ways.

The difference between my brother and I was that I was going to do it *anyhow*.

Some people say when we're born, we're each "dealt a hand of cards." And we're supposed to play that hand—without complaint.

I disagree.

I know none of us can ever get another hand. But what would happen if we played the hand *we wanted?*

I found out why all these accomplished sailors were attending the Basic Keelboat course, a curriculum designed for beginners. It turned out there was a series of courses and exams that are required by the American Sailing Association to become certified for bareboat charter. After completing Basic Keelboat, Coastal Cruising, Coastal Navigation, and Bareboat Chartering, and passing all the written and hands-on exams, the student would be able to lease a "bare" boat (no skipper or crew) from any of the charter companies that operated all over the world. The charter company supplied all the equipment and usually food, as well. All you had to do was fly out to the boat and sail away. But you need that A.S.A. certification first.

Bob began that first morning by sketching the points of sail: a run, a reach, a beam reach, close reach, and close hauled. It was all about the relative direction of the wind and which way you wanted to travel—and the fact that you could never sail *directly* upwind, so you had to steer the boat at least forty-five degrees or more "off" the wind. Later in the six-day course we learned about safety gear, maneuvers such as tacking and jibing, basic knots, how to raise, lower, and stow sails, the fundamentals of sail trim (adjusting the position of the sails for efficiency) and the rules of the road.

But it was hands-on action I needed most. The school owns a fleet of Santana-22 daysailers, and immediately after lunch Bob broke the class into groups of four, pairing each couple with another couple and the four single students in a boat of our own. Each daysailer also had an assigned instructor who would show us the ropes— literally.

"Cynthia, Kirsten, Alek, Glenn, you're in the *Orchid*, dock number five."

The ladies grimaced.

Once aboard our gleaming white training vessel, Alek took his best shot at trying to make smalltalk. Both women responded to his polite questions minimally. Then Cynthia turned to Kirsten.

"You know, I'm taking this course to get my certification, and that's really the only reason I'm here. I'm not really doing this to meet new people or anything like that."

"Same for me," Kirsten responded. "Seems like some guys try to use classes like this to get dates. I wish they would keep in mind this is not a dating club."

"I totally agree," nodded Cynthia. "It's a sailing school, not a dating club."

Alek and I exchanged knowing glances. I didn't think they needed to be so blunt about it. A bit rude, if you ask me.

Which brings us to the drive-by rejection. Where it all started.

I believe most folks are driven to pursue the dream of ocean cruising as a quest for freedom. This is confirmed in practically every written account, starting with Joshua Slocum's 1899 book, *Sailing Alone Around the World.*

Cruising sailors are free. Cruising is true *freedom.*

Cruising is a simple, stress-free lifestyle.

Regardless of whether anyone ever finds this to be true, that is the dream.

But it wasn't *my* dream. I already felt entirely free on dry land. I was too free, in fact: over forty, with no dependents, not even a girlfriend, no children, no real estate, no obligations. Incredibly, I felt the opposite urge of nearly every other man my age. Instead of seeking freedom, I sought *encumbrances.*

I didn't realize it at the time, but this craving for encumbrances was symptomatic of a longing to become something I was not. My first choice was to become a husband and a father.

And it was time to accept that was not going to happen, and to move on to some other option.

You're saying: Wait a minute. This is supposed to be a book about a sailing journey, right? Why is this guy harping about his lack of a love life?

It's simple. No issue with women, no voyage.

The money would have been spent, as normal people are prone to do, on the down payment for a house.

I had plenty of freedom. I was already making a six-figure salary in a fairly simple and easy job, with no debt, no legal problems, and a nest egg in the bank. I didn't need or want to go to sea on a "quest for freedom."

My quest was to transform myself into something I was not.

I understood I wasn't going to become a husband and a father. That conclusion was a long time coming. For years I had been in denial about a simple fact: It was extremely unlikely that the sort of woman I found attractive would want to form a long-term commitment with me. There was something out of calibration deep inside my head. I'm one of those men who are attracted only to women out of my league.

I can hear my dear mother: *But you're not ugly!*

No. But I am guilty of an Appearance Crime worse than ugliness. I am a *diminutive* man. Five-feet and five and a half inches, tiny hands, short arms, and practically nonexistent shoulders. My body has no *physical presence*. And that's the worst thing a man can lack. The truth is, ugliness, at least in a man, has a certain bad-boy, Quasimodo kind of appeal to many women. But to be small? Small with a chubby-cheeked face? I was both diminutive and fat at the same time, a bit of anatomical magic I somehow pulled off without trying.

Many men afflicted with the same sort of petite, pudgy, un-athletic body "solve" the problem by dating women at their own level of hotness: unattractive. I won't do that. I can't do that. Call me shallow, call me superficial, call me whatever you want—I feel attracted only to women who are smart, physically fit, considerate, feminine, and *pretty*. The Roseanne Barrs of the world have zero appeal to me. And I will not force myself to date women who have zero appeal. That is not an option, even if it means never becoming a husband and father. And I guess it does.

Looks are only part of the equation, you say. *What you really lack is self-confidence! You should be more confident because women will be attracted to that confidence!*

The popular misconception is that we small, flabby men "lack self-confidence," and this is our real obstacle. But as any dweeb can tell you, we are characteristically ruled by a startling and irrational *overconfidence* that convinces us, at least in our younger years, that we possess a rare type of animal magnetism that—once the woman *really* gets to know us—will make her forget all about those tall, strong, handsome suitors. Because we're smart, and interested in them, and just plain *nice*.

Reality taught us other lessons. For me, the wonderful myth "you'll meet someone perfect for you if you just keep trying" took two whole decades to die. For many years I played the hand I was dealt and went on as many dates as I could possibly get. Almost all of them were blind dates— fix-ups through friends and coworkers. Before the Internet era, I used the infamous *Washingtonian Magazine* "in search of" classified ads, and then later, Match.com and eHarmony.

I was in denial for over twenty years. The overwhelming majority of my first dates did not result in a second date, and in those rare cases that did, the "relationship" never lasted more than a few weeks before it faded with the plea, "Let's both see other people."

It took the drive-by rejection to snap me out of my delusions and force me to face reality.

Her name was Melanie. I met her through Match.com. She was an art teacher at a private high school in Palo Alto. Her dream was to travel to Rome, Turin, Venice, and other spots in the classical world to experience the beauty and the history with "someone special." Well, I was into that. We enjoyed several pleasant phone conversations of the kind that didn't need to end. We both loved children, and wanted to have them someday. We discovered we were both raised as Catholics in the Northeast and we both went to college in the Midwest. Melanie was easy to talk with, and best of all, she shared my eclectic sense of humor.

I invited her out for coffee. We agreed to meet at a nearby Starbucks at 5:30 Wednesday afternoon. I got there a bit early and waited at one of the wrought-iron tables outside the cafe.

Right on time, a car turned into the shopping strip parking lot. The vehicle slowed as it approached and I could see *it was her,* my artist, my lover of classical beauty and sculpture and history. She was driving at a crawl, looking, looking... She saw me, looked right at me, drove up as close as possible, stopped, and inspected me up and down. I smiled. I was raising my arm, and my mouth was open to say hi, when her head snapped forward and she hit the accelerator. She pulled away, turned out of the parking lot, rolled back on to the street, and was gone.

That is a drive-by rejection. A service I offered my dates, allowing them to reject me without the inconvenience of having to get out of their vehicle.

I went back to my one-bedroom apartment feeling like a different man than the one who had left half an hour earlier. Now I understood more clearly. I had been deceiving myself and wasting time. Wasting too much time. To make it real, I shut down my accounts on Match.com and eHarmony and spent the rest of the night poring over websites about sailing.

Long-distance ocean sailing.

It's a Blunderful Life

Sailing a real boat turned out to be a lot harder than reading books on how to sail a boat.

One of the things we nerds have in common is a lack of hand–eye coordination. My theory is that most people are born with brains that are pretty good at dealing with the physical world around them and also good at understanding abstract concepts. A minority of people, however, are born with brains particularly suited to dealing with the physical world. They move with grace, they excel in sports. They're the Little League outfielders who can catch a pop fly without really trying.

That's not me.

We nerds can never *quite* figure out how to smoothly catch that fly ball—after some frantic footwork, we're lucky to catch it at all. We're clumsy, awkward, accident-prone, always the last person picked for the team. But on abstract subjects we beat the jocks cold. We love physics and math and computer programming. We're daydreamers, practical jokers, *Monty Python* fans.

I wasn't much surprised when I found nearly every aspect of sailing challenging, especially steering and docking. A few years earlier I had earned my private pilot's license. The average number of flying hours to a first solo flight is about twenty-five. I did not solo until I had sixty-eight hours in the cockpit. The national average flight time to obtain a license was sixty-six hours. I wasn't recommended for my license examination until I had one hundred thirteen hours.

Those flight instructors can spot a nerd when they see one.

But I *did* get my license, and my FAA examiner declared my knowledge level "spectacular."

My instructors at Spinnaker Sailing School weren't about to go that far. I was learning, keeping up, and so far I hadn't damaged any property—but we still had a few more classes to go.

Every Saturday morning for six weeks, we gathered around the conference table for a few hours of theoretical lecture led by an old salt. We learned the points of sail, sail trim, how to turn the boat with the bow cutting across the direction of the wind (tacking) and how to turn when the stern cut across the wind (jibing). We covered safety equipment and emergency procedures, such as MOB (man overboard) and the basics of how to dock and undock a twenty-two food daysailer with an outboard motor and a tiller.

At noon Alek and I would break out our respective bag lunches and chow down, overlooking the marina and Redwood City harbor. As someone who had first gotten involved in boating as a job, and not as a family activity financed by affluent parents, Alek seemed like the only student who didn't hold my inexperience and lack of skill against me.

"I'd better start seriously looking for my own boat," I told him one Saturday, "if I'm ever going to, you know, sail around the world."

Alek smiled and shook his head in amusement. "Don't you think you should get some experience around the Bay first?"

"That's the trouble," I replied. "Without a boat, how am I going to get experience? And without experience, who would let me sail their boat?"

Alek finished his sandwich. "You are making this harder than it is, my friend. I know somebody who just got his sloop, thirty-two feet, and I am sometimes his crew. We sail Sundays mostly, sometimes Friday. You interested in maybe crewing on this boat, yes?"

"Hell yes!" I shot back. Thirty-two feet. Ten feet longer than the little training sloops we used at Spinnaker. That's getting close to the boat size I would need for my circumnavigation—thirty-eight to forty-five feet.

"Good. I ask him, but I'm sure it will be okay."

With a few Saturday afternoons of actual, hands-on sailing under my belt, I began to feel more confident about buying a boat, or at least test sailing a few models. If I wanted a blue-water vessel in the forty-foot range, it would have to be at least twenty years old to fit in my price range, as my funds were limited and I needed to plan carefully in order to have enough cash to outfit the boat, bankroll the actual circumnavigation, and then get re-settled when I returned to the United States. A fixer-upper was fine: By making the necessary repairs and upgrades, I would learn about the boat's inner workings and become an expert in what made her tick.

My strategy was to consider at least fifty boats, test sail at least a dozen, make an offer on five or six, and only agree to a deal if I could buy the boat at a massive discount offered by a highly motivated seller. The process might take months, but that was okay because I could use some time: I had started going to my apartment building's gym three or four times a week and lifting free weights. Spinnaker Sailing School showed me that sailing did not require a lot of strength, but I figured I'd better be prepared physically for whatever excitement the sea had in store.

Each night after work I'd devour books on sailboat maintenance, diesel engines, electrical systems, and the finer points of keeping water out of a boat. I focused on the different kinds of hulls and what makes a small sailboat seaworthy. I assumed, for now, that I would do this alone; and according to the books, when a sailor voyaging alone encountered heavy weather, fatigue and the danger of being swept overboard sometimes required putting the boat into a "hands off" condition, that is, doing absolutely nothing. It was known as lying ahull, and the experts said a heavy displacement, full-keeled boat would fare better than a sleek, modern hull. I decided that's what I would have: a heavy, full-keeled, traditional boat. A fin keel, they said, risked the boat breaching as it slid sideways down the face of a wave.

Breaching? That means the boat falls over on its side and maybe fills with water and swiftly sinks.

No fin keels for me.

Alek's friend with the thirty-two-foot sloop was an Irish-born attorney named Kevin Boyd. Kevin kept his boat, the *Serendipity,* north of San Francisco in Marin County. Alek and I rode up there one foggy Sunday morning with the intent of sailing under the Golden Gate Bridge, something neither of us had ever done.

Even if you've never been to the Bay Area, you've seen Marin County in countless movies. Picture the green or amber hills on the far side of the Golden Gate, commonly with an ethereal fog layer spilling down from their tops like fingers of milk. Kevin's boat was docked at a place called Loch Lomond Marina, nestled in the bluffs of San Raphael. Alek led the way down a wooden dock.

"I bought myself a boat as a present to celebrate graduation from law school," Kevin told me as he pumped my hand.

"Exactly what the world needs," I blurted out, already regretting my sarcasm. "Another lawyer!"

If Kevin was insulted, he didn't show it. He was much younger than Alek or I, as fit as Alek, and his pride of ownership showed as he took me on a quick tour of his boat. She was an Ericson sloop, fin-keeled—what is sometimes called a racer-cruiser. In theory, such a boat can sail anywhere in the world, but in practice her gear is lightly constructed to keep the cost down. Most owners used boats like this for coastal trips.

Kevin started the inboard diesel engine while Alek and I positioned ourselves on the dock to handle the lines. I was intensely interested in Kevin's technique for getting the boat away from the slip and out to the Bay. Like all marinas, Loch Lomond was constructed with an absolute minimum amount of space between the docks, which means more boats and more money in slip fees. To my inexperienced eyes, it looked like there wasn't enough room to back the boat out and turn her ninety degrees toward open water.

Kevin gave the order, "Cast off!" and all I needed to do was unwrap my stern line from the dock cleat, throw it aboard, and step onto the boat. Alek had the more physically demanding job of guiding the bow away from the pier and then pulling himself aboard across a three-foot gap over the water.

These guys made it look easy. Kevin took the wheel and put the transmission in reverse, backing the stern toward the opposite dock, which to me seemed dangerously close. He coolly slipped the engine into neutral and let the boat's inertia pull her out some more, and then quickly spun the wheel so the stern began drifting to starboard. The boats on the opposite dock were coming closer. Kevin saw this, spun the wheel the other way and slipped the transmission into forward. The boat stopped, sat motionless for just a second, then pulled forward.

I coiled my dock line. "You're pretty good at handling her."

"Thanks, mate. My father had a thirty-five-foot ketch, taught me the basics when I was young."

We motored out of the marina and found the upper San Francisco Bay without a trace of breeze, not uncommon in the morning. Kevin cut the engine and we drifted. The three of us lounged in the sun, sipping bottles of *Stella*.

"So, Glenn, Alek tells me you have an ambition to sail around the world."

"That's the plan."

"And how long have you been sailing?"

I knew this would happen. "Couple of months, I guess."

"Hope you're a quick learner."

"I want to get some heavy weather experience under my belt," I told him, trying to use some of the salty words I had picked up from books and sailing class. "I dunno, maybe state four seas. After I buy my own boat next month, would you be interested in taking her out of the Gate with me for a little excitement?"

The two men exchanged glances.

"Think you're ready for it?"

"One way to find out."

"You're a ballsy guy, I'll give you that. What kind of boat are you looking for?"

"A full-keel, heavy displacement cutter, around forty feet, something I could work on for a few months and outfit for cruising on my own."

Kevin nodded, impressed, or pretending to be. "You think big."

"I tell him, you know, start small," Alek chimed in. "But he's all ready for the big stuff."

"It's his neck," Kevin responded. To me: "Just beware of what a fifty-foot tall rig can do in a sudden puff of wind. I was on a racing crew last year and I saw three fingers pop out of a guy's hand and roll across the deck."

"Yeah?" I drained my beer, trying to sound unfazed. "How'd that happen?"

Kevin wrapped a piece of blue nylon line around his hand. "Did this with the jib sheet, didn't notice someone else uncoiled it from the winch so there was nothing between his hand and the sail. Puff of breeze, jib goes out..." He jerked the line. "Goodbye fingers."

"I'm here to get experience," I told him. "You see me wrapping a sheet around my hand, you got my permission to punch me in the face."

28

Kevin grinned and nodded.

"He's from Ireland," Alek warned. "He'll do it."

"Let me helm a bit when we're going out the Gate. Let me take her all the way back to the slip..."

"That I will do myself, thank you very much!"

Shortly later the wind did come up, and we sailed under the Golden Gate Bridge, turned around, and headed back to San Raphael. The Bay was kicking up whitecaps, and Kevin let me take the helm as we beat to windward under the bridge. Every ten minutes or so I'd bark, "Prepare to tack!" and my shipmates would take position at the main and jib sheets and we'd take the bow through the wind as a team. With the stiff wind and chop coming off of the Pacific, I noted it took near perfect timing and teamwork to pull off each tack and keep the boat from going "into irons," meaning the bow pointed into the wind and stopped, without steering.

How would I do it alone?

The time had come. Enough looking at boats on the Internet. I called a yacht broker, told him what I wanted, and set an appointment.

The broker, a tall, slender California-looking dude named Brad, had an office not far from Loch Lomond Marina. This was over thirty miles north and an hour's drive from my apartment in Sunnyvale, but it was where the sailing action was centered: the city, Marin County, Alameda. The smaller marinas near Spinnaker Sailing School and Redwood City were where Silicon Valley techies kept their showboats, and it was dead compared to the North Bay.

I was nervous when I shook hands with Brad, already wondering if I was making a huge financial mistake. I could tell he didn't think my pudgy physique was proper for a sailor, especially one keen on long-distance, blue-water cruising. I expected Brad to quiz me on my experience. He did no such thing. He was interested in my money, I figured, and not what happened to me and the boat after I signed on the dotted line.

Based on what I gleaned from the Internet, my circumnavigation of the planet would take three years and cost $70,000—not including the cost of purchasing and outfitting the yacht. For the boat, say $40,000 to purchase and $20,000 to outfit. I also wanted to allow at least $50,000 as a cushion for when I came back—to buy a car, furniture, clothes, and rent an apartment. That was all the money I had, gone. And once it was gone, I would not likely be coming into any more big piles of dough in my lifetime. That I had so much to begin with, I considered a fluke of nature.

A fluke of nature called the tech boom.

I was not a wealthy man. I owned no real estate and had no portfolios of stocks or bonds or funds, not even an IRA. Besides my trusty old Camry, whose book value was $6,500, I had no other assets.

A few years earlier I had been flat broke, renting a bedroom in someone else's townhouse at age thirty-eight. I had been the first person in my extended family to attend college, working full-time during the academic year and the summer. Bored with school, I joined the US Navy during my junior year and completed my degree while serving aboard a nuclear submarine. When I was discharged I knew one thing: I did not want anything to do with working in the nuclear power industry.

Which was the only real skill I possessed.

Thus began a ten-year period of drifting from one dead-end job to another, each year sinking my resume into a deeper pit. And make no mistake: The resume is king. With a little help from an untimely recession, I soon had a dismal job history as a bill collector, a taxi driver, a loan company employee, and (twice) as a pizza delivery driver extraordinaire. Plus, in what must have been an ill-advised attempt to prove I was "good with people" and hence not truly a nerd... an automobile salesman. During this long period of under-employment I spent countless evenings experimenting with computer-related subjects such as databases and networks. It didn't do me much good in the job market, at least not right away, but I found it interesting. In order to afford the books and software, I took a job working two evenings a week as a Wells Fargo security guard.

I had a poster of the wave-washed deck of an ocean sailing yacht pinned to the wall above my bed. It was a spectacle, but that poster did not make my plans feel *real*. I needed a tangible object, something I could hold in my hand, an actual piece of equipment I would need during my circumnavigation of the planet. As a pizza delivery driver I couldn't afford anything substantial, but there had to be something I could buy now.

I went into a West Marine boating store and found the right piece of gear in the navigation department: a Davis Instruments hand–bearing compass.

Once home I studied the compass and learned how to take a bearing. The compass was inside a clear plastic liquid-filled hemisphere mounted on a contoured handle of high-impact blue plastic. You aimed it and sighted at a distant object (say a lighthouse) and read off the magnetic bearing. With a chart, a navigator could use the bearing to plot a "line of position."

I purchased that hand–bearing compass six years before GPS became available and over ten years before people knew what it was. It set me back four hours of delivering pizzas. But it was to be my talisman, my symbol of a sailing journey that, however unlikely it seemed, would take place in reality—because I had already started gathering the necessary gear.

My errors of judgment and lack of practical strategy in the job market cost me many years of a better income in the prime of my life, but eventually I got my break. I began working as an office temp for $10.50 an hour and they sent me to the shipping department of a small, young software company called MicroStrategy. The shipping room was a shambles. I reorganized it, created an entire system for them, and found myself talking history and philosophy with the company president, whose office was two doors down. He hired me and doubled my pay, and for the first time in ten years I had paid vacations and health insurance.

The blue hand–bearing compass sat in a dresser drawer.

Brad seemed to know exactly what sort of boat I wanted. Or at least he thought so.

"Let me show you something on my hot sheet, something that came to mind when you said you wanted a motivated seller. Let me tell you, you won't find a more motivated seller than this guy."

I read the fact sheet about the boat as we drove across the marina parking lot. It was a forty-four foot cutter, full-keel, brand name "Bombay," which I had never heard of. List price? Just $25,000. My head was reeling. If I can get him down to $15,000 I'd have an extra $25,000 for my trip and unexpected expenses.

But the Bombay was an incredible wreck. It was filthy and rusted and stank like a jailhouse toilet. Brad mentioned the engine did not run, and the vessel would need to be towed away. The sooner the better. "Make an offer. Any offer."

I declined.

We headed back to his car and Brad showed me the fact sheet for another vessel, a thirty-eight-foot, full-keeled cutter named *Serenity*. The builder was Downeast Yachts, and if you included the enormous bowsprit, the boat was forty-four feet long overall. The sheet said the price had been "reduced" from $55,000 to $45,000 and the seller was *motivated*. My short apprenticeship in car sales taught me to take the "reduced" thing with a huge grain of salt.

Built in 1977. That did not make me optimistic.

I didn't really want to buy a boat on my first day looking, but I agreed to ride with Brad back across the Golden Gate to the Saint Francis Yacht Club in the Marina District of San Francisco—a high-rent area.

"The history of this vessel is pretty unusual," Brad told me as we descended to the docks. "It was bought by this lady lawyer about three years ago just so she could join the yacht club. Sure, that's right. Doesn't even like sailing, just wanted into the club, and you have to have a boat to get in. So she buys it and it sits here for three years. Don't be put off by the dust and grime. Now she's getting married and she wants out."

I saw the bowsprit first. It was pointed straight at my head. I walked up to it, and without thinking, placed my hand on the tip of the massive steel tube that formed the foundation of the sprit. At the tip of the tube, the extreme forward-most piece of the boat, was screwed a round silver medallion of a happy mermaid. I ran my fingers across it. For some reason I pushed the sprit back and forth just to feel the mass of the boat shift under my effort. The deck was as filthy as Brad promised, but looked to be solid and in good repair. Overall impression: a big, wide, solid, home.

Home. The boat felt like home.

We stepped aboard and I decided I liked the arrangement of the aft cockpit, really not a cockpit at all—a flush deck with a footwell. I thought it would be quite comfortable to lounge about that afterdeck, and I imagined what it would be like on a dark, starry night.

I made a show of inspecting the standing rigging and the engine. Despite having read all the books, I had no idea what to look for. I liked the teak sole belowdecks and the solid feel of all the wood. I couldn't see anything I did not like. It was the right size and type of boat, a bit older than I expected. It had a radar. The parts that were ancient and rusted (the stove, the head) I could replace. I figured it would take three to four months of hard work to get the *Serenity* upgraded and outfitted.

"This is a boat worth making an offer on," I told Brad, scarcely believing my own words. "Contingent on a test sail, of course." Yeah, I was considering the second boat I looked at.

"Of course. I think you'll love the way this boat sails. I sailed her myself last month when I accepted the listing."

The following Sunday morning I met Brad and his assistant at the Yacht Club. I showed up a half hour early so I could snap some pics of the boat—there was a good view from the pedestrian walkway above the marina.

I watched every detail as the two men got the vessel underway. The engine sounded rough to my untrained ears, but it did move the boat smartly. Brad was at the helm as we maneuvered through the tight confines of the yacht club, but once we got into the open water between the city and Alcatraz I took the wheel while Brad and his assistant raised sail. Almost on cue, a breeze sprung up and filled the mainsail. I felt a wonderful sensation under my feet as the deck responded and the boat moved forward. What an incredible, smooth, solid feeling.

"Fall off a bit," Brad suggested, and I turned the wheel a bit to port, away from the wind, allowing the sails to take a better shape and drive us through the water a bit faster. *Fall off*. I wouldn't have known what he was talking about two months ago. I began to feel like I was acquiring new skills. I began to feel like a sailor.

Yeah, I made an offer on the second boat I looked at.

The offer, of course, was contingent upon a successful marine survey report. A marine surveyor is an expert in boats, their value, and what can go wrong with them. We would have to haul the vessel out of the water (boatyard fee paid by me) so she could be inspected below the waterline. Brad offered to recommend a surveyor, but I declined: it was standard advice in the how-to-buy-a-boat books to find your own surveyor, so as not to encourage a conflict of interest between the surveyor's job and the broker's. It was too easy for a crooked broker to promise a crooked surveyor future customers in return for giving the boat a favorable report, which would speed the sale for the broker.

So I found my own guy, a sea dog named Walt with the obligatory grizzled beard. Found him on the Internet, of course.

Brad moved the *Serenity* to the boatyard and Walt and I met him there. Big mistake—the two hit it off right away, exchanging business cards and winks— this meant Walt now had an incentive to "highball" his appraisal of the boat's value or even downplay flaws in order to make the sale more likely.

Walt proceeded to examine the boat literally with a magnifying glass. He tapped the hull hundreds of times with a small ball-peen hammer, attempting to detect damage in the fiberglass laminate. He examined the engine, the stanchions, the ground tackle (anchors and chains) and the head. The propane system was so rusted he did not examine it, but instead marked it as not installed.

Then there was nothing to do but wait for the survey report. The boatyard would keep the boat out of the water for three days, and if I bought her, I would pay for a coat of anti-foul applied to the hull below the waterline.

My first offer had been for $34,000. The owner, through Brad, made a counteroffer of $42,000, citing that the price had *already* been reduced to $45,000 from $55,000. Brad accompanied the counteroffer with this e-mail message: "We can go back and forth forever so here's what I suggest. Let's cut to the chase and split the difference, make it $38,000 and be done." I agreed, and the second offer was accepted.

Meanwhile, the Internet told me two things, one good, one bad. Downeaster sailboats had a reputation of being solid and seaworthy but *slow*. That was okay by me, as I expected to take three years to sail around the world. The ocean around the southern tip of Africa worried me, as it had a reputation for fifty-foot "square" waves that would make a solid boat necessary.

The Internet also told me there were no thirty-eight-foot slips available in the Bay Area. The closest might be as far as Santa Cruz, a two–hour drive south. Fortunately, Kevin lined up a slip for me right at Loch Lomond; still a long drive, but at least I knew someone there.

The survey report came back and old Walt appraised *Serenity* at $57,000, which I didn't believe for a minute. He recommended I replace the entire electrical system (which I didn't think was a big deal), the bilge pumps, the deck stanchions, and the two spreaders near the top of the mast, which had been made from Sitka spruce but were now almost rotted away. He did not say anything about the engine.

Stomach aflutter, I cut a check.

Yeah, I bought the second boat I looked at.

The boatyard coated the hull and lowered the boat back into the water. I asked Kevin if he could serve as crew when I took her to Loch Lomond. He agreed, probably knowing I lacked the confidence to do it myself.

The day dawned completely wind-free. I met Kevin at the boat and I had brought my blue hand–bearing compass, now out in the sunshine after being tucked away for fifteen years.

"You brought a hand–bearing compass with you?"

"Yeah," I told him, holding it up. "This is my first piece of equipment, got it a long time ago, and now it's my first gear aboard."

I set the compass down inside the chart table. Now it was home, too.

How Hard Could This Be?

While at work, I created a spreadsheet schedule for getting *Serenity* seaworthy. It took a lot of time to make, but on the job at InfoData, I never had an issue with time. Time stood still.

Don't get me wrong. I have always liked the tech industry. The work is reasonably interesting and the pay and benefits are fair. I had wanted to work in the technology industry for many years after I left the US Navy, but it was tough to get started because I had no formal training in computers. When I first worked as a shipping coordinator at MicroStrategy, the company was filling all technical positions by hiring top grads from top schools, such as MIT, Dartmouth and Harvard. And the legal department put out a memo that any employee applying for an internal job must meet the same job requirements as any other applicant from outside the company.

Hate those memos.

I spent my days boxing software CDs and manuals, and stole a few minutes here and there to play with the company's "data warehouse" product, which was quite innovative and technical. I learned that the company ran a six-week "bootcamp" training course exclusively for new hires. For each new class of twelve students, I was responsible for distributing their technical manuals and CDs. One Friday afternoon I was setting out the materials for the class scheduled to begin Monday morning. Eleven students total, I was told. There was to be an empty desk.

In that empty desk I saw opportunity.

Going on the principle that it is easier to obtain forgiveness than permission, I told the bootcamp instructor that my supervisor had said it was okay for me to sit in on the class—if it was okay by her, of course. Five minutes later I mentioned to my supervisor that I had been invited to sit in on the next bootcamp class, if it was okay by her, of course.

It was okay by her.

But I would have to do my shipping job at the same time. I figured I could come in an hour or two early, box software during lunch, and stay an hour or two late each day. I would need my computer in the training room so I could answer e-mails all day too. I moved it myself. When I found it could not connect to the Internet from the training room, I ran into the company help desk department, breathless, and told them about an "emergency" problem that just came up: By orders of my supervisor, I needed my computer online in the training room, *today*. I mentioned the instructor's name, too, and a couple of executives I had never met for good measure. It became a top priority and I was connected in minutes.

Data warehouse bootcamp, MicroStrategy-style, was some of the hardest work I had ever done in my life. I couldn't do my shipping job at 5:00 p.m. because we would not be released until close to midnight. Each day was filled with lectures, quizzes, and exams, to culminate six weeks later in an individual project and presentation.

My fellow students, exclusively computer science and engineering graduates from some of the best universities in the nation, did not know what to make of me—the shipping coordinator, learning multidimensional modeling and star schema reporting with summary rollups and cross-attribute hash indexes. The company's flagship product operated by generating structured query language code that ran against relational databases that had been pre-formatted to supply detailed and accurate business reports. It was a rapidly growing field.

And, apparently, they did not yet teach it in colleges.

I held my own and no one kicked me out of the classroom.

I succeeded in my project and my supervisor assigned me to spend a couple of days training a new hire to replace me in the shipping department, after which time I was to be transferred to the tech support department and assume the duties of a support engineer, seated between a guy from MIT and a woman from Stanford. If she figured out what kind of stunt I had pulled, she didn't say a word.

But she did wink.

My job at MicroStrategy gave me an education, and after a year I graduated myself into a better job. I had developed a solid reputation by resolving about five times more issues per day than my colleagues, who, brilliant as they were, seemed more interested in studying and learning than doing tech support for customers.

I got my chance to join a Silicon Valley startup, a company called InfoData. I was employee number fifty and they offered me a generous stock option package and the chance to do different things. I leveraged my knowledge of MicroStrategy's software to understand what InfoData's products did and how to explain the details to customers. I must have done a good job explaining, because I ended up as an instructor. I spent half my time on the road, visiting customer sites and showing them how to use our software.

With the rising stock market, my employee options became extremely valuable, and soon, I was profiting more from the stock than my salary. I got rid of my clunker and got a new Camry, for cash. I fulfilled a long-term dream and earned a pilot's license and joined a flying club, accumulating over two hundred hours as pilot-in-command.

It was all great fun, but there remained my two *serious* personal goals:

1. Become a husband and father.

OR

2. Become a sailor and circumnavigate the globe.

So it was to be my second choice, and I felt grateful just to have the opportunity—launching me from pizza delivery driver to pilot and yachtsman in a few short years, all of it occurring after age thirty-five.

Only in America.

After four years with InfoData, I had packed another thirty pounds onto my small frame. I had gone from pudgy to *fat*.

Yes, I worked out at the company-paid gym, and my weekend sailing provided lots of exercise, too. I was still a fat guy, albeit a *strong* fat guy.

One Friday afternoon, five days after Kevin and I docked the boat at Loch Lomond, I sat in my cubicle covertly browsing sailboat hardware websites. The plan was to work on the boat every weekend, holiday, and vacation day until she was ready for ocean sailing.

Then, quit InfoData.

Single-hand her or recruit crew? How many crew? The prospect of going alone worried me. It multiplied the danger and sounded pretty lonely. But the prospect of sharing close quarters, for weeks at a time, with strangers. . .

These thoughts tumbled through my mind on that Friday afternoon as I alternated between fantasies of the voyage and puzzlement over what I would accomplish tomorrow, my first day of boat work.

My cell buzzed. On the screen: *San Rafael, California*. The marina. . .

"Mister Damato?" asked an authoritative female voice. I was almost afraid to acknowledge it was me. "Mister Damato, you will need to move your boat to another slip immediately."

"Really?" I felt a bit of blood pressure drop from my head.

"Yes, really. The slip you are occupying is too small for the size of your vessel. You're in a thirty-eight foot slip and you need at least a forty-four foot slip."

"But my boat is a Downeast thirty-eight."

"That may be," she replied. "But your bowsprit makes

your overall length much longer than thirty-eight feet. Your bowsprit is jutting over the dock and it's a safety hazard. Someone's likely to smash their head on it, especially a child. We need to relocate your boat immediately. Immediately today. We have an open slip for you that will fit your boat, but it must be moved now."

A touch of panic swept over me. "I see what you're saying. Can you maybe adjust the dock lines a bit, move it back a few feet for me?"

"Can't do it," came the quick reply. "Your stern would jut into the waterway."

"All right. I'll take care of it today. I promise."

I hung up and called Kevin. Voice-mail. I called Alek. Voice-mail.

Should I call the marina back and say I could not move the boat today after all? No way. I remember Kevin telling me about the marina managers: "They're nice people. But they know they're operating a business. And they run the place like a business." I wasn't about to let them know I was unable to move my boat on my own. With dock space so hard to come by, who would blame them for kicking me out due to gross incompetence?

I wondered if I could call Spinnaker and ask if any of the instructors could give me an impromptu boat handling lesson. I didn't like that idea. First, they didn't hang around there weekdays. Second, it was lame. I bought the boat. I was her owner. Her master. I needed to move her a few hundred feet, in a marina, not even out in the Bay. I had watched Kevin handle his boat dozens of times. This last Sunday, when we were bringing *Serenity* from the boatyard to her new slip in Loch Lomond, we took it slow and Kevin gave me pointers and guided me right into the dock, a smooth landing. Sure, there was absolutely *zero wind,* and he was telling me *exactly* what to do with the wheel and the throttle every instant—but we made it, didn't we?

Look, I told myself. I can land an airplane, can't I? How hard could this be?

I dashed up to Marin County as fast as the Friday afternoon traffic would allow. It was a pretty day, gloriously sunny, and as I drove over the Golden Gate Bridge I could see that the Bay was covered in whitecaps. I'd have to carefully compensate for the wind as I moved the boat.

Just think ahead, and compensate. We airplane pilots do that all the time.

As soon as I stepped out of the Camry I was struck in the face with a howling gust. I ran into the marina office and the woman, now much friendlier, showed me exactly where my new slip was located and how much more per month it would cost.

I walked the docks and surveyed the situation. All I had to do was back my boat out of the current slip, turn around, motor between the docks a couple of hundred feet, turn toward the new slip, approach, make another ninety-degree turn into the new slip, and use reverse to stop the boat as I had watched Kevin do. It would be a tad trickier because I had no line handlers. I would have to be nimble, jumping aboard with the lines myself, throwing them out on the dock and tying up on arrival.

There was precious little maneuvering room.

Transmission in neutral. Power breakers shut. Cooling

water hull valve open. I pressed the button to start the diesel, a decades-old thirty-one-horsepower job made by a company called Farymann. Cooling water sputtering from the exhaust: check.

As the engine warmed up I began untying the dock lines. I removed two and left two ready to go and put my fenders on deck as well. I boarded, stood on the stern and looked up and down the narrow strip of water between the docks and visualized how I would compensate for the breeze, which seemed to be getting stronger by the minute. *Just take it slow,* I told myself. *This is not rocket science.* I had gotten A's and B's in college physics. I could figure this out.

I swallowed, leaped onto the dock, untied the remaining lines and threw them on the boat. The vessel was now *free.* I clutched the wheel and looked behind me. The other boats seemed absurdly close.

I pulled the transmission into reverse. *Cla-klink!*

Serenity began moving backwards. Crooked. The hull began rubbing against the dock. The bowsprit pulled way to the right, for no apparent reason. I turned the wheel— turned it not caring which way I was turning it and not having any understanding what effect it would have. I just knew I needed to *do something.* The transmission remained engaged in reverse and the boat was gaining backwards momentum.

The wind took hold.

My stern was moving rapidly to starboard. I spun the wheel the other way. Then to the left. No, the right. The bow struck my dock. I started turning the wheel the *other* direction.

Meanwhile, the boat gained backwards momentum.

I could feel my brain freezing up.

I looked behind me, and the nearby docked boats were coming at me *fast*. Bowsprits, davits, sterns, hulls, all rapidly coming closer. I cut the wheel again, and my brain froze into a solid block of ice.

Impact was now mathematically inevitable, so I stood there, dumb as a bucket of dirt, waiting for it, dreading it, without so much as pushing the transmission into neutral or even forward.

That would have been a good idea.

BANG! CRACK! BANG! CRUNCH! SCREEEEECH!

The ugly sounds of wood and fiberglass and metal being destroyed.

Serenity stopped, but just for a second. The wind asserted itself anew, began pushing the bow over toward the few boats still left untouched. My IQ suddenly went up a notch and I put the engine into neutral, straightened the rudder, and tried to *think* what to do next.

The marina had been quiet a minute before, but now people appeared and came running from several directions, drawn by the wrecking sounds. They stared, fascinated.

If I didn't do something soon the wind was going to turn my hull completely around and I would be trapped, unless I knew how to drive the thing backwards, which I didn't. I didn't even know how to drive it *forward*.

Small groups of people had assembled at various viewing points up and down the docks. They watched in silence. A man pushed my stern davits away from the other boat's bowsprit I had just crushed, maybe to be helpful, maybe to keep me from doing more damage.

Free again, I pushed the transmission into forward and

pushed the throttle lever just a bit more open, providing more power. I didn't understand it at the time, but I had been moving too slowly for the rudder to have steerage effect. Strictly speaking I *did* understand it, as they had taught me this at Spinnaker, but the knowledge didn't come forth when I needed it.

In order to be controllable, the boat needs water moving past the rudder. At this point, I didn't think I'd ever need that information again, as I could see my career as a yachtsman coming to an inglorious end.

I still needed to guide *Serenity* to the new slip. Somehow the boat pointed in the right direction and began picking up a couple of knots of speed. I was back in control, for now. As I piloted the boat away from the old slip, people began walking, tracking me, maybe wondering if I was attempting a yachting hit-and-run.

"I'm coming back!" I shouted. "Just relocating!"

No one answered or took their eyes from me—they simply watched, wondering what would happen next.

I was coming up on the first turn. I remembered that this boat carried twenty thousand pounds of inertia, and cut the wheel a bit earlier than my gut told me to. That worked pretty well. The boat's mass, plus the wind, made it feel like I was driving an eighteen-wheel trailer truck on wet ice, with no breaks, with a thirty-one horsepower engine, in a thirty-knot wind. What I learned so far: boats move *sideways*. In fact, full-keeled boats like to move sideways better than fin-keeled boats and thus are considered trickier to handle at slow speeds in tight confines.

Another turn, and I was coming up on my new slip. Men, women, and children continued to chase me—no one wanted to miss the best show of the day.

Getting into the new slip would require a ninety-degree turn to port, and there was hardly any room to do it. I got over on my right as far as I dared, and a cry of, "*Watch it watch it watch it!*" erupted from the spectators. I had almost swiped against another boat.

There it was, my new slip. I had to gauge when to cut the wheel. I meant to put the engine into neutral as I had seen Kevin do, but in my desire to cut the wheel at the exact right moment I had forgotten.

As a result, *Serenity* had a bit too much speed going into the turn.

Which was too bad.

BOOM! CRACK! CRUNCH! SCREEEECH!

My bowsprit plowed into another boat, the one next to my new slip, a sort of houseboat. I had taken out a couple of structural pieces supporting an awning. My own bowsprit was bent out of alignment for a few seconds, and when it snapped back into position, the forestay pulsed like a huge violin string, which sent visible waves and vibrations through the mast and all the standing rigging.

The good news was the collision had taken off my excess momentum and my boat was now in her new slip.

A couple of men swiftly positioned themselves on my dock and motioned for me to throw them my lines, which I did. They expertly tied me up. No one had said a word. I cut the engine.

I had caused separate accidents and damage getting out of my old slip and getting into my new slip. Was that some kind of record for bad boat handling? Had I made history today? No one was talking. I jumped down on the dock and adjusted the lines to allow room for my fenders.

The excitement over, people began drifting away. Then I saw him: the one guy not headed back to his own boat. He was old and had a sickly pallor about him. He was short, too—shorter than me by a couple of inches. He had a scruffy gray beard and stood there in greasy mechanic's coveralls, puffing a cigarette, watching me.

Every marina has them: the old salt, the know-it-all. I guessed he wanted to kindly share some of his wisdom with me. To be honest, I needed someone to talk to.

"I had to move it today," I offered as a way of launching the conversation. "The marina, they said . . ."

"Yeah, I know."

"My first boat, actually. First time moving it, too."

"Is that a God–damned fact?"

He began inspecting my boat from the outside. We looked for damage to the bowsprit and the stern, found none. Apparently, my own boat was unscathed. We could not find so much as a scratch.

Strange.

I had to leave a note on the other boats I had hit. I grabbed a pen and paper and the scruffy pirate-looking man—Duffy was his name—came along to hear my story. I was a software instructor, I explained, just got certified in basic keelboat sailing, never owned any kind of boat before. But I didn't have much choice but to buy a large boat, you see, because my ambition was to quit my job and sail around the world.

Duffy listened without saying a word. We hiked across the marina so I could leave notes for the boat owners— only two boats damaged, it turned out, not as bad as I thought. One of them had a beautiful handcrafted teak bowsprit, probably the most gorgeous piece of workmanship in the marina until *Serenity* and I got to it. Now it was a hideous tangle of smashed and splintered wood, fit to be hauled straight to the dumpster.

By the time we got back to the new slip, Duffy had listened to three cigarettes' worth of background about me, my situation, my plans, my misjudgments today about the wind and which way to turn the wheel and how much power to add and when. When he had heard all I had to tell, Duffy took the cigarette out of his mouth, placed one hand on my shoulder, looked me in the eye and said, "Son, do yourself a favor. Sell this boat now, before you hurt yourself."

On the long, traffic-congested drive back home, I had time to reflect on my plans. I regretted starting. My mind ran over all the other things I could have done instead, should have done instead. Projects that were cheaper and easier, truly made sense, and would have yielded more desirable results.

For example, maybe it was not too late to find someone, fall in love, get married, and raise a family of my own. I couldn't do much about my height, but maybe I could hire a personal trainer and *really* get serious about re-inventing my physique. He would motivate me to get the job done, even if it took four hours a day in the gym and a diet of nothing but protein shakes made with skim milk. After a year of that, I'd look *amazing*. No more drive-by rejections, that's for sure.

Why hadn't I done that, something realistic and practical, instead of this crazy, futile boat idea?

Or I could just quit InfoData now and move to

Hollywood and *somehow* break in as a screenwriter. Take acting lessons. Meet starlets. Once I was an established Hollywood screenwriter, the dates with sexy young actresses were sure to follow.

But instead, I'm crashing this gigantic Tupperware bowl around, destroying other people's property and costing myself a tremendous amount of time and a good chunk of my net worth.

For what?

What would I do now? How could I take that huge boat out for a sail if I couldn't even travel fifty feet without catastrophe? How could I be so *stupid?*

Theory Versus Practice

Duffy could go to hell. I wasn't selling the boat.

Instead, every Thursday and Friday, I listed the jobs I wanted to accomplish over the weekend. I made up a shopping list of tools, equipment, and supplies I would need—which was always longer than I anticipated. My face became familiar to the floor clerks at Palo Alto West Marine. Fortunately, there was also a locally-owned hardware store near the marina in San Rafael and they were able to provide knowledgeable advice on what I needed.

My work began at the crack of dawn every Saturday morning. Loch Lomond was less than forty miles north of my apartment in Sunnyvale, but a big segment of the journey was not on the highway. San Franciscans had long ago figured out how to fight the system, preventing the construction of freeway overpasses in their tiny neighborhoods; anyone needing to travel from Silicon Valley to Marin County had to bull straight through the city and tolerate nearly a hundred traffic lights.

Once parked at Loch Lomond I would say hello to my neighbors and open up the boat. I would work nonstop through the daylight hours, minus a brief lunch break and a few pauses for small talk with passersby.

The first Saturday I didn't know where to start. I

examined the running rigging (the halyards that raise the sails and the sheets that control the sails and boom) and found it worn and stiff. After all, Brad the broker had told me, "One of the things you want to do is replace all the running rigging as soon as possible." I would have to measure everything and buy replacements, so I opted to save the task for next weekend. I'll have to measure all the old rigging to buy the correct lengths.

Wait—if I pull it down, how will I get the new lines to the top of the mast? I had a total of four halyards that went all the way to the top, fifty feet above the water's surface, wrapped around a block (sailor talk for a heavy-duty rope pulley) and came back down again. I'd have to estimate the length and then replace the old lines by tying the ends to the new lines and hauling them up and over the blocks.

One of the things I liked about the design and appearance of the Downeaster 38 was the flush deck, a single surface from the bow to the stern, broken only by the raised cabin top and a footwell that held the wheel. Quite a salty layout, I thought. Today, Day One, that deck was covered in dry seagull crap and a fine powder of automobile exhaust particulates. I should clean it off first thing. But how? A garden hose? Would have to buy one next week, too.

Duffy came sauntering down the dock, puffing on one of his customary cigarettes. In a way I was glad to see him, as he could see for himself that I had no intention of following his advice. He silently inspected the boat.

"Mind if I ask you," he called out, exhaling a huge cloud of tobacco breath in my general direction, "what you paid for your cutter?"

"I got a deal. Thirty-eight."

"Thirty eight hundred?"

I looked at him. "Thousand."

He puffed for a while longer while I puttered about the deck.

"Permission to come aboard?"

I hesitated, then told myself that anything this guy had to say to me was probably something worth hearing. Despite the sarcasm and personal digs, he knew what he was talking about, or at least it seemed that way to me.

"Do you have a boat here in the marina?"

He pointed down the dock at an enormous white catamaran. For an instant I thought he was busting my chops.

"Wow. Quite a boat. Forty feet?"

"Fifty-two."

Duffy pointed his cigarette at the mess that covered my decks. "I got a pressure washer you can borrow."

"Thank you. Want to see belowdecks?"

We descended a five-foot wooden companionway ladder. The main salon took up most of the boat's interior. There was a tiny galley on the port side, with an ancient propane oven, a grimy sink, and a couple of built-in iceboxes that I hoped could be converted to refrigeration. There was no pressure water system—two foot pumps near the cabin sole sent fresh or salt water to the sink. Or at least they were supposed to. I pumped both and nothing happened.

Duffy mumbled, "Yeah."

On the starboard side, opposite the galley, was a large chart table with a quarterberth that served as a seat. I lifted the tabletop and spied my trusty blue sight resting amid old pencil stubs and assorted junk.

I showed him through the salon to the folding dinette table. There were foam cushions on both sides that doubled as berths. Farther forward was an enclosed head with a toilet: gross, smelly, bone dry. The most forward section of the hull was occupied by an enclosed cabin guarded by a brass plaque: *Captain's Quarters*.

I opened the door and a stink hit me right away. A filthy public restroom. Old urine, old crap, and old toilet paper. The smell wasn't strong, but its nature was disgusting and unmistakable. I hadn't smelled it *before* I bought the boat.

"Smell that?" I asked. "Funny, it's not coming from the head."

Duffy didn't respond, just turned around and puffed. The restroom smell bothered me. I'd have to investigate, and soon. I didn't want to be breathing it for long, especially if I were ever to sleep aboard. I opened a couple of lockers. Garbage, garbage everywhere.

"I'm going to have to get rid of a lot of this junk before I start outfitting," I said, trying my best to sound like a sailor.

"How's the engine?"

"Runs like a top."

"Then you got yourself a good solid boat here. You got a good price."

"Thanks. Just got to learn a bit of boat handling, right?"

He gave me an icy stare, and we were done talking for the day.

* * *

There was the matter of the three boats I had damaged. I decided I would file an insurance claim on the most expensive claimant, the gorgeous teak bowsprit I had reduced to toothpicks. The marina required that all tenants carry at least $500,000 in liability insurance. I couldn't file a claim for *damaging three boats in one day*, before I'd had the boat for a week. They would cancel me for sure, I'd be unable to open a policy with another company, and I'd be expelled from Loch Lomond with nowhere to go. The other two boats I would pay to repair from my own pocket.

I located and apologized to the owners and told them I was lining up contractors to perform repairs to their satisfaction. I needed to hire a fiberglass shop and a welder and a carpenter and a painter—virtually my own private boatyard. And none of it for my own boat. The owners were laid-back and surprisingly understanding, but each gave me a hard glint from their eyes: Do not let this happen again.

Duffy's pressure washer blew most of the accumulated grime off my deck. He warned me to start with low pressure and gradually increase it, to prevent damaging the non-skid sand embedded in my deck, a nice feature not common in more modern boats. I didn't listen, and was rewarded with a few permanent and ugly swirls etched in by the water jet.

I fell into a routine. Every Saturday, Sunday, and holiday I spent on the boat from midmorning to sunset. I was driving home each day—a waste of six hours' road time each weekend. I replaced the running rigging. After that, I spent just about all my time chasing cosmetics. Irrational as it sounds, I behaved as if the *appearance* of the boat was more important than seaworthiness. So I cleaned and scrubbed and started the big job of cleaning out the lockers.

The cap rails—the edge of the deck where it joins to the hull—were topped with four inch–wide solid teak boards. This was good. Problem was, they hadn't been varnished in years, and the California sun (even in the foggy Bay Area) had burned away most of the previous coats, leaving hideous blisters and pockmarks. So I went varnish shopping and began the restoration process. This meant many hours in uncomfortable positions, scraping off what was left of the previous coats, power sanding, and then hand sanding. Then came six coats of varnish, which each required sanding beforehand. When I was done, the cap rails (probably about eighty-five feet total if you consider the curve of the deck) glistened in the sunshine and drew many complements. What I did not know, but most everyone else did, was that the beautiful shine would not last a month. Plus, it left the rails slippery. Not good. Later, when I was older and wiser, I left all the cap rails bare wood. It meant better footing and zero maintenance, and didn't look too bad, either.

At the end of each day my body ached from head to foot. I would trudge through the marina grocery market and pick up dinner and an iced tea for the drive home, then repeat the process over the next morning.

People became accustomed to seeing me around the marina. Duffy and his wife Tara invited me aboard their new catamaran, *Nightingale,* a reprieve from my boat work. I learned that Duffy Saunders had owned and managed a major commercial laundry in San Francisco, had recently retired, and was planning a South Pacific cruise with Tara. I didn't ask why they didn't just up and leave *now*.

Kevin was busy with his new law firm job and rarely came by the marina, but when he did, I would show him my latest improvements to *Serenity,* and he would nod in approval.

As the summer wore on, the filthy restroom smell coming from the forward part of the boat grew steadily stronger. I procrastinated on locating the source—maybe I was a bit afraid of what I would find, or maybe I just got used to it. I figured it was probably the holding tank or maybe the sanitary hoses themselves, and I wasn't ready to deal with a mess like that just yet.

One Saturday afternoon Duffy came by and said, "Your boat cried herself to sleep last night."

I put down my paintbrush. "Excuse me?"

"She's been neglected."

"I'm here all the time—"

"No matter. A boat like this, she needs to be taken out into her element regularly. You haven't taken this boat off the dock once in almost two months." He had me there. "You don't give a boat what she needs—wind in her sails —she'll get all screwy on you, and that will be the end of it."

"Yeah. Well. I'm going to get myself some boat handling lessons—"

"And I've been watching you drive in every weekend morning from . . . where did you say you lived, Sunnyvale? Why don't you just sleep aboard, avoid that long drive?"

"Absolutely. I definitely will sooner or later."

"Why not tonight?"

"Not quite finished with the interior. The cushions are totally mildewed underneath, and there's this smell coming out of the forward—"

Duffy laughed. "A *smell?*"

"A really nasty stink."

"You gotta be kiddin' me."

"Once I get it cleaned out. . ."

Duffy shook his head, lit a cigarette.

"Okay, I admit, I'm a bit spoiled. I like a nice, antiseptic, clean-smelling sleeping environment. Like a Hilton hotel."

He exhaled slowly. "Then you shoulda bought yourself a Hilton boat."

I picked myself off the deck and wiped the accumulated sweat from my face.

"You're supposed to be some kind of Navy nuclear submarine guy, right?"

Duffy and Tara had asked me where I learned how to swing a wrench, and I told them about my time aboard the USS *Atlanta*.

"So stop being a wuss and sleep with her before you hurt her feelings so bad she'll hate you for life. A boat is no different from a woman." He kicked the gunwales. "Five thousand years' worth of human experience and know-how went into this boat and you better believe that's what makes her human. Treat her right and she'll treat you right. Treat her like a dog . . ."

"I don't want to smash up any more boats. Can you blame me for that?"

"Then like I said before, you better sell her. I mean, think about it. What the hell good is a boat tied to the dock? You take her out, what's the worst that could happen? The worst that could happen is the fucker will sink on you. Ain't that right?"

"Yeah, that's right."

"And that's no worse than tied up to the dock. So sail her or sell her, what's it gonna be?"

"Would you give me a couple of pointers getting her in and out without hitting anything?"

"You sleep with her, I'll show you how to get her in and out or your slip."

I went below, determined to find and fix the source of the stench that day.

A marine head is a simple contraption, really just a bowl and a hand pump, with connections for hoses to take water in and shoot waste out. It's the rest of the sanitation system that causes the problems. To be legal inside a harbor or marina, the boat needs a holding system—generally a metal or fiberglass tank and associated thick plastic hoses.

I could not find *Serenity's* holding tank.

By process of elimination I determined that it must be deep, deep in the forepeak, the narrow forward-most section of the hull. I removed all the foam cushions from the V-shaped captain's quarters. That revealed the cover to a sail locker. I pulled out four densely packed nylon sacks holding tightly rolled sails: a yankee jib, a storm-cut mainsail, and two sizes of staysails.

With every bag I pulled, the stench got worse. Under the sails was another solid plywood cover. I removed it. The smell maxed out and I knew it was the source. Someone had constructed a *wooden* holding tank of 3/8–

inch thick plywood, sheathed in a single layer of fiberglass. In all my readings about boat systems, I never heard of such a tank. But here it was. A wooden holding tank, apparently filled with raw sewage and who knows what else.

I would have to get rid of it, somehow. All of it, the whole thing—otherwise that smell would be with me forever.

I couldn't drain it from the hoses connected to the tank because they were clogged. Maybe I could remove the tank whole, and cart it away? Not a chance: it was connected to the hull, and its sides and bottom were out of view and out of reach. All I could access was the trapezoidal top.

At least it was thin wood.

I wrapped a rag around my face, which I hoped would attenuate the obnoxious odor and keep the liquid off my face. I used a key saw to open up a six-inch hole and a wave of putridity nearly knocked me backwards. It was worse than I thought. The tank—a plywood box, really—was filled to the top with a thick, dark, gray fluid that for all I knew represented the remains of food eaten and digested during the Reagan administration.

I walked out of the boat gagging, and drove to the hardware store for a full-enclosure painter's respirator mask. I also purchased a Sawzall I had been considering, which is like a mini-chainsaw. I knew what needed to be done, and it wasn't going to be easy, or pleasant.

Respirator on, I cut the entire tank top away. I began swiftly scooping bucketfuls of filth into a larger five-gallon bucket. The mask helped, but the stench was so powerful and so disgusting that I retched with every bucket I dumped. It was splashing on the sole, on the bulkheads, on my arms and legs. And there were at least thirty gallons in there.

When the first bucket was full, I hauled the bucket down the dock, across the parking lot, down another dock to the pump-out station, where I sucked it away with a black vacuum pump. Repeat six times.

When the tank was reasonably empty I used the Sawzall to separate the sides and bottom, and then I carried each part to the dumpster. The stink was now all over the dock and everyone knew what it was—except, they assured me, they had never smelled waste so pungent. Well, their sewage hadn't been properly aged.

Seagulls were coming in from miles around.

By the time I was done, there was sewage all over the boat and my clothes. After cleaning up the boat, I hosed myself down head-to-foot right there on the dock. The smell would soon be gone, but if someone had told me that this ordeal was *not* as disgusting as it could possibly get, I wouldn't have believed him. As time would tell, I would have been wrong.

With Duffy's coaching, I was able to get *Serenity* in and out of her slip many times in the coming weeks without hitting so much as a piling. I now understood *prop walk*, the tendency of a boat's propeller to pull the stern port or starboard depending on which way it was turning, plus the simple fact that controlling twenty thousand pounds of inertia required forethought. I learned to *never* leave the engine in gear for more than a few seconds in tight quarters, lest the boat gather too much momentum. I learned how to compensate for the wind and tidal currents in the marina, both of which were often strong.

I found a perfect boat slip, too. It was much closer to home and work. It was at Bair Island Marina, just one highway exit from InfoData, and best of all, the marina was surrounded by an apartment complex. I could live at the same place as the boat.

Kevin agreed to serve as crew in sailing *Serenity* from Loch Lomond to Bair Island, a forty-mile trip we figured would take less than a full day. We would sleep in our respective boats on Friday night, rise at the crack of dawn, and get underway. I left my Camry at Bair Island and took the train to San Francisco's Financial District, where Kevin picked me up after work. We had dinner with Duffy and Tara in their catamaran, which was more like a spaceship than a sailboat. After a couple of rounds of scotch, my three companions quizzed me about my desire to walk away from my well-paying job and sail for three years.

"I want to do something with my life," I stammered. "Do something . . . be something."

"You couldn't think of something easier?" asked Kevin, and we all laughed.

"No fun," I offered in the way of explanation. "It has to be hard, or what's the point? Becoming is the best part. Being alive is becoming. Being is becoming."

I was up before the sun. It was a cold morning and the docks were coated with a thin crust of frost. *Serenity* had no head, so I walked out to the marina lavatory. It was a gorgeous star-filled night and the nearby Richmond Bridge was lit up like a Christmas tree.

While walking back from the lavatory I looked up and wondered why only *half* of the Richmond Bridge was visible. How could there be half a bridge? Then I saw it: an enormous wall of fog was moving in from the sea. It was vast and looked incredibly surrealistic, like one of those computer generated end-of-the-world tsunamis in the movies.

By first light we had enough visibility to get out of the marina, but just barely, and the fog was getting worse.

"Fog generally burns off later in the day," I told Kevin.

"So you want to wait?"

"Well, it might not burn off till noon, and if we wait that long we'll be getting into Bair Harbor at nightfall, and you know what they say—never make a night entry. But once we get out, it should get better. I think we should leave now before it gets worse."

"You're not making any sense." Kevin rubbed his eyes. Both of us were short of sleep after that evening with Duffy and Tara. "What sort of nav gear do you have aboard?"

"GPS, compass, radar, Bay charts."

"We should be all right. You can use the experience, anyhow."

We cast off to an eerily silent Loch Lomond. The visibility seemed to drop by the minute. I could see well enough to guide us out of the marina, but just beyond the entrance was a dense wall of gray. I had my handheld GPS ready. I figured I could use it to point us in the right direction and find our way to Bair Island Marina regardless of poor visibility. I mean, the GPS tells you exactly where you are, right?

The entrance to Loch Lomond is odd. There is a narrow

channel, about half a mile long, marked on each side with wooden pilings. And when I say narrow, I mean it: about seventy feet wide, with the pilings a couple of hundred feet apart.

Into the gray we went. We could see maybe thirty feet in any direction. The sunlight was so diffuse it made distinguishing direction impossible. To my horror, the channel was not on my GPS map. I could see *where* we were, but not whether or not we were in the channel between the pilings. The smart thing to do would have been to turn around and tie up at the fuel dock until it cleared up. But I'm not that smart. I tried to use the GPS to maintain our heading between the pilings. I noted that our position hadn't changed in a while. I looked at the water next to the boat and it was motionless.

In salty nautical terms, we had run aground. We were stuck.

I figured we were right on the edge of the channel, *barely* resting on the mud, because our impact had been so gentle we hadn't felt it. But we had to get off *now* because I knew the tide was running out. I opened the throttle. Kevin turned, perplexed.

"We're stuck, I'm trying to get off . . ."

I put the throttle to the max. Behind me the prop churned up a huge bubbles of black mud. Kevin shook his head, sat back down. "That's not what you're supposed to do according to the book."

But we were moving again. We were back in the channel, and it was just a matter of keeping the boat between the pilings. Easy in theory, extremely difficult in practice. There were two problems: (1) I could only see one piling at a time, and (2) they were not located directly across from each other—they were staggered.

One plus two equals stuck in the mud again three minutes later.

I opened up the throttle, again. Big black mud bubbles, again. No dice—we were *really* stuck this time.

Kevin waved his arms. "You're gonna draw mud into the cooling line! Cut the engine!"

I did so. We assessed the situation in perfect foggy silence. The fog seemed to eat up sound; I didn't know such quiet existed.

Finally Kevin said, "We're listing slightly to port, so the water's probably deeper there. What we're gonna have to do is put the boom out, put something heavy over the starboard side, and maybe float her off."

I knew we had to get off immediately, as the water was getting shallower as the tide went out. We didn't have enough time for such a scheme, and if we didn't get off now we'd be stuck here for nine or ten hours. We'd have to go back to the dock in the December darkness.

The sound of an engine approaching, and voices.

I screamed into the general direction of the sound, "Help! Mayday! Over here!"

Kevin threw me a look as if I were nuts.

A little white fishing skiff materialized in the mist. The engine idled, one of the sweetest sounds I had ever heard: they were slowing. Two fishermen peered at us. I grabbed a dock line and waved it in the air.

"Can you tow us off? *PLEASE*, can you tow us off?"

Without a word, they maneuvered closer and motioned for the line. I tossed it while shouting many, many thanks into the air. They pulled us off the mud in ten seconds. In another half an hour, we may have been stuck too firmly.

"We were lucky twice so far," Kevin observed. "Wanna make it three?"

Once we were past the Loch Lomond channel the rest of the Bay was plenty deep enough. About thirty-five nautical miles separated us from Bair Island. At five knots (about jogging speed) we'd be there by four o'clock. With the GPS I could correct our heading and navigate between the landmarks: the Richmond Bridge, Angel Island, Alcatraz Island, and the San Francisco waterfront. Kevin and I alternated at the wheel. We were motoring past some of the most spectacular scenery in the world, and we couldn't see thirty feet. It didn't feel like we were in San Francisco Bay at all, but rather an eerie sailor's purgatory.

We were approaching the Oakland Bay Bridge. Once past that, there would be almost twenty miles of open water without having to change heading. Once we got past the bridge, I planned to set a GPS waypoint just outside the Bair Island Marina entrance and steer straight for that.

Thinking about the bridge, I suddenly realized we had something else to worry about: There were several large steel towers and one massive cement monolith holding up the Bay Bridge. *Where were these towers?* They were not shown on the GPS chart. If I didn't know where these towers were, we could smack right into one. Visibility remained no more than thirty feet. We were moving eight or nine feet per second. Once the base of a bridge tower became visible, I would have three seconds, four at the most, to turn the boat—or we'd smash into it.

This was a serious problem.

Radar! I turned on the radar, which had a twenty-four mile range. The bridge towers should be visible there. Except that the radar wouldn't light up. I asked Kevin to check the breaker. No go. I asked for my multimeter and checked that it was getting voltage. It was.

Well, it worked just fine when we took the boat up to Loch Lomond.

We were within a mile of the bridge. I consulted with Kevin: "We have two choices. We can motor around in circles and wait for the fog to clear. As it is, we'll get in a couple of hours before dark."

"I don't think it's going to clear."

"Me, neither. What I think would be better is if I reduce our speed to just enough to steer the boat, probably three knots, and you can get out on the bowsprit and be lookout for a bridge tower. If you see one, yell and I'll turn."

"You know how to port around?

"Yeah. I'll throttle up, turn full rudder port or starboard, then the other way . . ."

"So our stern won't hit. Okay, sounds like a plan."

The odds were in our favor. There were five towers on the west span of the bridge, but only three in the deep water zone we were traversing. One was the massive concrete tower about a hundred feet wide. The other two were steel, and about a quarter mile of water separated these obstacles. I estimated there was only one chance in ten of hitting the bridge even if Kevin's attention wandered.

I throttled down and watched the compass to make sure I was still able to steer the boat. The GPS reported our speed over the bottom was slightly less than three knots. Kevin and I peered into the haze, searching for any sign of steel or cement. We could hear the rumble of cars and trucks barreling down the highway hundreds of feet over our heads. After a tense couple of minutes the GPS told me we were past the bridge.

Kevin went below to get a cup of coffee. I opened the throttle back to five knots. Relieved that we had nothing but twenty miles of open water in front of us, I *released the wheel*, sat down on the deck and began hunting for the GPS menu option to set a waypoint, which took a bit longer than I expected, but no matter: the water ahead of us was clear.

I finally figured out how to set the waypoint and activated it—which confused me, because it was telling me the waypoint was *behind me*, which was impossible. Ah, I know: I was holding the unit upside down. I flipped it over. Hmmm.

I looked up and saw dozens of truck tires fastened to pilings, rapidly approaching the starboard bow.

I yelled, "Holy shit!" and spun the wheel to the left as fast as I could. The boat lurched. The tires and the pilings, forming a sort of bumper around the steel bridge tower, came closer . . . closer . . . then glided past the starboard side with less than ten feet to spare.

Alarmed, Kevin stuck his head out of the companionway just in time to see the steel tower gracefully slide past.

"What the hell . . . ?"

Heart pounding from the adrenaline rush, I steadied the wheel and stammered, "We almost hit the bridge!"

"I can see that! How the hell did that happen?"

Then it dawned on me. "We must have just gone around in a big circle."

Unpleasant pause.

"You have got to be kidding me."

I looked at the GPS. "I got distracted. I figured we'd go more or less straight."

It had taken just a minute or so to motor a hundred and eighty degrees and come close to smashing up the boat. The rudder must have been slightly off center. Because the sunlight was uniform in every direction, I couldn't tell we were turning around. Sure, the deck compass must have been spinning, but I didn't notice.

Even with the tires acting as bumpers, the side of *Serenity's* hull would have had to absorb twenty thousand pounds of inertia moving at six miles per hour. That's how boat hulls cave in and boats sink.

"Third lucky break in one day," Kevin said. "Let's be extra careful because I think we've called in all the favors the Bay gods are going to grant us today."

We reached Bair Island Marina, the sunbeams bursting through the mist just as we entered the Redwood City channel.

Serenity was now located in an ideal spot. I could store some gear and tools in my apartment. I could work on the boat almost every day! Which was good, because shortly after I brought the boat to Redwood City I found out exactly how much work it would require.

We had a major rainstorm, the kind of storm known in the Bay area as a Pineapple Express. It poured all night, the first big rainfall since I bought *Serenity*. I had made sure that every port and vent and other opening was closed before the storm began. I had read that boats have a tendency to let water in, and I figured the storm would be beneficial because it would show me if I had any leaks.

The following morning, I opened the companionway hatch and got one of the biggest shocks of my life. There were two inches of water on the cabin sole. I descended the ladder and saw that everything—and I do mean every single item in the boat—was soaking wet. Several expensive power tools, drenched. Manuals, charts, electronics, all saturated. I dared not turn on the main breaker. I opened a few lockers. An inch of water lay on the bottom. All the bunk cushions were sopping wet, explaining the copious amounts of mildew I had found earlier. It was as if someone had walked around with a garden hose for an hour or so, wetting down the interior until the bilge was full.

Panic rose in the back of my throat. This boat was unlivable. Uninhabitable. How could I possibly take this boat to the South Seas—some of the rainiest places in the world—and live aboard? It stormed quite often in the Bay Area between December and March, once or twice a month. How would I even work on the boat?

How could I make such a stupid mistake, opening a vast hole to swallow up my time and money and leave nothing but a pile of waterlogged junk?

Dust Monkey

When I first bought *Serenity* I made a list of what I needed to do. It was mostly appearance-oriented work. Now I made another list, a serious list of what was required to make the boat habitable and seaworthy.

First, there was the water. I combed the Internet for information on keeping the interior of a boat dry. There was a vast body of knowledge on this subject, a lot of it revolving around a marine adhesive sealant manufactured by the 3M Corporation called "5200." Boat owners sang its praises. I bought ten big tubes. Now what was I supposed to do with it?

Most of the rainwater was flowing in through the boat's windows. *Serenity* had six old-fashioned rectangular bronze portholes and four much larger Plexiglas "windows" on the aft part of the cabin near the galley and nav station. I removed a couple of the bronze ports from the cabin side, a simple-sounding job that in reality took hours. I resealed the ports with plenty of 5200, following the directions exactly.

The rains came. The ports leaked. The boat flooded.

The big Plexiglas windows were something else. They were yellowed and scratched and needed replacement, as they leaked a lot of water, too. Yet as I soon realized, replacing them wouldn't do much good, and more drastic, time-consuming, and expensive work was needed.

I slowly discovered that one or more of the previous owners had simply drilled holes in the deck as needed. You can't do that on a boat—it's going to leak. Now I was stuck with it. Each hole used to mount hardware and handholds would have to be filled with epoxy and re-drilled, and then the fitting would need to be re-bedded with 5200.

And then there were the batteries.

There were four of them sitting on a platform just aft of the engine—big, heavy, Group 27 wet cells, old and at the end of their lives. Each was held down with a nylon strap screwed into the fiberglass. That was fine for Bay sailing, but I planned to take *Serenity* to the "roaring forties" south of Cape Town, where there was a good chance of a knockdown or capsize. The batteries had to be contained, restrained, and mounted properly. I designed and built a proper plywood battery box to keep the new batteries firmly in place. I sheathed it with epoxy and fiberglass.

The next problem was this: How would I fasten that big box down to the engine room platform? Screws or bolts would not do—I could not get to the underside of the shelf at all to use any sort of washer and nut to hold the bolts in place. The box with the batteries and cables would weigh just under four hundred pounds. I wanted a *guarantee* it would not tear free even if *Serenity* capsized— as she might very well do a few times while rounding the southern tip of Africa in the notorious Roaring Forties.

I bought myself a power grinder and a supply of dust masks. I crept behind the engine and, stooping, proceeded to grind off the surface "gelcoat," that smooth and glossy (but brittle and weak) coating that you see on the outside of all fiberglass products. I had to grind off a big rectangle maybe five by three feet. This took hours, and produced an ultra-fine power of white plastic that coated everything inside the boat and the still waters of the marina. Even with the face mask I figured I might be breathing enough microscopic particles to give me lung cancer or some horrible respiratory disease years down the line . . . and there would be no one to sue.

Once down to the bare fiberglass I covered the rectangle with a thick mixture of epoxy and plastic filler power, then bedded down the whole battery box. It would not come loose, ever.

If you're wondering where I'm getting all this epoxy, I'm not using those little plastic tubes you can pick up in a grocery or hardware store. I used gallon-sized cans of resin and hardener sold by marine supply stores for fiberglass repair work—evidently, people with old fiberglass boats buy the stuff in super jumbo family size quantities.

Bair Island was a yuppie's marina, full of sleek white powerboats and even a mini recreational tugboat that obviously never tugged anything in its life, but probably set some guy back several hundred thousand dollars.

The marina manager, a pleasant middle–aged woman who went by the nickname Tweety, didn't mind my doing boat work as long as I didn't get any materials in the water or on someone else's boat. I often saw her husband Jon coming and going in a pickup truck marked "Professional Marine Repairs—Certified Diesel Mechanic." I asked if he'd care to take a look at *Serenity's* diesel and give me his opinion about a problem I observed.

"When I got the boat last year it seemed to run perfect," I told him. He stood with me, surveying the boat in his mechanic's coveralls. "But then it began smoking every time it runs. Just a light smoke at first, but it's gotten thicker. An oil mist in the air, too."

"Let's start her up."

With the engine running just a few revs over idle, Jon pointed out the thin oil sheen covering the entire yellow engine. He sniffed. He removed the oil dipstick—a puff of oily vapor burst forth. After a minute the acrid smoke began accumulating.

"Smell it?"

"Yeah."

Jon poked around a bit and then we shut her down.

"Farymann makes a fine engine. This one is blowing oil past the cylinders. If you don't run it a while the tar buildup will reduce the oil blow for a while but mark my word it will come back. It's robbing you of compression and power, and hurting your fuel efficiency,"

Not to mention stinking up the whole boat when the engine was at half–speed or higher.

"So how do we fix her?"

"Well, it needs to be rebuilt." Pause. Grimace. "Farymann is a good brand but they shut down their marine division a long time ago. You'll need new cylinder heads and studs, for openers. Got the parts manual?"

I did, and Jon marked off all the parts needed to put the engine back into working order. Most of them were *big*. My heart sank. I couldn't continue to run such a smoky engine, but I had figured the cause was just something that a mechanic could fix or adjust. Diesels were supposed to be rugged. Maybe they were, bit this one had been assembled when Gerald Ford was president.

I wrote down the part numbers and descriptions, and that night I pored over Google and eBay, looking for sources. I found plenty of forum entries where other people, including Downeast sailboat owners, complained about the impossibility of finding Farymann parts.

There was one hope: a shop in southern California, DieselWorks, that bragged on their website they could locate Farymann marine diesel parts. I called them the next morning with my parts list. They said "can do" and quoted me $950, and estimated four to six weeks for delivery.

Meanwhile, Alek and I sailed Kevin's boat every chance we got. One particularly sunny and windy Saturday we beat up and down the San Francisco waterfront, the thirty-two-foot hull slamming down into the waves and sending showers of salt spray everywhere. That was the last time I went sailing without foulies. My sweatshirt and sweatpants were soaked, but I stoically remained on deck, shivering while my two companions were relatively warm and snug in their head-to-toe waterproof bib coveralls. Kevin wisely told me to get below before I came down with hypothermia.

Things hadn't changed much at Loch Lomond. Duffy still strode about with his inevitable cigarette, poking his nose into other people's business. I told him about my leaks and my plans to fix them.

"I'm going to have to replace all six ports with new ones that I can bed properly. Then for those four huge Plexiglas windows, I'm going to get rid of them completely. I found a couple of articles on how to fiberglass over big window holes. Once I paint the cabin it will be like they never existed. Then I'll put in four new bronze ports in their place."

Duffy tossed me his sourest expression. "Don't do that. You're gonna have an ugly-ass scar on your cabin and people are going to wonder what the hell happened."

The work went on. My life alternated between teaching classes for InfoData, *Serenity* upgrades, and an occasional sail with Alek and Kevin. I became the boat work guru, and it wasn't long before Kevin was consulting *me* about repair jobs for *Serendipity*.

I ordered ten solid bronze opening ports, the best on the market, from a manufacturer with a reputation for watertight integrity. They cost $200 each, and the hardware, tools and 5200 required to bed them added another $300 to the total. But the real kicker was the labor involved. Each of the old ports had to be removed, the fiberglass hole enlarged slightly, and the edges filled with epoxy putty to give the mounting screws a solid foundation. Each of the ten ports required twelve counter-sunk holes drilled in precise position.

Do the math.

When the California rainy season ended in May, I removed all four old Plexiglas windows, leaving four gaping rectangular holes in my cabin. Going by a detailed procedure I found on the net, I installed an outer mold of eighth-inch plywood over each hole, coating the inside of the plywood with mold release. Then I began "laying up" the new cabin sides from spun fiberglass cloth and epoxy.

Each hole required about a dozen outer layers of fiberglass cloth and epoxy, followed by an inner foam core, then about seven layers of fiberglass for the interior side.

Sanding the outside took weeks. Tweety eyed me suspiciously and made sure I wasn't spreading fiberglass dust into the water or on other people's boats, which meant I could sand only on wind-free days and had to vacuum up my mess as I sanded.

But when I painted the outside of the cabin, *it was perfect*. It looked as if the holes had never been there—there was not the slightest trace. It was also strong—probably the strongest part of the boat. I didn't have to worry about those square forty-foot waves off of the Cape of Good Hope smashing in the Plexiglas.

Jon complimented the work. People asked me how much would I charge to do fiberglass work on their boats. I had to turn them down, due to time constraints.

The summer wore on. I tackled one job after another:

First, I replaced each of the twelve deck stanchions. They were leaking and weak. I replaced the lifelines with new stainless-steel lines custom made at a local rigging shop.

Second, I removed the entire sanitary system, including all plastic hoses (which were clogged with fecal matter) and the ancient, inoperative marine head. Duffy told me the secret to pulling the hoses off the fittings: You have to heat them with a hair dryer.

Per the surveyor's recommendations, I removed the entire propane system including the tanks, the lines, the regulators, and the entire stove. All were corroded and unsafe, and would have to be replaced.

I cleaned and re-painted every locker on the boat.

Next, the fresh water system consisted of two steel tanks at the bottom of the boat, plus old plastic hoses and manual pumps that did not work. I replaced all the plumbing, including the fill hose leading to a deck fitting, but the tanks were something else. I could not see inside them; water tanks should have inspection plates on the top, but these had none. For all I knew, there could be anything inside those 1970s vintage tanks, up to and including the remains of Jimmy Hoffa. I would need to cut an inspection hole, clean them out, then install a cover. Eventually.

Other things I would need to do "eventually" included replacing all the seating cushions and covers, the diesel fuel filter, the standing rigging cables, the two rotted Sitka spruce mast spreaders, the running lights on the mast; and then install a battery charger, solar cell, and maybe a wind generator, a refrigeration system, a new radar that worked, and various electronic gear at the nav station: a long-distance single-sideband shortwave radio, GPS chartplotter, depth sounder, knot meter, and finally, an autopilot of some kind.

That list was not the end. Many of those items, such as replacing the standing rigging, would require a stay in the boatyard. That would have to wait until a couple of months before departure.

The next rainy season hit the Bay Area. This time, only a few drops found their way below. I pronounced all ten new ports waterproof. The forward deck hatch, an old wooden affair that appeared none too strong, definitely leaked and would need complete replacement.

I didn't understand that it was pretty easy for a boat to be dry while tied up to a dock. At sea, a fiberglass hull twists and flexes several inches in every direction, opening tiny gaps and seams and letting water into the interior.

My colleagues at InfoData laughed at my idea to buy a boat and sail around the world. As soon as they understood that I meant what I said, the laughter came to a halt, replaced by troubled frowns. They weren't as much concerned for my safety as for my mental health.

In the summertime our department holds a weeklong meeting in some venue like Las Vegas or Tahoe or Orlando. Each evening the dozen of us software instructors would assemble at a restaurant chosen by our manager, Peter Gibbons, and enjoy a good meal and the opportunity to chat and catch up on subjects—*any* subjects—that had nothing to do with InfoData or our software.

Most topics that would have generated a semblance of interesting conversation (politics, religion, gender relations and the like) were tactically *verboten*. What did that leave? Golf? The kids? Mortgages? The other instructors were predictably homogenous white-collar technology workers, and everyone's stories were pretty much the same: each of my colleagues were married, had one, two or three children, and lived in an overpriced McMansion on a cookie-cutter subdivision. Yes, custom granite countertops all around.

They were lean and fit due to a regular jogging or

handball schedule, and everyone (the men at least) loved golf, although they did not have the time to play as much as they'd like, what with the kids and all. Their (unspoken) life ambition was to be promoted to management, in order to do less actual work, and acquire a larger house, eventually building a solid portfolio that will enable them and their spouse to retire by age sixty—when it will be time to *really* work on that golf swing.

Given this sea of banal harmony, our group generally relied on me to provide entertaining accounts of things I did on the weekends that did not involve mowing a lawn or driving kids to birthday parties. I had mentioned my plans to circumnavigate to my colleague Bob Porter, and I sensed it was only a matter of minutes before he brought it up with everyone else—not because he thought it was interesting, but because it was, well, freaky.

"To sail off into the sunset . . ." Bob began shortly after the potato skins arrived. "Every man's dream. Glenn may someday buy a boat and sail off on us."

"Well, I actually did buy the boat. Showed you pictures, remember?"

"Oh, wow, that's right. My bad. You actually bought your boat." Heads were turning. "And how much did it cost, if I may ask?"

"You may. A bit north of forty grand."

People whistled, shook their heads in bemusement. I could have reminded them I had pre-IPO stock options and did not go into debt to acquire *Serenity*.

"How big a boat are we talking about here?"

"*Serenity* is a forty-four foot cutter, thirty-eight on deck. Twenty thousand pounds displacement."

"I suppose you need a big boat," Bob announced to the

table, "To sail all the way around the world, huh?"

"You got that right."

Our manager, Peter Gibbons, piped in. "You didn't mention anything about this to me. How long is it going to take?"

"To circumnavigate? About three years."

The reaction across our table was pure shock and awe. Peter peered at me intensely, trying to figure out if I was serious or not.

"A boat at sea averages three or four knots, considering days with light winds. In a typical circumnavigation, a boat spends two or three days in port for every day at sea, maybe more. Three years is considered typical—some people take a lot longer."

Bob shot back, "What are you gonna *eat*?"

"*Serenity* has a galley with a stove, an oven, and a refrigerator," I replied. When I get a chance to install those things, I added silently. "Plus plenty of storage space. You provision in port, and cook and eat pretty much as you do in a house, except that you might go three or four weeks between trips to the market, so you're eating more canned stuff."

More whistles and chuckles of amazement. I was sort of amazed that they were amazed. Bob Porter and Peter Gibbons and the rest of my fellow software instructors—Dottie, Bert, Gene, Indra, Scott, Patrick, David and Vernon—were all serious, hard-working professionals performing an unglamorous and rather thankless job during a recession, when many people not too different from themselves were hopelessly unemployed. The concept of someone my age, far too young to retire, quitting for a three-year hiatus from the job market. . . *That* they found mind-bending.

"We'll have to talk about this further," said Peter. "When do you plan to leave?"

"Outfitting is taking longer than I planned," I told him. And that was certainly the bald truth. "So I'm not sure. But I'm shooting for October. I'm going to be recruiting crew soon and I'll entice them with a trip to Hawaii."

"Crew? You're not doing this on your own?"

"I could sail the boat on my own," I replied, leaving out the fact that single-handing scared me. "But I want to build up some experience at sea first. So I want to take one or two other people on the first leg, at least. Get them to help outfit *Serenity* so they feel committed to the boat."

"Got this all figured out, huh?" interjected Bob. "Forty thousand. You should have invested that money—the market's performing well right now."

"Money is migrating from real estate . . ." Patrick chimed in, and they were off—talking about their investment portfolios.

None of my colleagues would have thought twice about spending forty thousand dollars or more to renovate a kitchen or install a backyard pool. But those items are "investments." A necessary part of a "managed" life. Each of them had gotten married at the nominal point in their lives—mid-twenties—had two-point-one children, and planned their lives a decade or more in advance. They were disciplined—but to me, their lives lacked passion, other than the acute anticipation of moving into a larger and swankier house in a couple of years. They accepted the conventional wisdom that the appreciation on their current house would pay for an upgrade to the next—in the long run.

Did anyone explain to them that if they kept doing that, they would never see any cash—ever? It would always be tied up in the house. And give the modern real estate market, they had no guarantee of even that much.

Funny thing was, more than anyone here, I physically resembled the classic couch potato, comfy and overfed. My job spoiled me. It gave me a generous pay and benefits package, plus full-blown creature comforts no matter where I was—home or on a business trip in a hotel. Except for a few minutes during landing and takeoff, I could get anything I wanted to eat or drink at any instant. Everything I could see and touch and smell was clean and dry. At night I adjusted the air conditioning to sixty-six degrees and I didn't like it at all at sixty-eight. I slept on a soft, flat, clean, dry bed that didn't pitch or roll or jerk back and forth.

I took all these things for granted.

"They say you don't regret the things you do," I told my InfoData colleagues that night at dinner. "You regret the things you didn't do. So yeah, I'm going."

Peter gently whispered, "It's a nice dream, and we all need our dreams. But I don't think you'd leave your job for a boat. Why not take shorter sails while on vacation? My brother-in-law is a federal prosecutor in Los Angeles and that's what he and his wife do—weekend sails to Catalina. Said they would take us along sometime. Don't you think that makes a lot more sense? I mean, sailing around the world? Three years? You really don't want to do that, do you?"

I could tell by his grin it was a purely rhetorical question.

*   *   *

After a couple of months, DieselWorks sent me *some* of the parts I needed for the Farymann rebuild, but not all of them. The parts they did send me were perfect. But I could not rebuild the engine until I had all the parts. I called the owner weekly and he assured me the other parts would arrive soon. *Serenity* had sat dockside for almost six months total. If I wanted to go sailing, I would need to run the engine, and that would fill the cabin with smoke and a fine oil mist that seemed to be getting worse. Jon said *do not* run the engine until it was rebuilt.

Three months, no parts.

Four months, no parts.

I had to accept the reality that the owner could not find the parts and he was hoping I would keep waiting, on the outside chance that he would find them. I suspected my $950.00 was gone. I called and said I could not wait any longer and offered to return the parts they had sent in exchange for my $950.00. To my surprise he agreed, less the amount he had spent on shipping.

So what about that Farymann?

It was a useless chunk of iron. How much would a new engine cost, including labor? My head spun. Outfitting *Serenity* already cost over ten thousand dollars more than I had planned, and I had a long way to go: the boatyard, additional ground tackle, the autopilot, and an oven, propane system, and refrigerator. I ran some numbers, then stopped.

Maybe I couldn't do this. It was just too expensive. I had only so much money, and when it was gone, it was gone. I had sold all my stock options. I owned no real estate—just some savings accounts and CDs earning a pittance in interest. Unsure of what to do, I stopped working on the boat. Temporarily. I began catching up on my Netflix queue. I went on long hikes across the San Francisco waterfront, ignoring the hundreds of sailboats in the marina. It troubled me.

As I drifted back into my pre-boat routine, it occurred to me that I might not make the trip at all. I had tried, but in my naiveté, wound up with an exorbitant vessel that was not suitable for voyaging, and never would be. I ran through some mental images of the last year: the surveyor getting friendly with the broker. My damaging three boats in one day. The close call with the Bay Bridge tower. Ripping out hundreds of pounds of corroded gear. The extensive "to do" list and even longer "to buy" list, both growing *longer* as the months slipped by and my cash reserve dwindled.

Peter Gibbons' smirky admonishment, *You really don't want to do that, do you?*

One evening while watching reruns of *South Park,* my cell buzzed.

It was Tara Saunders, Duffy's wife. She sounded unusually cheerful. She and Duffy would be down in the Peninsula on Sunday—would I be around? Could they maybe drop by and see the progress I've been making on *Serenity?*

"We miss that boat. And you!" she said.

They came over to my apartment and I could see Duffy was in poor health. He was more stooped than normal, and pale, and he wasn't smoking. He spoke little. I hugged them both, as is the California style. We had homemade Italian manicotti and Duffy took a "beauty rest" nap on my sofa, which I assured him did no good whatsoever.

They inspected *Serenity* bow to stern. Duffy was particularly pleased with the seaworthiness of the new ports. I described all that I was going to do, inviting an order to get off my ass and do it. I pointed to the overhead (ceiling) and told them I had torn down all the old gray vinyl so I could do a better job mounting critical deck hardware such as vents, handholds, and blocks. Now the bare fiberglass was exposed, and it was ugly.

"I'm going to put up insulation with contact cement and build a wooden covering with pine slats. It'll look great."

"You don't want all that weight up there," Duffy growled.

I told them about the engine. I left unsaid whether I'd replace it. I showed them the blue hand–bearing compass I had bought during my pizza delivery days, symbolizing a promise to myself of someday owning an oceangoing yacht and embarking on a voyage.

I told them about my coworkers' laughter.

"People don't know what they're missing," Tara consoled me.

By the time they left Bair Island, I understood that Duffy was truly sick and this was likely a goodbye visit. This couple had purchased their boat a few years ago with the dream of sailing the Pacific, and it seemed that now they would never depart.

Duffy looked me in the eyes and said, "You'll do fine."

* * *

So if I was going to do this, I needed a clean-running engine that was reliable, safe, and easy to service. I talked to Jon about the cost and timeframe of putting in a new engine.

"I'm a Yanmar distributor," he told me. "Ballpark, you're looking at $11,000 with labor, and it will take a couple of weeks, assuming the 3YM30 isn't back ordered."

We installed the new engine right on the dock, without having to cut any holes in the cabin top. With the greasy old Farymann removed, I was able to completely clean and re-organize the engine room, including fabricating new electrical busses. Before Jon installed the Yanmar, I installed a new fuel line, including a top-of-the-line fuel filter and water remover that set me back $300. The transmission would not be perfectly aligned with the propeller shaft for another few months, when the boat was taken out of the water in the boatyard. Little did I know it, but I would also end up having the yard install a new shaft, a new mechanical seal, and a new bronze three-blade propeller.

The Yanmar took a big bite out of my circumnavigation fund, but I began to feel more optimistic about the voyage. I no longer had to worry about a decades-old engine going bad on me at the worst possible moment. Diesel engines are simple machines, requiring only fuel, air, and cooling water to run—no spark plugs, ignition system, or electronics—which is what makes them ideal for the marine environment. They are far more efficient than a gasoline engine, too.

I had a seventy-five gallon fuel tank. I could motor for three days and travel over five hundred miles between fill-ups. Provided I had smooth water, with no wind or waves.

Kevin called three weeks later to let me know Duffy had passed away due to lung cancer. We had a memorial service at Loch Lomond, where everyone took turns describing how they met him and recounting their favorite stories. I told them I probably would have placed *Serenity* up for sale a long time ago had it not been for Duffy. Tara gave me a long hug and wished me following seas.

Home, I began another list. I still had a *long* way to go— install equipment, construct the overhead, recruit crew, hire the boatyard to do their work. At least another six months. But there was something I wanted to do *now*, something that would not wait another damned minute. I logged into my e-mail and drafted a message to Peter Gibbons.

My years at InfoData have been professionally and personally rewarding, The time has come, however, to pursue my lifelong dream of sailing around the world. My last day with the company will be August 15.

Orphans Preferred

I could sail *Serenity* across oceans alone. Other people had done it. It's just that I preferred having a crew—*strongly* preferred. I had no delusions about my level of experience or the inherent danger of voyaging on the open sea, where, if you were alone, a broken leg or fall overboard was a death sentence. This was no suicide mission.

Who could I get to crew, and how could I find them? My strategy was to recruit at the six-month point, which was now. Two reasons: I needed as much help as possible, and if the person was willing to help me work on *Serenity* without pay, they would be vested in the boat and would be less likely to change their minds two days beforehand and leave on another yacht. Plus, this would give my prospective crew members and me a chance to get to know each other.

I needed at least one, hopefully two, and now was the time to bring them aboard.

There were hundreds of boats advertising for crew at any given time, and likely more boats than sailors. I wanted my ad to stand out but not scare anyone off. Knowing sailors, I decided to go with a humorous approach—sort of a play on both the legendary Ernest Shackleton Antarctic expedition crew advertisement and the Pony Express "Riders Wanted" poster. I placed the following ad on Craigslist and in the main Bay Area sailing publication, *Latitude 38:*

Sailing crew wanted for long, hazardous journey. Hawaii, Tahiti, Australia, possibly beyond. No pay. Poor food. Surly shipmates. Constant danger. Safe return doubtful. Orphans preferred.

The ad ended with my cell number. I deliberately left out a departure date on the assumption that more people would call to find out, and I could talk to them; even if our schedules conflicted, they might put me in touch with someone else. While I waited for my cell to buzz, I cleaned up *Serenity* and did as much as possible to make her appear like a complete, well-found vessel. It did not take long to get that first call.

A woman's voice: "Are you the skipper?"

"Yes..."

"Great. My name is Gail, and I loved your little ad there. Pretty funny."

"Thanks. Can you tell me a little..."

"How long have you been sailing?"

"Me? Oh, a little over a year. I hold..."

"Excuse me. Did you say a year? One year? Total?"

"Yes, but I've been sailing a lot..."

"Where to?"

"Uhm, Redwood to around Lock Lomond Marina, if you know where that is. I've sailed out the Gate. Around Alcatraz..."

"Wait, wait, wait. Out the Gate? How about beyond the Gate? How many ocean passages have you made?"

"None yet. But I'm a fast learner."

She laughed. My instinct told me she was more laughing with me than at me, but that may have been a self-delusion. "Hey, sorry, but I'm looking for passage with an experienced skipper."

"How much experience have *you* had?"

"Plenty. My dad sailed a Hans Christian cutter and he taught me when I was like nine. But it doesn't matter, because a boat can only have one skipper, and he or she needs to be experienced. You're going to make a thousand mistakes, and I don't want to be your guinea pig."

Wow. Pretty blunt. I guessed she was right. Did I want to maybe consider letting someone else skipper *Serenity*? That idea had no appeal to me. I felt that with all the trouble and expense and work and agony I was going through, I had *earned* the right to be skipper, provided I wasn't some kind of arrogant ass unwilling to learn as I go.

More calls came in, two or three a night for a week. Surprisingly, most of the callers were women. I had expected them to be interested in finding out more about the boat. It quickly became apparent they were more interested in *me*—my sailing résumé. And I did not have one. Some did ask about the vessel, but each told me they would get back to me and hung up.

Finally, one person agreed to check out the vessel. The next Saturday I rose early and spruced up the topsides, paying special attention to making my rope coils and everything else look salty, based on what I learned at *Spinnaker Sailing*. At ten o'clock sharp I met Kerry at the marina gate and made small talk as we walked down the dock. She was in her thirties, tanned and cute and outdoorsy. I noticed she looked me up and down and seemed disappointed with what she saw, exactly as did ninety percent of my many blind dates in the past. But this was not a date—it was business, and I decided I did not care.

We met Jon and I mentioned that he and I had just re-powered the boat with a brand new Yanmar. To my delight Jon bobbed his head at me, winked and said, "Pretty good mechanic."

But it didn't do much good. Kerry allowed me to show her the boat, asked few questions and left, shyly explaining she had many other boats to consider.

A gruff-voiced man called who was more interested in telling me about his Army Ranger experience than anything else. He had held the rank of major, now recently divorced, looking for passage to a South Seas adventure. He was happy to hear I was an ex-Navy submarine sailor. I told him I had no blue water sailing experience.

"That's not material to me, and do you know why? Character and attitude count more than experience. Always have, always will. And the fact that you're ex-military, that tells me you carry a lot more maturity and fortitude than these lousy bums who always had it easy. No matter what happens out there, your attitude will be, 'This too will pass.'"

Gruff Man made an appointment to check out the boat but he didn't show or return my calls. I dunno. Maybe he was suddenly called in from retirement for a secret mission to Afghanistan.

Many calls, no prospects. After a while, the calls dwindled and I wondered what to do. Kevin and Alek said they would put the word out and give me their recommendations, but I didn't hear back.

Late one Saturday afternoon I was wrapping up the day's work and I heard someone calling my name from the dock. I poked my head topsides: a gnomish, barrel-chested man waved. He was about sixty and covered with fine gray hairs over his entire body, which I could see quite well because he was shirtless.

"Glenn, we meet at last!" He pumped my hand firmly.

"Do I know you?"

"You do not, so let me correct that right now. My name is Bruce Morrison and I have been searching for you far and wide. You know that ad you put out? Well, I lost it! I lost your number! I remembered it was a Redwood City exchange so I went to every marina around here and asked for the fella looking for sailing crew. Tweety, your wonderful harbormaster, told me your name and sent me down here."

I saw Tweety watching closely from outside her office a couple of hundred feet away. We waved.

"You lost the number? Why didn't you just get a back issue from the library?"

"Couldn't find one!"

I could think of lots of reasons to be suspicious of Shirtless Bruce. With all the dozens and dozens of ads for crew at any given time, why get obsessed over one of them? I mean, it wasn't that funny.

"Okay, man. Let me show you the boat."

It turned out he was an old Navy man himself—somehow that did not surprise me—and he had owned his own small sloop, sailing the Atlantic seaboard and the Puget Sound for many years, doing odd jobs. Shirtless was the first of many single-handed cruisers I would meet, men (always men) who lived alone in small, Spartan vessels and lived hand-to-mouth for years at a time. Although he did not say it, he was the type of person who would claim, "I live by my wits." To me, this could truly mean, "I can't stay in one place very long before the locals get wise to me and run me out."

I like almost everyone I meet, but Shirtless Bruce was an exception. I could not figure out exactly why. It did not help that he was shedding fine gray hairs all over the interior of Serenity. And why walk around shirtless anyhow? It wasn't a particularly hot day, and there was no beach within thirty miles.

Shirtless insisted I dine with him at a nearby seafood restaurant, his treat. I knew the old "I forgot my wallet" routine, but I resigned myself to just get it over with even if I ended up paying—it would take just as long to go to pick up groceries for myself and cook. We stopped at his pickup for a shirt.

He was shocked (*shocked!*) that I did not like seafood—seafood of any kind. Not even the smell. I just didn't eat it. He called the waiter over and instructed him to bring me a single filet of salmon, grilled with a little oil, and a slice of lemon on the side.

"You are about to find out how good fish can be."

But I wouldn't have any of it. I shook my head to the waiter.

Bruce responded, "I hereby pledge it will be my mission to get you to try fish, at least once."

We finished dinner comparing notes on our Navy days. I expected him to ask when he could sail *Serenity* or at least meet other prospective crew members, but we parted ways without exchanging phone numbers. Apparently, he had rejected *me*.

The month of departure was approaching, and I had not found my crew or even arranged a boatyard week. Then I had an idea. As part of my self-education, I had been reading *Latitude 38* every month and I knew they often printed letters to the editor, which asked for advice about nautical matters, particularly ones of local interest. What if I asked them for the best way for an inexperienced skipper to recruit crew? The most they could do was laugh and throw it away.

But they did no such thing. A couple of weeks after I sent them my note, they re-printed my letter and their reply in *Latitude 38*:

I'M TOLD THAT NO ONE WILL CREW WITH ME

I would like to solicit opinions on how I, a well-prepared but inexperienced boat owner, can attract crew for extended offshore passages.

I call myself a boat owner rather than a skipper because some who may know me better than I know myself think I'm unworthy of the title. I am a 44-year-old single man who has recently bought and upgraded my first boat, a Downeast 38 cutter that I purchased a bit more than a year ago. I spent six years in the submarine service of the US Navy as a mechanic. As such, in addition to understanding watch standing, I'm quite handy with tools and have repaired or replaced every major system on my boat, and know her backwards and forwards. My time in the Navy means that I understand the importance of spare parts, contingency planning and damage control. I've spent tens of thousands of dollars beyond the purchase price of my boat to make her as safe and seaworthy as I know how.

As for sailing, my job commitments and extensive boat work have prevented me from making any offshore passages—on my boat or any other boat. So far, I've been a Bay sailor, taking my boat out on 8 to 13-hour jaunts from Redwood Creek to as far as Mile Rock, under as wide a variety of conditions as you can find on the Bay. Meanwhile, I've been hitting the books and learning as much as I can about ocean weather routing, first aid, anchoring scenarios, emergency procedures—you name it. I hold three American Sailing Association certifications.

I'm planning a South Pacific cruise—Hawaii, Tahiti, Fiji, New Zealand—starting this October. If I'm still having fun after a year, I might circumnavigate. I've begun my search for crew—I would like three, including myself— and that's where I'm having a problem. All the prospects naturally want to know how many offshore passages I've made, and to where. The answer is zero. At least not counting the Navy. Adios, prospective crew member.

The consensus seems to be that someone who has never made an offshore passage in a sailboat has absolutely no business listing himself on a skippers' list. This, it seems to some, is tantamount to false advertising. No matter that I have successfully skippered on many Bay sails, I'm told that it's different from sailing on the ocean, and therefore doesn't count. The word is, no one in their right mind would crew for me, because only a feather-merchant melon-farmer would dream of going offshore for the first time on his own boat.

I know, I know, the solution is to bring experienced people. But apparently that doesn't matter—even the experienced people seem to want a skipper who has more experience than they do. When I was a student aircraft pilot, I was legally permitted to fly solo when I had obtained a rudimentary level of knowledge and experience —even though I had only been flying for a few weeks. I know that flying is not cruising, but at a certain level the analogy is valid—you do not have to be Barnacle Bob with 37 years of sailing wisdom to be safe. We licensed pilots are taught to compensate for lack of experience by being conservative, and that mindset has made me a safe Bay sailor.

Based on the reactions I've gotten so far, I'm wondering if, come October, my choices will be to single hand or not go on my proposed voyage at all. I believe that part of the issue is that there are many more crew slots than serious prospective crew, so they have the edge and can pick and choose exactly the set of circumstances under which to voyage. I would take off from work and crew offshore with other people for a while if I could, but that's not an option. Any ideas for a well-prepared but untested skipper-wannabe in search of crew?

Glenn Damato
Serenity, Downeast 38
Redwood City

Glenn—Relax. As long as you change one thing, we'll bet a quarter that come October you won't be looking for crew, but rather picking among those who would like to crew for you.

The little thing you've got to change is your plan to sail

to Hawaii in October and then on to Tahiti. October–November is too late in the year to safely sail to Hawaii or even be likely to have a good trip. And once you're there, you're faced with thousands of nasty upwind miles in strong winds and big seas to reach French Polynesia. We've had Changes reports from both the SC 52 Kiapa and the Wylie 39 Punk Dolphin recounting this very problem. Offshore sailors quickly learn the benefits and comforts of sailing with the wind rather than into it.

There are good reasons why just about all West Coast sailors who cross the Pacific start from Mexico. And there are particularly good reasons for novice offshore sailors to do it. Sailing on the ocean is very different from sailing on flat water, no matter how strong the winds might be. Everything—standing, steering, reefing, eating, sleeping —is more challenging, and even more so at night. Sailing on the ocean is not overly difficult, but it takes getting used to.

We think the best way for people to get used to ocean sailing is gradually. For Northern California sailors who haven't had time to sail offshore prior to the start of their cruise, we highly recommend that the first sail be 15 miles down to Half Moon Bay in fair weather. This would be followed by day sails to Santa Cruz, Monterey, San Simeon and Morro Bay. From there, you could try an overnighter around Pt. Conception to Santa Barbara. With a little experience under your belt, you could follow that up with some time on the hook out at Santa Cruz Island. From there you gradually become more ambitious. This is a much better introduction to offshore sailing and cruising than just taking off across the open ocean to Hawaii.

It would be a big help if you could complete this coastal

cruising and be in San Diego at the end October in time for the start of the Baja Ha-Ha. We say this not because the Ha-Ha needs any more entries, but because many more prospective crew want to do the Ha-Ha than sail down the Mexican coast on a solitary boat. For example, had you been in San Diego two days before the starts of the last two Ha-Has, you could have easily signed on two or more eager crew for the event. There were capable-looking folks who were very disappointed not to have found berths.

The main reason you should relax is that based on what you've told us, you've got a lot going for you. At the top of the list, you seem to be honest. You describe your sailing experience accurately and don't fudge the fact you haven't been offshore. That's a great start.

The business about being a mechanic, having plenty of spare parts, and knowing your boat backwards and forwards is huge. This will score big points with potential crew who know what they should be asking about.

You've also completed ASA sailing courses, and availed yourself of other appropriate training. And, you're a pilot. This will suggest to prospective crew that you're at least reasonably intelligent and not an irresponsible yahoo. And that even though you haven't done any offshore sailing, you've experienced facing challenges with your life in the balance.

Our advice is to attend the Crew List Parties and work the Crew Lists, while continuing to present yourself just as you have to us—a guy with many things going for him, but without any offshore experience. If you do this, and change your itinerary so that you start by cruising down the coast to Mexico as most other folks do, you won't have any trouble finding crew.

Caution: Don't make the all-too-common first-timer's mistake of trying to find crew for the whole trip. Realistically, every crewing arrangement should be viewed as being nothing more than one port to the next. If the experience is good, you keep going together. If it is bad, you go your separate ways. With a little experience, you'll discover that this kind of an arrangement is of much greater importance to the boat owner than to roving crew. So trust us, if you've got a good program and are easy to get along with, you shouldn't have a problem finding crew anywhere.

Lastly, if you're at the helm of your boat, you're the skipper, no matter how little or how much experience you have. You don't, of course, want to introduce yourself as "Capt. Glenn," which would be pretentious. But you don't seem like the kind of person to do that.

I was elated with *Latitude 38's* detailed and thoughtful response. It was packed with information and I found it uplifting. For the first time in weeks I was optimistic again.

So it would be Mexico! I began drafting another ad. I didn't have to. The day *Latitude 38* published the letter my phone hardly stop ringing. By the time I got home my answering machine was almost full—and they had not published my phone number. Apparently people were getting it from 4-1-1. I had to take down names and phone numbers and put them in a spreadsheet to contact later.

One man told me he was a retired NASA engineer. That got my attention. An experienced sailor, too, and a former boat owner who had sailed the Gulf of Mexico for years. Divorced. Ex-US Marine. His dream was to circumnavigate, and at age sixty-two he figured he'd better get on with it. We made an arrangement to tour the boat that same day.

At first glance Doug Chessman did not have the look of a US Marine. He was paunchy, and about the same height as me. I didn't know the Marines accepted men that short.

He closed the door of his white Ford pickup truck and looked me over head-to-toe as he strode across the marina parking lot. As we shook hands he whacked my soft, fat belly with the back of his other hand.

"And I was worried about me."

I liked this guy already. He seemed genuinely impressed with *Serenity*. More importantly, he was interested in the systems and the work I had done so far. I showed him what was next on the hotlist: the fresh water system and tanks, bilge pumps, and some sort of permanent head. As it was, when we took *Serenity* out for a day sail, we urinated in bottles or over the side.

Once we toured the boat in detail, Doug and I sat down on the after deck and he leveled with me.

"Money is tight. I'm staying with my daughter for the time being. Are you looking for someone who can contribute to the cost of food and maintenance and moorings and such?"

"No, Doug, I'm going to cover that out of my pocket. Whenever we eat, on the boat or at a cafe, it's my dime. But you can earn your keep by helping me with the work that still needs to be done. And I mean just that—help me.

I don't expect you to put in more hours than I do. There's a lot to do I haven't even mentioned. If we're going to leave this year, we have a ton of work ahead of us."

"Glenn, this is music to my ears. This is what I live for. Did you say we're putting in a fresh water system next? When can I start?"

No question, Doug was raring to go. But there was a loose end I wanted to talk about here and now, something I had read about in a book about long distance cruising.

"One more question for you, Doug. You're interested in going the whole distance?"

"Absolutely."

"What kind of health insurance do you carry?"

Doug was perplexed for a moment. I probably should have asked in a more tactful way.

"I don't have any insurance. Like I said, money is pretty tight. I'm too young for Medicare. I take care of myself and I'm in excellent health so I don't anticipate any problems in that area."

"I see. The reason I asked is that some of the countries we'll be visiting, like French Polynesia, require that every crew member carry proof of health insurance or put up a bond."

He cast his eyes to the deck.

"Well, that's not something I could afford."

"Okay, I understand." I regretted bringing up the subject. Sure, it was a prudent thing to discuss, but let's face it: The people willing to jump aboard *Serenity* and go cruising with me were unlikely to be affluent types with all their financial ducks in a row. If they were that sort, they'd have their own boat.

"I just needed to find out in advance so we can clear

into ports."

"Is it going to be a problem?"

"No. The most important thing for both of us is to be willing and able. Now let me show you what the potable water system looks like."

We consulted about the stainless steel fresh water tanks. I needed to cut circular holes in both of them so we could inspect and clear the interior. But my efforts so far had gotten nowhere. I had drilled a few holes, which is really tough in stainless, and tried to make a cut with the Sawzall, but made no progress.

"What we need is a welder."

"Really?"

"Piece of cake, my friend."

The next day Jon cut me two perfect six-inch holes in each tank. "Call me when you have a job I'm gonna charge you for," he said.

We pumped out the old water and inspected the tanks. They had some old welding grit but otherwise they were clean. We made plans to install a massive rubber water bladder in the bilge forward of the tanks so we would have a total fresh water capacity of one hundred and sixty gallons.

Doug took the initiative with the fresh water system. He suggested that he buy all the necessary parts and hoses and hardware, per my specifications, and be reimbursed. As anyone who has ever done house or boat renovations knows, this can be one of the most time-consuming aspects of any job. We gathered the parts for the bilge pumping system, battery charger, and new fuse panel. Doug did not cotton to all the disorganized cabling and wires snaking through the boat, but he agreed it would require an inordinate amount of time and money to rewire the entire vessel.

I called the San Francisco Boatworks and set a date for haul-out. Doug located a metal fabrication shop that fabricated for me out of solid aluminum two exact reproductions of our Sitka spruce mast spreaders—for a flat $500. Doug picked them up, and we would install them when the boatyard removed the main mast and laid it down on the ground.

We agreed that a third crew member would be ideal— maybe even a fourth. *Serenity* offered plenty of interior space for four, and our at-sea routine would be easier with at least one more person. At sea, someone needs to be on watch at all times, round the clock. The boat never stops. Someone needs to be awake and on deck in order to spot shipping traffic, weather changes, and unforeseen hazards that may come in out of nowhere. If it were just Doug and myself, we would each be on watch fifty percent of the time: four hours on, four hours off for example, or six and six. I knew from my time in the Navy, this "port and starboard" watch schedule was far tougher than it sounds and it wears a body down in no time.

I began going over the spreadsheet with all the names and numbers of people who had called after the *Latitude 38* letter came out. After a couple of no answers and a couple cheerful rejections along the lines, "Thanks, but I found a berth," I came to the name of Joyce Zimmerman.

She answered immediately and came across all gung-ho. "I need to get in as much sea time as I can because I'm going up for my captain's license next year. I'm a part-time instructor at Neptune so I have the experience and the skills. It's just a matter of getting in that documented blue water time. I need thirty-four days of underway time to hit my three sixty-five, so I won't be sailing around the world, just Mexico for the season."

That was fine with me, because at the end of the season, around April, Doug and I would have more experience for the passage to Hawaii. And we'd have several months to recruit a third crew member.

Joyce asked questions about *Serenity*, one of the few people to do so over the phone. "She's a heavy displacement full-keel cutter. Forty-four feet overall with the sprit, thirty-eight on deck, and we're about to go into the yard, where we're getting a new prop, new shaft, new standing rigging. And . . ." I laid this on her with relish, "we just re-powered with a brand-spankin'-new Yanmar."

Joyce immediately came over to meet me and inspect the boat. She had the hard-edged look of a pioneer woman. I could easily envision her as the licensed captain of a commercial vessel, such as a fishing boat or a yacht for charter. Her no-nonsense demeanor contrasted with her Berkeley hippie style of dress: psychedelic tie-dyed t-shirt, faded jeans, Birkenstock sandals.

"You're just like I pictured you from the letter," she told me as we shook hands for the first time.

"Yeah. Pudgy little couch potato, right?"

"If you're going to sea, you're no couch potato. Let me ask you: Are you planning to do the Ha-Ha?"

"You mean the Baja Ha-Ha rally?" I had heard of it; a sailing rally that begins in San Diego in late October and ends at the tip of the Baja peninsula. "Well, no."

"Why the hell not?"

"Haven't really given it much thought. There's a lot of boats, right?"

"About a hundred and fifty on up."

"Yeah. Well, I didn't really picture myself sailing with a huge fleet of other boats. Not very idyllic, right?"

Joyce gave me her look. I didn't know it yet, but I would be seeing a lot of that look in the future. Imagine a cross between your second-grade teacher and your mom when she knows you have just told her a fib.

"What are you talking about, idyllic? How much more idyllic can you get than cruising Baja Mexico? There's safety in numbers, ever hear of that?"

"Sounds sort of crowded to me. Tell you what, let me look into it."

"You really should."

The thought of heading south as part of a rally did not appeal to me. For one, they put you on a schedule. The rally sets the stops you make. It sounded like a lot of red tape to me, and I couldn't think of a single major benefit.

Joyce and I toured the boat and her knowledge and experience quickly became apparent. I explained some of the special features in the running rigging and she nodded, saying, "You certainly sound like an instructor."

We went below and she moved throughout the main cabin while extending her arms in various directions, testing to see how much solid stuff was around to grab.

"You'll need more handholds," she concluded. She pointed to three spots on the overhead and the bulkhead near the companionway ladder. "Here, here, and here. Big handholds bolted down tight. Otherwise you're going to get thrown around this cabin. It can get like a roller coaster out there. You need solid handholds everywhere, otherwise somebody's gonna get hurt, and it ain't gonna be me."

We moved forward.

"You don't even have a head?"

"That's one of the jobs Doug and I are going to accomplish over the next few weeks."

"You better get going. You told me you're going to put in an autopilot, a refrigerator, a stove, a propane system, a chartplotter, a radar . . . How many guys you have working with you, ten?"

"Doug and I are pretty efficient. We do the work of ten ordinary men."

We moved into the forward cabin and I repositioned myself to show Joyce the storage lockers port and starboard. She swiftly and smoothly maneuvered herself so that I was not between her and the one door to the tiny cabin. Fair enough; I was a man she had just met, and she wanted to make sure I didn't try any maneuvers of my own. In truth, sex and romance weren't on my mind. Joyce was much older than me, fifty-five I would learn later. She had lived in San Francisco and Berkeley her entire adult life, and I could imagine that back in the 1970s, with her vibrant red hair and sky-blue eyes, she must have been stunning.

We went topside. "I love your boat," Joyce told me. "I much prefer a heavy, solid boat over these featherweight Hunters and crap people sail. You'll see what I mean when you get out there. Put those handholds in, and meanwhile, I will think about it and let you know."

Joyce left as stridently as she arrived, sandals click-clacking across the wooden dock.

* * *

Less than twenty-four hours later, my cell buzzed and it was Joyce.

"You got those handholds in?"

"Ah, no, but I plan to shortly. It's a good idea."

"Get them in. Second question. I found out I have a berth with a couple of dear friends of mine and their boat is doing the Ha-Ha. All things considered I prefer your boat because it's more solid and nowhere near as crowded and I won't have to listen to Larry's damn country music all day and night. Wait a minute. You're not going to play any cowboy songs, are you?"

"Absolutely not."

"But I will put up with his damn music if I need to because he's doing the Ha-Ha. Are you willing to do the Ha-Ha?"

I thought fast. Joyce had tons of knowledge and experience. I wanted her on board *Serenity*. Hell, she may even be right about this rally thing.

"I've been thinking about that. I think it makes a lot of sense. The answer is yes, *Serenity* will join the Baja Ha-Ha."

"Okay, we got a deal."

"Now let me ask you something. Do you have any sort of special diet—vegetarian, for example?"

Silence. I could almost feel that look coming through the cell.

"No. Why did you ask?"

"Oh, I just wanted to make sure . . . just wanted to see if you were a vegetarian or vegan or anything like that."

I could hear her snort through the phone.

"So you're on board?"

"I just told you I was."

"Come on over sometime this weekend and meet Doug. Did I mention that he's a retired space shuttle engineer and a mechanical genius?"

"You did. About four times. It doesn't matter. Once we're out there for a while we're all going to hate each other."

Now I had a crew of two—both experienced sailors, one highly capable technically and the other a part-time instructor at Neptune, one of those posh yuppie sailing schools near Tiburon. My attitude about this nascent adventure soared, and I began to believe, deep down, we were genuinely going to somehow pull it off.

Part II

BREAKING OUT

State of Grace

What's a boat without a head? Sailors need a place to do their business. Thing is, on a sailboat, there's no easy or cheap or foolproof way to accommodate the call of nature.

Most marine toilets are plastic bowls where the water and waste are pumped in and out—and I do mean *pumped*, up and down, with a hand pump. Your biological refuse goes through a plastic hose either directly overboard, or into a plastic holding tank that must be used when you are within three miles of land.

Sounds straightforward. Yet marine heads have earned a well-deserved reputation of being fragile, smelly, unreliable, and downright ornery. The hand pump and hoses often clog with toilet paper or fecal matter or both, requiring disassembly. Sound nice? In port, the waste accumulates in the holding tank, which sooner or later has to be pumped out. This requires moving the boat to a marina pump-out station or calling a service, which costs money. And the holding tank usually reeks. The plastic cannot keep the odor at bay, especially in tropical warmth.

Other systems are available, such as "macerator" models that chop it all up, but they're expensive, heavy, have a huge footprint, and use copious amounts of electricity.

If you think about it, putting a big tank of raw sewage

inside your boat and sailing around with it sloshing back and forth is a little loopy. I figured there had to be a better way, and after some searching I found it.

I brought Joyce and Doug aboard *Serenity* and beckoned them to follow me below.

"Know how sailboat heads reek to high heaven? Get clogged and break down?"

"Some of them," replied Joyce.

"Did you put a holding tank in the forepeak like you said?" asked Doug.

I turned and stopped, blocking them from the forward cabin until I was ready to unveil the big surprise.

"We're not going to have a holding tank at all."

Joyce shook her head. "What are you talking about?"

"We're not going to haul around a giant tank of crap and piss so it can rot away and stink up the boat."

"Why not? Everyone else does."

"I read about something new in *Practical Sailor* magazine. They recommended it as a viable solution as a marine toilet. Other sailors have blogged about it and . . ."

Joyce shoved me aside and yanked open the door to the head. She gawked, open-mouthed, unable to contemplate exactly what she was looking at.

"It's a composting head. It will not clog, ever. No hoses, no pumps, no valves, no tanks. Takes up less space, it's lighter, and people who have used one say there is very little smell."

Joyce was speechless. Doug examined the device with curiosity, opened the lid, turned the metal crank jutting from the side.

"I get it. We crap, it drops to the bottom container there, and it composts."

Joyce rested her chin on her hand. "And *that's* not gonna stink?"

"No, it will not. Holding tanks and hoses stink because the waste decomposes anaerobically, without air. With a composting head, you put some peat moss in the bottom here." I uncovered the round plastic base and showed them the brown, crumbly stuff, which resembled topsoil. "Every time you go, you give the crank two turns. That mixes and aerates everything." I stroked the plastic air vent running from the base to the overhead. "It's vented so the air flow is going outward, so what little smell there is, goes outside. The company that makes it calls it the AirHead."

"Maybe they're talking about their customers," Joyce mumbled.

"This is basically a good old-fashioned outhouse." Doug pointed out. "For a boat."

"And you urinate into there, too?" Joyce asked.

"Well, no . . ." I opened the front section of the AirHead to reveal a sort of plastic jug jutting from the front of the unit like a pregnant belly.

"You're not gonna tell me . . ."

"The way it works is, the bowl has a special rim that direct urine into this container. We empty the container over the side, or into a marina toilet. Piss and water have to be kept out of the peat. The whole point is to dry out the solid waste. The peat increases the surface area so it dries fast, and dried crap takes up a lot less volume than fresh."

Joyce snickered. "Whoever designed that didn't know a thing about the female anatomy."

"Oh, it works with females."

I could tell from his impish grin Doug was intrigued with the concept, albeit not entirely convinced. "We'll find out quick enough when we start using it."

"I been using it for a week. Every morning I've been tramping out here with my newspaper and making a deposit. Smell anything?"

Doug leaned forward, sniffed. "Nothing much."

"Damn right. Just dirt. People say this thing works like a top. Turns crap into dirt real fast. Practically no smell."

"But we gotta empty the piss bottle."

"Off going watch will be responsible for that."

Doug positioned himself atop the unit. "So you make your deposit just like this, no water or nothing?"

"Well, you need these."

I opened a cabinet and pulled out a stack of coffee filters.

"You put one of these in first. You do your business in the filter. Then open the trap door and it drops down into the base. You give the crank handle two turns."

Silence, then Joyce laughed out loud. It wasn't a happy laugh.

"You want us to crap into coffee filters?"

"Well, yeah. Keeps the doo doo from sticking to the sides of the bowl. It's not a big deal."

Doug fingered the filters as if he had never seen one before. "I'll give you this much. You're willing to try new things. But maybe that plywood holding tank you were telling me about disturbed you more than you think."

"Worse comes to worst," Joyce said, "we'll all be going into a bucket. Not like I haven't done it before."

It looked like they were buying it. Sure, I could have asked for their opinions *before* purchasing and installing the AirHead. But I really, truly felt that the benefits overwhelmed the potential drawbacks. As they say, it's easier to obtain forgiveness than permission.

The notion of a composting toilet on a sailboat is not a bad idea, and it has a lot of potential when you consider that the alternatives are even more repulsive. As time would reveal, there were still a few kinks to work out. For example, the designer of the AirHead did not anticipate two things: (1) crew members who drink about three gallons of hot tea per hour, and (2) a starboard tack, which makes the boat—and the AirHead—lean sharply leftward with the wind.

On a foggy Saturday morning, Doug and I motored *Serenity* to the San Francisco Boatworks and watched as a mobile crane lifted her from the water and set her atop a pair of wooden supports. Out of her element, *Serenity* appeared as helpless and vulnerable as a beached whale. The boat had last been hauled for her pre-purchase inspection two years ago, and now, a boatyard worker immediately started his work with a high pressure hose to wash the accumulated seaweed and barnacles off the hull.

The one week we planned to spend in the boatyard was crucial for a late October departure. Previously, I planned to sail from the Bay "after the hurricane season," but because I had promised Joyce we would enter the Baja Ha-Ha rally, we were now on a *schedule*. My last day at InfoData was August 15. I gave my landlord notice that I would leave my apartment September 30. I had planned to live aboard *Serenity* for a month or two, either anchored off Sausalito or at a marina if I could find one that allowed it; Bair Island permitted sleeping aboard only on weekends.

The Baja Ha-Ha left San Diego on October 29. We had to be there before that date, no matter what—those were the conditions Joyce had set forth in exchange for her presence aboard *Serenity* and the hence the benefit of her experience. San Francisco Bay to San Diego—how far was that in sailing miles, which are never a straight-line distance? If it was five hundred nautical miles, I figured a five-day passage in a heavy displacement boat, possibly six or seven. Then we'd need time in San Diego. The Ha-Ha rally is a major social event among many West Coast sailors. Joyce needed to attend two parties before the rally departed. She was looking to network with next year in mind, when she would be looking for a job as a new-minted commercial captain.

Serenity had five months to get ready. If you've ever outfitted a cruising sailboat, you'll know that's a squeeze. For one, I was still working full-time at InfoData, including business trips and a mandatory, weeklong company meeting. Second, there was Zeno. Maybe you've heard of Zeno's Paradox. Zeno was an ancient Greek philosopher who imagined what would happen if the fastest runner in Greece ran a race against a tortoise. Suppose the tortoise convinced the runner that before he ran even one foot, he would first have to run half of that distance—six inches. But before he could cover six inches of distance, he had to move half of *that* distance, three inches. But in order to move three inches . . .

You get the picture. The tortoise convinced the poor runner that in order to move *any* distance, no matter how small, he would have to *first* cover half of that distance. No matter what, there would always be a smaller distance to be covered first, and since it is logically impossible to complete any given task if there always remains an essential task that must be accomplished first, well, you hardly ever do anything. The runner could not move at all. The tortoise won the race.

Zeno was probably a boat owner.

Every boat work project, no matter how minor, is preceded by many tasks that must be finished first. Each of those tasks is preceded by smaller tasks, all of which must be accomplished first. Each of *those* tasks...

I assigned Doug the project of installing our large electric bilge pump. Before it was installed, we needed to connect and run the discharge hose. Before we did that, we needed to purchase the hose and hose clamps. Before we did that, we would research the correct type of hose to use, and test to see whether the hull fitting requires an adapter. And, we needed to measure the exact run distance to ensure we buy enough hose without wasting money. Then, we'd need to make the purchases. Before we did that we'd need to drive to West Marine. But before *that* we needed to hit the john and check our e-mail.

Even the most straightforward-seeming jobs, which I would have guesstimated as three hours of work, tops, blossomed into scores of sub-tasks that ate up the entire day and spilled well into the next. I looked at the list of jobs we needed to accomplish by the middle of October. Despite my taking vacation time for the week and Doug pledging to assist me for seven consecutive days sunrise to sundown, we would not finish, not even close.

I sat down with Doug at the chart table and looked him in the eye.

"I want you to know it's been a pleasure working with you..."

A dark mist of disappointment swept over the man's face.

"No, no, Doug, it's not like we're parting ways or anything. I'm just trying to say you've done an outstanding job and working with you totally rocks. I wanted to get that straight between us before I talk to you about the future."

"Okay."

I spread out the job list. Doug mumbled something like, "Hurmph."

"These are jobs we need to complete by October, and everything from here on up is a boatyard event. We need to get the cables for the new radar and running lights routed through the mast while they have the mast lying on the ground."

"Yeah. And attach the spreaders."

"And the new blocks. Then we have the depth transducer. The radio ground plate. The bilge pump. The chain plates, before they get the mast back up. And so on. Then, over the next few months, install solar panels, a wind turbine, single sideband radio, autopilot, stove, propane system and tanks, refrigeration system, water generator, water bladder, forward hatch, two new anchors and tackle, the new cushions and covers... Well, we're not gonna make it. Not at the rate we've been going."

"I know it."

"But we can, if we make a couple of basic changes. I think we should work independently."

I could see by the look in his eye he did not cotton to that idea.

"I think if we work independently we can get much more accomplished in each day."

"Some of these job require two people…"

"Sure, for a short period of time, so we'll help each other when we need to, absolutely. But let's face it, most of what we do is one-man stuff."

I didn't want to say it directly, but most of the time we spent talking or watching each other work. We were practically a two-man Department of Highway Maintenance.

Doug sort of grimaced and sighed. "I can see what you mean."

I knew that Doug was on this adventure in part for the human company. In many ways he was like me: a physically small man, no girlfriend, probably not too good with the ladies, didn't follow sports, wasn't a drinking man or an athlete. Women go shopping with each other, but what are men like us supposed to do? We'd been working together and developing mutual respect, and now, I was driving a wedge into a friendly working relationship.

I didn't see any other way.

"Once we get caught up, we'll be working always as a team," I told him. "And I look forward to that. One other thing we both need to do. Focus on efficiency. Not get caught up in, well, perfectionism."

Doug knew what I meant. He did great work, sometimes *too* great, when good-enough was all *Serenity* needed. Yesterday we built a wooden mounting base for the mast's new anchor light. The base was just a block of wood, but one side had to curve to fit flush with the mast. Also, it needed four holes to fit the holes already in the mast, and its surface needed to be precisely flat so the light would shine horizontally and not slightly upwards or downwards.

When we were finished and the six-inch block of wood was coated with epoxy for preservation, it was a sight to behold. In fact, it was mathematically *perfect*.

But it had taken us the entire day.

"Yeah, all right, let's do crappy work."

"That's not what I'm saying. I'm saying let's not spend time on appearances, on qualities that don't affect safety or function. For example, today you're going to install the big bilge pump. We agreed on how to do it—mount it on that two-by-four and mount the top of that onto another piece of wood bolted to the inside of the sink cabinet. But when you attach that piece, just epoxy it into place with the filler like I showed you. Don't worry about craftsmanship—no one is going to see it. Just make it *strong* so it won't come apart."

Doug nodded. He did not like this approach, but the tyranny of the calendar gave us no choice.

We finished our boatyard tasks without a minute to spare. While the mast was down I removed all the standing rigging (steel cables and turnbuckles that keep the mast in place against the wind) and brought it to a rigging shop in Alameda so they could duplicate everything. The rigging was twenty-five years old and past its service life for blue water sailing, where gales and even routine weather can subject the mast to tremendous forces. A sailboat demasted at sea is usually a total loss—you might as well sink it, because towing a boat thousands of miles is not financially viable.

The boatyard did admirable work, with one exception. I gave the standing rigging a 360-degree visual inspection and felt each cable for tension. Then I went into the office and told them, "The starboard upper is not all the way in the spreader." They fixed it right away, probably thinking I was some sort of salty sea dog to notice this problem and express it so exactly. The boatyard also gave us a new prop and shaft, and recommended I have the rudder replaced because the extreme top was delaminating. I declined, and instead simply filled it with epoxy resin.

On Wednesday afternoon Doug and I took a break for a couple of hours to swing by the Alameda Boat Show. We were mostly interested in gear. Doug sorely desired to have worldwide Internet access installed aboard *Serenity*, so we could blog our passages in near real time. We talked about it while driving across the Oakland Bay Bridge.

"I looked into it, and it costs thousands of dollars for the hardware and a couple of hundred dollars a month for the subscription. There are data transfer limits, and they're quite low. Plus, the speed is about the same as a modem. It's not like the Wi-Fi at Starbucks."

"I went on a cruise with my son last year," Doug replied. "And the ship had Internet and it was pretty fast."

"Well sure. That's on a huge ship with massive antennas and tons of money from all those tickets people pay for. Me, I'm no Rockefeller. I dropped about half of my total cash on the boat so far. It's going to cost around seventy thousand dollars, all told, to sail around the world in three years, assuming no major breakdowns. And I'm going to need some money to get settled once we get back —you know, buy a car, rent an apartment, get some furniture, find a job. I don't think it's wise to take on a major expense unless it's a safety requirement."

"You don't think having e-mail would make us safer?"

"Doug. Dude. Come on. I spent forty-five hundred on a single-sideband radio and almost another thousand on the antennae insulators and ground plate. That's our long distance communication line. We can send an international mayday, get medical advice, weather maps . . ."

"I just think it would be nice to have e-mail at sea."

"I agree, but I'm not made of money. We can try sending sailmail with my laptop and the SSB."

We went straight to the boat show exhibit hall. The first equipment we checked out was the "Portland Pudgy," a fairly new type of eight-foot dinghy. Every cruising sailboat needs some sort of tender craft, a ferry to take crew and supplies back and forth between the anchored boat and land. Many cruisers use inflatable Zodiac rafts and an outboard, which becomes the cruising families' minivan. But we were not a family, and we wanted something simpler that we could row. "Hard" dinghies made of wood or fiberglass had a reputation for being far more durable than the best rubber inflatables, and if it were row-able, we would not need to store an outboard and gasoline on board. Joyce concurred with this approach.

The Portland Pudgy was different from the other hard dinks on the market. I discovered a review in *Practical Sailor* magazine and it struck me as a well-thought-out product. It was made from rotomolded polyethylene and it was unsinkable: The entire hull is double and the bottom filled with closed-cell foam so a hole won't flood the dink. The sides were divided into waterproof storage compartments. Based on the durable construction and 557-pound capacity, it could be used as a life raft for three or four adults (a tight fit but better than drowning). The company sold a sailing kit with a mast and sail and rudder, and special equipment to allow use of the Pudgy as a life raft: a boarding ladder, a canopy, and a sea anchor. It even had a built-in compass and lighting system.

You can't sail a rubber raft.

We both wanted to see a real Portland Pudgy before I bought one. The main downside was that it cost three times the price of a basic eight-foot fiberglass dink. But it could double as a life raft, which costs $6,000. Nevertheless, I knew what Doug was thinking: For the price difference between a Pudgy and a regular dink, we could have Internet.

I ordered one on the spot, in international yellow.

Doug announced, "We'll call it Ducky. Reminds me of one of those yellow floating bathtub ducks."

On the way out of the boat show, we spotted a booth full of books. Standing at it were Lin and Larry Pardey, selling their world-renowned guides and tapes on safe and economical long-distance cruising. With his white beard, Larry looked exactly like Ernest Hemingway. I shook his hand and told him, "I really enjoyed *The Self Sufficient Sailor* and I got a tremendous amount of useful information out of it. Your books have a lot more practical value than the others I've come across."

He beamed at me and said, "I like you."

The boatyard presented me with a five-figure bill, and after I paid it, the crane lowered *Serenity* back into the water. The bottom of our hull had been completely cleaned, painted, and given two coats of anti-foul paint, which would reduce the growth of barnacles and weed for about two years.

Doug and I boarded and took half an hour searching for any leaks from the spots where work was performed: the depth sounder, the SSB ground plate, and the new mechanical shaft seal. When we were satisfied that *Serenity* was secured for sea, we started the diesel and motored back to Bair Island. After a grueling week of boat work, the three-hour trip in the sunshine was a welcome respite.

We docked and went over our work plan for the coming week: continue installing insulation and wood paneling on the interior overhead, install the main solar panel across the stern davits, and begin work on the propane system and the new forward hatch to replace a weak wooden and Plexiglas hatch. By that evening, I noticed a new voice-mail on my cell, from Joyce. Strange, I thought; she could have reached me directly at any time during that day.

Suspecting something was amiss, I played the message.

"Glenn, this is Joyce. I'm afraid I have some bad news. A family emergency has come up and I might have to cancel all my plans to cruise in Mexico this fall. I'm really sorry. It's a bummer for you and me both. It's a long story but my damn sister is screwing with me on an inheritance we're supposed to get from our aunt, so I don't think it's smart for me to leave the States for at least a few months. This is all still up in the air so I will keep you posted. Bye."

Huh. Didn't make a lot of sense. Our cruise was five months away, so I didn't understand how she could be so predictive about her ability to crew. I knew I wouldn't get much sleep that night unless I ironed this out, so I called back.

"Like I told you," she said, "it's up in the air. I just do not know. If she continues to screw with me, I probably can't go. I just wanted to let you know what was up sooner rather than later."

"I appreciate that, and I'm not trying to be nosy about your family business, but you seemed pretty definitive in your message. So, do I need to replace you?"

She sidestepped the question. "You're going to need to recruit one other crew anyhow, and she needs to be a female."

"We have three..."

"Which ain't enough. Trust me, you want four or more,

in case somebody gets incapacitated. You need to find us another crew member anyhow, and I'll tell you right now, I'm not going to be on a boat where I am outnumbered three men against me, so she needs to be female."

"Yeah. Well, I might just get two then."

"Whatever. And I been thinking. I have a couple more requirements before we leave. You got something to write with? Our sail inventory doesn't cut it. We need a big genoa, a storm jib, and a working jib to replace that Yankee up there now, which won't drive your boat close-hauled in any kind of sea. Last but not least, a lightweight spinnaker."

"I don't even know how to use a spinnaker."

"Then learn, doo-doo head. I have a friend who loves to fly his spinnaker every chance he gets. He'll give you a lesson if I ask him to, for free. I mean, you have a good spinnaker pole, so why the hell not get a spinnaker?"

"Yeah, yeah, yeah…" My head was spinning.

"One more thing. I want you to get at least some blue-water experience as crew before you take that boat through the Gate as skipper."

"Joyce, we have so much work to do…"

"Will you shut up for a minute? You can spare one weekend, can't you? I know students at Neptune who need crew for their bareboat charter certification practical. Two days out. You gotta pay your share of the rental and the food, but it will be two days of experience more than nothing."

"Okay. I'll do it. But I need your help in getting that fourth crew on board, especially if it *must* be a female of the species, per your requirements. It will be a lot easier for you to do it than me. You're a girl, too, right? Put an ad on Craigslist."

"You do what I told you, keep your end of the bargain, and I'll find our fourth."

"Preferably somebody who wants to do a South Pacific trip. Big tits, too. Can you write that down?"

I had told Peter Gibbons my last day at InfoData would be August 15, and that day arrived as any other. I could scarcely believe it. I taught my last software class, and cleaned out my cubicle. I had an appointment to take my laptop up to Human Resources at 2:00 for my final interview and final paycheck.

Just before lunch, I wrote an e-mail with the subject line, "Goodbye InfoData Friends" and addressed it to the mailing list for the entire company. Here is the body of the message:

Life is all about new challenges, and for me it is time to pursue a different kind of challenge.

I'm not going to work for some other company. There's no other company I'd rather work for. Instead, I am embarking on an adventure—a circumnavigation of the world on my own sailboat. This has been a lifelong goal for me, and I am humbled to have the opportunity.

I know lots of tech workers in the Bay Area, and after listening to them, I can confidently say that we have a special place here at InfoData. It's been my good fortune to be on the InfoData team and to work with the people here—truly among the smartest and coolest I have ever had the pleasure of knowing. Thank you all for allowing me to contribute in my own way, for helping me learn, for forgiving my mistakes, and for tolerating my idiosyncrasies over the past six years.

Don't let anyone tell you that what you want to do is "unrealistic." You and your actions determine what becomes real and what remains fantasy.

God bless you all and may your wildest dreams come true.

Glenn Damato

There weren't many people to send me off that day because, given the nature of our department, my colleagues were on the road at customer sites teaching classes. I expected maybe a dozen "so long old chap, see ya" responses to my note. That didn't happen. I received over a hundred e-mails that last afternoon, most from people I had never met face-to-face. Many asked for a regular update on the journey. Some asked if they could come along.

And just like that, I joined the ranks of the unemployed.

A week before school started and family vacation season officially ended, my younger brother Paul and his family visited me in California. I believe they wondered if this would be the last time they saw me alive.

Paul and Katie had been married for fifteen years and had three boys: Tyler, thirteen, Brian, eleven, and Chris, seven. Paul had not attended college but he and his wife strove to be upwardly mobile. They had a McMansion in suburban Virginia Beach and a couple of smaller rental properties. An air conditioning technician by trade, Paul ran his own small business with about a dozen employees. Time was in short supply, and from my perspective, he rarely did anything for fun.

"My kids are my fun," he told me once. "I take Tyler to football practice. I take Brian to a Boy Scout meeting. There. That's my fun."

No question about it: a day sail aboard *Serenity* was in order. I checked the tide tables and identified the date in late August we could leave Bair Island with the ebb flow shortly after sunrise and return with the flood current before dark. Conditions permitting, we could sail under the Golden Gate Bridge at slack water.

Both Doug and Joyce were available to crew on that date. The only thing that worried me was the possibility of seven-year-old Chris slipping under the lifelines around the edge of the deck and going overboard. I had planned to put in port and starboard jacklines anyhow, so Doug picked up the hardware and we sank four large, industrial-strength padeyes into the deck, fore and aft. Then we ran two lengths of nylon webbing (a strong ribbon) between the pad eyes and tied them off *tight*. I bought one child-sized and four adult-sized harnesses and tethers that would clip to the jacklines while at sea. The idea was to prevent anyone from falling overboard. If that happened, the rest of the crew might be belowdecks and no one would know you're gone.

Not a pleasant way to spend a vacation.

Paul's family arrived and we did the requisite things when East Coasters visit the Bay Area: took the Alcatraz tour, rode the San Francisco cable cars, stuffed ourselves on Mandarin food in Chinatown.

The next day, I showed them the boat.

Paul and Katie both wore a look that melded disappointment and worry. I think they expected a sleek, sparkling white and chrome yacht where a butler would serve them wine and cheese. *Serenity* was a working blue-water sailboat, decades old and with the attendant dings and scratches. The boatyard had improved her seaworthiness, but did scant for her appearance, which didn't bother any of her crew but gave these landlubbers pause.

I methodically showed Tyler and Brian the proper way to board and disembark from a yacht tied to a slip.

"Put one hand I here and grab this cable," I said, clutching the starboard outer stay. "Then put one leg on deck and pull yourself up like this…"

Once on deck, I said, "When you want to get off the boat, do not jump. I'm serious—do not jump off onto the dock because your foot could easily get caught on something." I pointed out the edge of the gunwale. "If that happens, there is *nothing* for you to grab on to. You will fall forward and your face is gonna *smack* into the cement. You can break your nose, your jaw, lose some teeth, dislocate your shoulder or break your arm. So don't jump. Instead, grab this stay, put one foot on the dock, then the other foot."

I demonstrated twice.

Everyone got a quick tour belowdecks, including the AirHead, which to my surprise did not elicit any reaction from the adults. A few minutes later I found out why. Paul took me aside on the dock and said, "I know you had your heart set on taking us sailing, but Katie and I discussed it and we're going to have to call it off. Thirteen hours is just too long. What if the kids get sick?"

"You're so full of shit, bro. You just don't want to see them sad because they're missing their morning cartoons. Look, we're going, all of us, and that's the end of that."

He shook his head. "It's too dangerous. Too far."

"It's about time you all did something you haven't done a thousand times. I suppose you plan on taking the kids to a theme park instead."

"Well, yeah."

"Forget it. I'm getting you all up at six sharp tomorrow. We're sailing under the Gate. You're going to love it."

I went to talk to Katie. As I suspected, she was moderately and cautiously in favor of the sail rather than another day at a theme park. I showed her the safety harness I bought for Chris and that sealed the deal.

As we left, Brian took a *flying jump* from the deck to the dock.

We left the dock at the crack of dawn. Doug, Joyce, and I got *Serenity* underway like a crackerjack team of sailors. We motored down the Redwood City channel and to our surprise, the wind came up.

"We can raise sail instead of running the stinkpot!" exclaimed Joyce. "Oh, happy day!"

I assigned Tyler and Brian straightforward tasks to help us raise the mainsail and pull the jib out of the roller. With Joyce at the helm, *Serenity* went on a beam reach and I cut the diesel.

Ten minutes later, the wind died.

"This is common in this part of the Bay this time of the

day," I explained. We lowered sail and I asked Doug to start the engine. I wanted to get him used to doing it on his own because Jon had instructed us that it was best to press the starting button as briefly as possible. Holding it down could burn out the starter or shorten its life.

Doug pressed the button but I don't think he held it down long enough. The diesel rumbled but did not start.

"Try it again. Hold it down a bit longer."

Doug pressed the button. Nothing.

"Uhm, it's not working."

This got everyone's undivided attention, pronto: Joyce, Paul, and Katie.

I stepped into the cockpit and pressed the button. There was no response from the engine. I did hear a slight "click" coming from the engine room.

"Engine's dead," I announced. "I'm going to go see what's up."

I already knew pretty much what was going on. Poor Doug looked like a puppy who pissed the carpet. He called after me, "I'm sorry, Glenn."

Without an engine we would have to call for a tow back to the dock. The day was done.

"Don't worry about it, Doug."

I postulated that the started fuse had popped. How did I know this? A diesel is a simple machine that needs only three things to start: fuel, air, and electricity to turn it over the first few revolutions. A diesel does not even have an ignition system or spark plugs. The compression ignites the fuel every stroke.

Our diesel was just running ten minutes ago. It definitely had a supply of fuel and air. The fact that it did not turn over proved the starter was not working. It was either burned out or it was not getting electricity. I doubted one button press could burn it out.

I looked at the fuse and it was blown. This was a huge fuse, a hundred amps, and I had meant to get some spares but we had none yet. So I had two choices: call for a tow, or bypass the fuse. I guessed that it had blown because Doug held the button down so briefly that the starter did not turn at all, and he had tried two or three times when it only looked like once.

After I bridged the fuse with a thick cable the engine started. I showed Doug that the button had to be held down for a second or two until the engine caught, then released immediately.

Later, he took me aside in private and said, "Joyce was really impressed how you fixed the engine."

"Oh, it was nothing. The engine wasn't broken."

"Regardless, she was blown away with how fast you found the problem and got it started. Nice going, skipper."

We sailed under the Golden Gate Bridge. It was a gorgeous, breezy, sun-drenched day on the Bay, just peppy enough to make for exciting sailing. As we approached the Gate on a close reach, I beckoned for Tyler to come into the cockpit. The tall, lanky thirteen year old had never sailed a boat—hadn't done anything, really, except play video games and supervised sports.

"Tyler. You're going to take the helm. I'll show you how to do it." His face brightened. I pointed at the deep red bridge that was almost upon us.

"Are you man enough to sail under that bridge?"

He grinned, nodded and took the wheel. I noticed

Joyce grimacing and shaking her head. I had been unjustly identified as a male chauvinist.

We docked smoothly at dusk, and my crew expertly tied us up and battened down our vessel. Paul and Katie expressed their thanks for what they felt was a perfect day. Everyone had relaxed, saw the sights, learned a bit about what makes a sailboat tick. We ended the day by enjoying a leisurely and well-deserved Italian dinner at a local bistro.

"Good luck finding yourself." Paul told me over his cappuccino.

"Bro, I'm not doing this to find myself," I answered back, a bit more loose-lipped than usual thanks to a couple of glasses of merlot. "I'm doing it to become."

"Become what?"

"Damned if I know. I'll find out when it happens."

Shakedown

I had no idea that joining a sailing rally involved so much paperwork.

The Baja Ha-Ha is an annual event that starts in San Diego and ends at Cabo San Lucas, Mexico, the southern tip of the Baja Peninsula. Each October, a couple of hundred boats make the 750-mile trip. The pace is leisurely, allowing the fleet to anchor at two fishing villages along the way, and take a total of twelve days to complete the trip. The Rally Committee organizes the boats into classes, and each class has a first, second, and third place. The rally is for fun, though, not competition. Every boat that doesn't come in first or second ends up "tied for third" with all the others.

I downloaded a "Skipper's Waiver" form, which had to be signed and delivered with the $375 entry fee by September 10. It was a dense, two-page document headlined, "Assumption of Risks, Waiver, Release and Indemnity Agreement—This form is a contract." It was essentially a promise that your boat was safe and seaworthy and well equipped, and in a worst-case scenario, a promise not to sue anyone associated with the rally, particularly not *Latitude 38*.

The Frequently Asked Questions form was an entertaining read. Question *numero uno* was: "Is the Ha-Ha a good event for novice skippers to try their hands at ocean sailing?"

The answer given: "No. The Ha-Ha is for experienced sailors who would have been willing to sail from San Diego to Cabo San Lucas on their own, anyway. The Ha-Ha is definitely not an offshore babysitting or hand-holding service."

Every one of the nine answers ended with the following sentence:

"The Ha-Ha is a high risk activity open only to those gladly willing to risk injury and death in the pursuit of adventure."

Sounded good to me. I signed the form and sent it off.

Before we even contemplated taking *Serenity* beyond the Gate and into the open sea, Doug and I had plenty of work to finish. Much of it we hadn't even started.

Every cruising boat with a limited number of crew needs some sort of autopilot—a means for the boat to steer itself on a pre-selected magnetic course without someone standing at the wheel. It's theoretically possible for the person on watch to hand steer, but in reality, doing so is exhausting, and it means the watchstander is going to need help doing everything else, such as every sail trim and log entry. In effect, everyone is on watch all the time. Not gonna work.

Trouble was, sailboat autopilots had even worse reputations for mechanical breakdown and general unreliability than marine heads. Some cruisers bring two complete units—and they cost big bucks. I Googled this subject for months and found the following: Most of the ordinary autopilots sold by the big marine hardware chain stores are cheaply constructed with plastic gears and other marginal parts intended to jack up the per-unit profit. I could use a windvane instead, which is a bulky steel construction that attaches to your stern and steers the boat relative to the wind—but they, too, are pricey and prone to failure, and only work when there is relative wind.

My other option was to buy a commercial autopilot, which tended to be hydraulic rather than use gears and pinions. These units were intended to steer large metal boats, anywhere from fishing trawlers to cruise ships, and most of them were bulky, heavy, and expensive—but *reliable*. Fortunately, there was a small company near Seattle that manufactured and sold commercial-grade hydraulic autopilots in a size suitable for sailboats in the forty- to fifty-foot range: W-H Autopilots. They cost two to three times the price of a consumer-grade plastic system, but after discussing it with Doug, we agreed it would be a sound investment. We might end up crossing the Pacific with just the two of us on board, and sailing two thousand miles from land with a broken autopilot is no way to live.

Besides the price, there was a catch: "Professional" installation was required. For the price, you got the control unit, an electronic compass, and a hydraulic cylinder, pump, accumulator, and sensing mechanism so the unit could track the rudder's position. That's it. It was up to us to figure out how to install and test the system, and it didn't look too tolerant of errors.

"This is my cup of tea," Doug told me while looking over the W-H supplied schematics. "I built hydraulic systems at NASA."

"Can you make the hoses?" I asked. "They don't give

you the hoses to connect the components."

"Hmm. That, I haven't done but I have a feel for what's involved. Do they at least give us the lengths?"

"No, only the fitting specs. The lengths will depend on exactly where we mount the components."

The hydraulic cylinder needed to be *firmly* bolted to a solid part of the boat, to brace against hundreds of pounds of force it may generate to hold the rudder in place against heavy seas. We decided the unit would be housed in the aft cockpit lazarette, next to the rudder quadrant. I set to work creating a heavy-duty wood and epoxy base for the unit, as well as wiring the cable and fuse for the pump. When the components were mounted, we cut lengths of inexpensive plastic tubing to serve as mock-ups for the required nine hydraulic hoses. The lengths of the plastic tubes gave us the correct length of each hydraulic hose.

Doug found a small company willing to fabricate the hoses and the end fittings for us quickly, on short notice, for a reasonable price. To expedite things he drove a hundred miles to their shop and returned the same day with the hardware. Every hose fit perfectly.

We filled the system with hydraulic fluid, bled the air, powered her up, and calibrated the compass, which was mounted on the overhead at the exact center of the boat. We swung the quadrant to both sides and carefully tweaked the mechanical alignment of all the moving parts.

Now came the test. Out on the Bay, I pulled the cockpit lever that mechanically engaged the rudder quadrant with the autopilot.

I let go of the wheel.

Doug and I stood holding our breath, wondering if the thing would indeed *work,* somehow skeptical that it would.

The bow ever so slightly drifted to starboard. From the lazarette the motor *growled,* the wheel jerked three inches, and the boat snapped back on course.

It was amazing. We shouted with ecstasy and pounded each other on the back. Other men behaved in a similar fashion when their football team scores a touchdown. But this was something *we did.*

The work never let up. We were on a marathon, a relentless and plodding race against time.

Our bright yellow Portland Pudgy dinghy, *Ducky,* arrived at a shipping center and we picked her up in Doug's truck. At eight feet and 128 pounds, she was too big for UPS. We wheeled her down the dock and went for a test row around the marina, greatly amusing Tweety with the sight of two grown men in a little yellow boat. We practiced raising the dink from the water to the deck, which was tougher than either of us expected. In the marina, with the boat rock-steady, it was barely within our physical ability to manhandle *Ducky* into place—how would we do it at anchor, with the boat pitching and rolling?

Besides the alternator on the diesel, we had two means of charging the ship's batteries: a large solar panel mounted across the stern davits (on a custom frame that Doug fabricated from scrap metal) and a wind turbine generator. The turbine was mounted on a vertical pole aft of the cockpit that was braced by two other poles. I installed the cabling and the voltage regulator.

Next we installed a stainless steel gimbaling propane stove and oven, with a brace bar in the front to give the cook something solid to grab onto. I installed a GPS chartplotter at the nav station and Doug mounted our Emergency Position Indicating Radio Beacon, a battery-powered device about the size of a half-gallon carton of milk. If the boat sank or burned at sea, we could activate the EPIRB and it would broadcast our position anywhere in the world. This was no guarantee of rescue, of course. Ninety-nine percent of the time we would be far beyond the jurisdiction of the US Coast Guard or the rescue services of any country. Most likely, the closest commercial ship would re-route to our last known position, make a big circle to look for us, and leave. But that gave us a better chance than having no EPIRB at all.

As promised to Joyce, I spent one weekend as crew aboard a forty-foot Beneteau, and following that I contacted Spinnaker Sailing and arranged a half-day of boat handling tutoring with one of their instructors.

At first I resisted the idea. "I think I can dock and undock fairly well."

"You don't know jack. I want to make sure you're prepared for some of the situations you're going to find sooner or later while cruising. Now call them and book the lessons."

I spent an afternoon in Redwood City harbor with Spinnaker instructor Leslie Waters practicing several boat maneuvers and techniques I never knew existed. Leslie taught me how to keep the boat in one location—stationkeeping—against the direction of the wind or current. We did anchor setting and recovery, approaching a dock with and against the wind, and how to drive the boat backwards.

Yes, *backwards*. Not just a few feet as in a car, but as far as I wanted, at jogging speed. You stood in front of the wheel and faced backwards. You moved the wheel slightly one way or the other—the trick was to get a feel for the sensitivity and how much rudder it took to make a course correction. Like riding a bicycle, it's almost impossible at first, but with practice it got easier.

"Neat trick," I told Leslie. "But I can't imagine the circumstances that would require motoring backwards."

He gave a knowing smile. "Oh, you'll be surprised at what can come up."

Meanwhile, Doug was taking care of one of our final habitability jobs: the interior seat and bunk cushions. We had measured the shape and dimensions of the old, mildewed cushions and cut replacements from new foam. Doug had found a local company, one woman really, who agreed to create new zippered slipcovers for an extraordinarily affordable price.

I discovered that Doug was negotiating these excellent price deals by simply explaining to people we were getting a boat ready to sail around the world on a tight budget.

We now had a livable, seaworthy cruising vessel. All that remained was to install the refrigeration system and cold plate, install the reverse osmosis watermaker (which could be done in Mexico) and load on board a couple of new anchors and their rodes.

And we were done.

One final, main task lay before us: a shakedown cruise. We needed to test the *entire* vessel, in moderate ocean conditions, day and night, for at least forty-eight hours. If anything didn't work right or revealed an unknown flaw, there was still time to come back to the marina and fix it.

"We need to pick a weekend with moderate seas and winds within thirty or forty miles offshore. It would be a waste of time to do it in light seas, and we don't want heavy seas either."

The following Thursday afternoon Joyce called and said there was a system passing three hundred miles offshore and it was expected to generate moderate seas through the weekend, probably twelve to fifteen foot swells and twenty-knot winds, perfect for a shakedown. She was available, and Doug was always ready.

I had one serious concern before we left. We were going to be *way* offshore, and I was responsible for having a contingency plan in case of emergency. Boats did sink, and boats did burn. The ocean is full of large floating debris (like cargo hold lids) that can punch a hole in a small craft and sink it in two minutes. The Portland Pudgy people marketed their product as a lifeboat, but I could see for myself that it could not hold the three of us safely in any kind of sea. I told Doug I would have to make a quick run to West Marine and snag an inflatable raft we could keep on deck, ready to go. Doug offered the use of his old Zodiac instead. Before our real departure, I would have to order a genuine, certified emergency raft.

Friday morning, we made a provision run to and returned with enough food for seven meals plus assorted snacks of yogurt, candy, fruit and nuts. The plan was to leave the dock before noon and be out of the Gate and offshore by sundown. We would spend all of Saturday sailing a wide arc maybe forty miles off the coast, and then be back inside San Francisco Bay at dawn on Sunday, returning to Bair Island early Sunday afternoon.

As I had asked him to do, Doug purchased a set of foul weather gear for himself—weatherproof overalls, jacket, hood, sea boots and cold-weather sailing gloves. As we sailed past Alcatraz Island, the wind and the swells suddenly picked up and you could *feel* the storm system, even though it was several hundred miles to the west. The day was bright and cloudless, but it was evident the ocean would offer a real test of every component.

I put forth the rule that once past the Gate, everyone was to wear their harness and clip to the jackline while on deck. I also suggested a watch schedule of four hours on, eight hours off, and Joyce said three hours on was more reasonable at night. I agreed.

We sailed under the Golden Gate Bridge and the wind and waves really picked up. A "swell" is different from a wave, as it is smooth and the top does not break, as beach type waves generally do. *Serenity* was now seeing ten-foot swells, maybe seventy feet apart, hitting her right on the nose. The bow began pitching into each new swell with a violent *thud,* but it didn't seem to slow her much. We were headed due west on a close reach, and the autopilot was performing superbly, exceeding Joyce's expectations.

I went below to visit the head. Our head was near the bow, which is not a comfortable place to be when the boat was slamming into swells. I did my business as quickly as I could, as being confined to such a tiny space while being yanked up and down several feet was making me nauseous. I left the head and made a beeline for the companionway. I could feel my mouth filling with saliva and I grudgingly accepted what was about to happen. I climbed the ladder, forced myself to hook my harness tether to the jackline, grabbed the starboard lifeline, and heaved my guts overboard.

Nothing came out. Another loud heave, nothing out. A third heave, and this time my mouth filled with a thin, sour trickle of stomach residue, not even any honest vomit.

I sat down on the deck and wiped my mouth with my jacket sleeve. Joyce and Doug were at the other end of the after deck, observing.

I managed to whimper, "Dry heaves suck."

Joyce frowned. Doug said, "We thought you were joking!"

"No joke. Head made me sick."

I drank some bottled water and that began to settle my stomach. I had long ago digested my lunch, which made throwing up impossible, even though my stomach muscles now ached from the effort. I knew I was somewhat susceptible to seasickness from my time in the Navy, as even submarines do surface transits and are subjected to rolls. I also knew I was not debilitated by seasickness as some people were—like most, I found the sensation miserable but I could function; I had remembered to hook on my tether.

"Look at the horizon." Joyce suggested. "Better yet, manually steer. You should get some practice doing that, anyhow."

I stood behind the wheel and pulled out the lever that disengaged the autopilot. We were on a course of 270 degrees, sailing north of the main shipping channel. This time of year the sun set almost due west, so I could steer by the sun without even looking at the compass.

After a few minutes' practice, I got the hang of anticipating and countering each swell. *Serenity* was sailing beautifully. Besides a freighter on the horizon, there were no other vessels in sight and the Golden Gate Bridge was a good twenty miles behind us. Even with the *mal de mer,* I began to relax and enjoy myself. I felt a rising euphoria. The sea was impossibly blue, the sunlight an incredible shade of orange yellow. It felt like I was seeing everything for the first time, or at least with a different pair of eyes. Without solid land around us, the world took on a new perspective, a new scale, a universe bounded only by a smooth horizon.

The three of us silently watched for marine life. We pointed to an occasional sea lion and a couple of porpoises that followed us for a few minutes. One of the porpoises surfaced and seemed to stare right at me, wondering why I was invading her territory.

As the sun neared the horizon dead ahead of us, Joyce and Doug went below to prepare dinner. That morning, on terra firma, we had planned some hearty meals—chicken and mashed potatoes were on the menu tonight. Joyce turned as she was going down the companionway.

"Think you'll be able to eat?"

"I think so. Feeling a lot better."

They were below for a long time. I got to watch the sun dip below the horizon alone. The sea took on an extraordinary deep indigo hue. Behind me, the hills of Marin County were just a thin and distant line on the horizon. I considered our course. We should keep westing until midnight, I decided, then turn south. That would put us maybe fifty miles offshore for the night. The air smelled *sweet,* maybe sweeter than I'd ever smelled in my life.

Joyce came topside, looking unhappy.

"Doug is very sick."

"What are you talking about? I thought you guys were making dinner."

"Read my lips. Doug is very, very sick. Let me take the helm and go see for yourself."

I found Doug folded into a fetal position in the starboard quarterberth, a plastic bucket clutched to his side. His eyes were shut but he was not asleep.

"Doug? Are you okay?"

"No, I am not."

"Doug, you gotta come topside. Get some fresh air, see the horizon. The colors, come up and see the colors! It's amazing out there."

"No, I can't."

"It will help, I promise. You'll feel much better."

"No. Please leave me alone."

"I can't leave you down here like this. You'll be going on watch soon."

He tried to open his eyes, found he'd rather not.

"Glenn, I'm sorry, but I can't do this."

I drew a blank. My own gut was churning anew.

"What do you mean?"

"I mean I can't do this. I'm not moving. I can't do it. I'm sorry, I just can't."

I went topside. Joyce and I sat in the twilight for a few minutes.

"He won't move. Won't budge from that spot. He's got that bucket and won't listen."

I engaged the autopilot and Joyce got us both some yogurt. I assumed dinner had been canceled. I didn't feel much like eating.

"We need to head back in."

"Oh, come on, Joyce. We just got out here. We need..."

"What the hell is the matter with you? Doug is extremely ill. Get it through your head—he is incapacitated. We need to get back inside the Gate."

"I think he'll be fine once he adjusts."

"He doesn't seem to want to do that."

"I don't understand." Now that it was sinking in, I was rapidly growing angry. "He told me he was an experienced sailor. Owned his own boat, he said. Sailed on the ocean."

"Let's head back in."

What could I do? I told myself I could reason with Doug later, maybe in the morning.

"All right. We're going to have to jibe. You got the main sheet?"

We did our first jibe at sea in the growing darkness. That involved maneuvering *Serenity* a hundred and eighty degrees so we were sailing downwind, the lights of San Francisco ahead of us.

Joyce and I ate cold snack food for dinner, and around 10:00 p.m. we sailed back under the Golden Gate Bridge. The wind vanished, so I started the diesel and we lowered the main and reeled in the jib. All the while Doug remained curled up on the quarterberth, still clutching his trusty bucket.

Motoring back to Bair Island would take six hours. It didn't make sense to anchor overnight because if we did, it would still take us all morning to get back. It made more sense to motor around Treasure Island until after midnight and then head south to arrive at the Redwood City channel at the crack of dawn, to avoid entering the harbor at night—always a risky proposition. We would alternate three hours on, three off. Even though the boat was not rocking, Doug did not budge from his spot.

It was an endless night. The sparkling city lights were pretty but I didn't enjoy them. The diesel exhaust, which smelled like adventure a few hours ago, was noxious to me now.

We had *Serenity* docked just after 6:00 a.m. It was a dull, gray Saturday. In its nineteen-hour shakedown, and the boat performed perfectly. Doug made his way back to his truck, saying nothing to either of us. I wanted to have a private talk with him, because I thought I could persuade him to give this another shot. Try Dramamine, maybe. Or one of those wrist bands.

"I'm sorry, it's not going to work."

"Just like that, you're through?"

"Yeah."

"I thought you had your own boat, sailed it on the ocean."

Doug paused. "I did. But it was the Gulf of Mexico."

"Didn't you live near the Kennedy Space Center?"

"I did. But I had my boat in Tampa. Sailed on the Gulf on the weekends. The Gulf is nothing like the Pacific. It's flat. Even when it's choppy, it's flat. No up and down, up and down like we had last night."

"I thought this was your dream."

"It was. But I can't do it. I'm sorry, I just can't."

I walked back to my apartment knowing that if Joyce's family situation deteriorated as she warned me, I now had zero crew members.

After a few hours' rest and some coffee, my head was clearer and I realized what I must do. From that point, I'd have to assume I would be alone for the trip—maybe the whole trip. Now that I had those few hours on the open ocean, I was confident I could survive. The boat worked.

The autopilot worked. It was the *people* who formed the weakest link. Single-handing still worried me, but I would have to go forward under the assumption that there was truly only one person I could count on: myself. If I made some mistakes and ended up a fatality, I was willing to accept that possibility. I would simply have to take extra care and be diligent, but I would never call it quits.

Force of Evil

The day after our shakedown-cruise-that-wasn't-a-shakedown-cruise, Doug sent me an e-mail of apology and assurance. He told me he would be glad to assist me on the final outfitting of *Serenity,* if I would allow him back on board. Provided we stayed in the Bay.

I responded there was nothing to apologize for. Some people are debilitated by sea sickness and there is no real cure. I started to write some suggestions he might consider trying that can relieve some of the symptoms—Dramamine, electric wrist-bands, ginger supplements. I erased it all. I knew from my years in the Navy that none of those remedies were all that effective. When we had to do a long surface transit, you could get a dose of Scopolamine if you wanted it (in the form of a transdermal patch applied behind your ear) and it helped a bit. For civilians, it required a prescription.

No matter—I could not rely on Doug. I thanked him for his offer and assured him I was still proud to call him my friend and asked when would he be available to help me install our new anchor rodes, knowing he had nothing better to do.

Joyce wrote me a note, too. Under the guiding principle, "when it rains, it pours," I expected her to, and I could almost predict the contents word-for-word. Things with her sister had turned for the worse. Legal matters. She explained a few scanty details. There was an inheritance involved, and her sister was trying to tie it all up in probate and challenge some aspects of the will. Joyce needed to be there at the hearing, which right now would probably take place as the Ha-Ha started. So sorry. But it was not *definite* she would not come. Meanwhile, she was pursuing some leads on prospective crew—which still had to be female, in case Joyce did come.

Sometimes a maybe can be worse than a no. I resigned myself to the increasingly probable specter of making my first offshore passage alone. The thought terrified me and excited me at the same time.

And wasn't that exactly why I was doing this?

I had to be out of my apartment by October first, just eight days away. Most of my furniture and housewares had already been carted off by the Salvation Army. I smiled at the thought of a needy Bay Area family receiving my big screen high-def television.

Doug and I had planned to complete additional boat work and provisioning, and then motor north and drop anchor off Sausalito, an affluent and sailing-intensive community in Marin County. We would be about a quarter of a mile off the docks, so we would have to be self-sufficient in every way: food, propane, electricity, laundry, even fresh water (hauled in five-gallon plastic jerrycans). Our sole link to shore would be *Ducky,* which we would row to and from the docks. Our tentative departure date was October 16, which would allow us almost two weeks to sail five hundred miles south to San Diego for the Ha-Ha. We wouldn't need all that time, of course—five days, probably, maybe fewer—so there would be plenty of time for last-minute outfitting and provisioning before we left the United States on a long haul.

Except now it would be *my* departure date. Single-handed sailors were not allowed to join the Ha-Ha, so I would no longer be tied to any sort of schedule. I would be free.

Technically, single-handed ocean voyaging is a violation of International Maritime Law, which requires all vessels operating in international waters to maintain a "safe watch" at all times. Thing is, the skipper is given a huge amount of leeway in deciding the exact definition of a "safe watch," and it is rare for the authorities (such as the Coast Guard) to declare a voyage manifestly unsafe and require the boat to return to shore.

Which meant I was free to risk my own neck if I so desired.

I went online and ordered a CARD system (Collision Avoidance Radar Detector), a device intended to improve the odds for single-handed sailors. Since it was not possible to stay awake at all times, I needed some sort of warning when a large, high-speed vessel, such as a trawler, cargo ship, or cruise ship, was bearing down on me on a collision course. If such a collision occurred (and they *do*— you *cannot* depend on the ship's officers to change course and avoid running you down) the tiny plastic boat would be cracked asunder and she would go down in seconds. The ship might have a couple of scratches in its paint.

The CARD was a small hemispherical antennae that connected to a control unit that sounded an alarm when it detected a radar signal from another vessel. Made for use in restricted visibility, it indicated the approximate direction from which the signal originated. Now I could nap, and if a ship was coming the CARD would wake me.

Two days remaining before I must vacate my apartment. I had gotten rid of almost everything except my bed, some kitchen gear, and a couple of dozen books I did not want to donate. Doug and I took a ride in his pickup truck to an Alameda rigging shop and we returned with two new anchor rodes plus two new anchors, a Danforth and a CQR. Both rodes consisted of two hundred feet of high-tensile stainless steel chain connected to three hundred feet of nylon cable. It took us a full day to methodically load the chains aboard, the working rode in a forward locker and the spare in the bilge where the infamous holding tank had been.

The day before I closed out my apartment for good, I found an e-mail with the subject line "Introduction." The contents were:

Dear Glenn,

My name is Megan Lynch and I received your name from Joyce Zimmerman.

I am an experienced offshore sailor and I am interested in possibly crewing on your boat.

I did my first Mexico cruise two years ago and I also participated in a Transpac as a deckhand and I have sailed and raced various boats over the past twelve years. I am also a licensed registered nurse. If you feel my qualifications are adequate please respond via e-mail or at the phone number below.

Sincerely,
Megan Lynch

I gulped and resisted the temptation to shoot back, "Hell, yes, your qualifications are adequate!" I dialed the number. Please, God, don't let this be another disappointment.

Megan was polite and she told me she wanted to come on board as soon as possible so she could help with the outfitting, as Joyce told her there was still a lot to do and not much time for doing it.

It turned out she had decided to take a leave of absence from work, six months and possibly longer, deliberately open-ended. She wanted to at least do a seasonal Mexico cruise and maybe the South Pacific. She had grown tired of a dull routine. As a sort of free agent nurse, she could leave and return to work pretty much as she wished.

I described our schedule and we made arrangements to meet up in Sausalito in six days. I would take her out to the boat in *Ducky* and she could help Doug and I with our final work, including installing a new refrigeration system. I asked for her advice on medical equipment and drugs.

By the time the twenty-minute call was over I was pretty much in love. It's a geek thing. My mind raced: She had made no mention of a boyfriend or fiancé, which she should have done if discussing her plans for the next six to twelve months.

Transpac crew. The Transpac was a well-known ocean race, and crews had to be top notch. Would I want a former Transpac crew aboard *Serenity*—a *female* crew member?

Yeah, I think so.

I called Joyce to thank her. The second sentence out of her mouth was, "She's thirty-five and single."

The following day I put my computer in the Camry's trunk and turned over my apartment keys to the rental office. *Serenity* was now my only home. She offered everything I needed and wanted, except Internet and a hot shower. For that, there was the marina restroom and my laptop at Starbucks. I thanked Tweety, who had given me permission to live aboard for the next four days, even though it was not the weekend and technically against the rules.

We needed to complete the new refrigerator compartment before we installed and tested the machinery itself. Refrigerators on small cruising yachts were controversial. They tended to use a tremendous amount of electricity and break down fairly often, requiring expensive repairs. But my research revealed there were two known causes for these problems. First, the "cold box" installed on all but the finest yachts were woefully inadequate in design and insulation. They let out too much heat. The manufacturer would try to cut production costs by using three inches of foam insulation and cheap, leaky, poorly insulated doors. To remedy this, I purchased several rectangular panels that encased vacuum insulation, incredibly efficient and equal to eight inches of foam. I also got a heavy-duty, vacuum-insulated, top-closing door. To accommodate these changes we had to tear out the entire old unit box and fabricate, paint, and install a whole new cold box. When we were done Doug did the new countertop and it looked like we paid a pro to do it.

I had sold the Camry to my InfoData colleague Bob Porter for a flat $6,000, with my old computer thrown in for good measure. It was for his son, who had just started his senior year in high school. It was in good condition, only five years old and had a full leather interior, so I knew I could have gotten a higher price—it's just that I didn't have the time to be showing it to people, with no guarantee anyone would buy it before we left. I needed to keep the car right up until the day before we left the marina. Bob accepted the pink slip and turned over the keys to young Joshua, who was pissed off because he felt a dark blue four-door sedan did not fully express his awesome and unique personal style.

I didn't own my first car until I was twenty-three. And I earned the money to pay for it.

On a hazy Wednesday morning we bade goodbye to Bair Island Marina and the safety of a dock. Doug wanted to stay aboard until the departure date. We motored north on autopilot. The closer to San Francisco we got, the colder and darker the weather became. It felt more like January than October. We chugged past Alcatraz and used the autopilot to come to starboard toward Richardson Bay and Sausalito. As Doug and I checked our ground tackle it occurred to me this was the first day of my life I did not have any sort of fixed address. For legal purposes, I was homeless. I didn't have any bills, either. Bank statements were going to my brother's house in Virginia.

There were about three dozen sailboats already anchored in the designated area. Doug took position on the bowsprit and I steered a big circle, looking for a good spot to anchor—the first time I had ever anchored without an instructor on board.

When boats anchor, they do not simply drop the gear straight down and leave it at that. In order to hold, an anchor needs to bite into a sandy or muddy bottom horizontally, so the chain must pull it horizontally, not straight up. This means any anchor chain should be four to ten times greater than the depth of the water beneath the boat; six or seven times were prudent. In order to anchor in the twenty-five feet of water we found in Richardson Bay, we would need to pay out around a hundred and fifty feet of chain.

I had briefed Doug on the procedure. I picked a spot we wanted to end up that wouldn't be near any other vessels. We motored to a position around five or six boat-lengths upwind of that spot, then I gave Doug the signal to drop the Danforth.

Splash!

We let the breeze pull us backwards as Doug shouted out the chain length as it played out. At one hundred and fifty feet, he engaged the clutch and the full momentum of the boat pulled on the chain and—I hoped—dug the anchor into the mud.

It worked. Perfectly. Except we had gone back too far and we were too close to another fellow's twenty-foot sloop. He stared at us and I gave the order to try again. This meant motoring back to the spot we dropped the Danforth and using the electric windlass to haul it straight up.

Our second attempt was perfect, plus we got some practice retrieving an anchor.

Day two was Megan Day. Doug thought she'd love our picturesque anchorage. We were surrounded by the hills and tony cottages of Tiburon. We could see Angel Island and a little bit of the Golden Gate Bridge—the foghorn had added to the nautical atmosphere all night long. The motion of the boat was gentle and it did not seem to affect Doug.

After breakfast I called Megan on my cell. She was already at the agreed spot, waiting and eager. Doug and I lowered *Ducky* into the water and I began to row toward the docks.

Already my stomach was aflutter, that familiar blind date feeling. I had *not* intended to turn this circumnavigation into a dating club; as the girls at Spinnaker Sailing pointed out, that's not what we're here for. But Fate seemed to have other plans. It would be ideal to meet a potential mate and have a shipboard romance and sail together to Tahiti and beyond. And when we returned...Who knows?

As the dock came closer, my logical old geek brain churned out the familiar thoughts. She almost certainly has a boyfriend. Probably a lean, healthy sailor whom she will want to join us in Mexico. Of course she doesn't want to mention him *now*. Or even if she happened not to have a boyfriend (maybe a breakup precipitated this trip?) she would take one look at me and become the picture of keen disappointment. I'd seen it so many times. I'd be an inch or two shorter than her, with narrow shoulders, short arms, tiny little hands and feet. A diminutive, chubby little twerp. Her hopes raised for *nothing*. Then I'd talk about ideas, which always bores people. She'd probably decide not to crew *Serenity* at all.

I tied up *Ducky,* climbed up to the dock, and looked around. In an instant I could see that all that emotional angst had been wasted. Megan was a big girl—and I mean *big*. Not simply overweight, but wholly obese. Huge. We waved, and as we got closer, I could see she was also plain and, well, masculine in her bearing and appearance. She reminded me of a tough Georgia good old boy I had served with in the Navy named Mike Bevins—could have been his twin sister, his equal in every way but gender.

We shook hands, made some friendly small talk and began the row back across the inlet. *Ducky* had a five-hundred and sixty pound rated capacity and I'm sure we pushed it to within a hundred pounds. I rowed, and she directed. Halfway there we passed an elderly couple rowing their own dink toward shore. They waved and smiled at us and just *stared* with great big wide grins at these two portly people in a bright yellow boat. *Isn't that just the sweetest thing you ever did see?*

I knew straight out, from the moment I first saw her, there was no possibility of Megan and I ever having any sort of physical relationship—at any point in the future, no matter what. Ever. I felt as attracted to her as I would to another man. At the same time, I was resigned not to hold her unfeminine, unsexy appearance against her. I would be gracious to her and welcome her as crew, because her qualifications were practically ideal. I mean, a nurse on board. What could beat that?

I know: an attractive young woman on board, without

a boyfriend—*that* would beat that. But it wasn't in the damned cards. I hadn't been dealt a good hand, but I didn't have to play it.

Megan and I installed the refrigeration equipment. The second problem found in most marine refrigeration installations is that people install the compressor and evaporator in the engine room, which is the hottest place on board—even when the engine is not running. But the compressor needs cool air as a heat sink, otherwise the chilling process is inefficient and the motor needs to run all the time, using up power and wearing out the moving parts.

I solved this by building a plywood housing around the refrigeration equipment and force-venting it with a fan and a deck-mounted mushroom vent.

We turned it on and the chiller plates got cold immediately. The three of us cheered and stuffed our new luxury machine with cans of Diet Coke and bottles of Becks beer.

"It has a freezer at the top," I told Megan. "We're going to have ice and ice cream!"

Doug and I settled into a routine that week. *Serenity* did not yet have a coffee pot, so each morning we rowed ashore and hit Starbucks. This allowed us to use our laptops to check e-mail and the news.

Megan had sent me an e-mail: "Glenn, I decided I want to be on your crew because you have a nice boat and I think you will be a responsible skipper."

I responded, "Welcome aboard. Please be ready to sail by the sixteenth."

We visited the local chandlery and stocked up on nautical charts. I snagged an old-fashioned stainless steel coffee pot, a percolator with one of those glass nobs at the top.

I told Doug, "Only makes four cups at a time, but it's metal—won't break no matter what."

We also picked up a shortwave radio operator's station license, which was necessary to transmit on the SSB radio, an emergency engine starting battery in case our main bank somehow discharged completely, and two powerful, rechargeable handheld spotlights.

Joyce called and told us she had nailed us a berth at an Alameda marina for the last five days before departure. She assured me this would make provisioning far easier, as there was a Lucky's Supermarket half a mile away and we could top off our fresh water and diesel fuel without shuttling jerrycans back and forth aboard *Ducky*. Thing was, there was exactly *one* slip left, and it was a cash-only deal, take it or leave it: five hundred dollars for five days, paid only to a specific fellow I could find in the office.

I paid. Turned out the cash-only "last slip" was at the pump-out station. We would spend our last days in the Bay Area watching and *smelling* a stream of boaters pumping raw sewage from their holding tanks.

Doug and I both needed a good hot shower. Our week anchored off Sausalito had shown me what it was like to live without the comfort of an apartment. We agreed to wash ourselves every day, but *Serenity* did not have an inside shower. We rigged a sun shower from the main boom and used half of it to take a not-really-a-shower shower in lukewarm water. We slept in sleeping bags, I in the forward quarters, Doug in the main cabin. We ate way too many meals ashore, at expensive cafes and bistros. Truth was, sharing the boat with someone I was not related to felt confining, even if we had worked together for several months. I had more room and more "privacy" in my Navy submarine, because everyone pretty much let everyone else be if they were off watch, and all meals were prepared for you. With one other person, everything was more complicated. What do we eat? Who cooks? Who cleans up, and how?

Doug tended to make a lot of noise as he ate. He *crunched* his ice with his teeth. Every time. *Every last cube.* When we did eat aboard, I played a DVD or *South Park* episode on my laptop loud enough to cover the sounds.

I probably hadn't bonded with the guy as much as I thought. Maybe that was why he was so quick to bail as soon as he found a reason.

We were down to two days before departure. Megan had joined us in Alameda and she and Joyce were getting along famously, like two reunited sisters. It turned out that Joyce had been one of Megan's long-ago sailing instructors.

West Marine had told me I could take delivery of my four-person certified life raft by today, but they had lied. Another week, so sorry. Trouble was, we could not delay departure by a week as we had to be in San Diego by October 26 to participate in the pre-rally events. Doug graciously allowed us to borrow his Zodiac, which we would keep inflated and lashed to the deck amidships, ready to supplement *Ducky* should we improbably end up with no boat under us. Offshore, about a hundred miles out, it could take hours for the Coast Guard to find us after a distress call. Survival would require keeping our bodies out of the frigid Pacific.

The store assured me our raft would be delivered to the San Diego West Marine so that we could pick it up before we left for Mexico. The raft cost $6,000 (goodbye, Camry money) and it would be in a compact case we could store in the port lazarette opposite the autopilot. When you throw it in the water, it automatically inflates. Doug gave me his address so I could deflate and ship his Zodiac back to his home.

The day before departure was reserved for provisioning with edibles. The four of us made multiple trips to Lucky's and began loading hundreds of pounds of cans, boxes, and containers aboard the boat. I put everything on my Master Card, which I had set up for autopay on the full balance from one of my bank accounts. While standing in the checkout line Joyce's cell buzzed and a few seconds later she let out a "Whooopie!" She profusely thanked the person on the other end.

"We are in luck," she said to Megan and I. "My good friend Richard can come with us as far as San Diego. Just happens to have a clear schedule and he's in the mood for sailing. We now have four people!"

"Is he experienced?"

Joyce sniffed. "What do you *think*? Of course he's

experienced. He has a boat in Hawaii, been sailing all his life."

Dinner over, it was time to say goodbye to Doug. We stood on terra firma and marveled at the boat and all that we had done over the last few months.

"There is no way this trip would be happening if not for you," I said. "Not a chance in hell."

Doug extended his hand and we shook. "My pleasure."

From our vantage point, it was clear *Serenity* was sitting quite low in the water, which we expected now that she was fully provisioned. Trouble was, the bow was sitting lower than the stern—too much weight forward.

"I'm going to have to do some rearranging. Probably move the reserve chain from the forward bilge to the center bilge and stick all the extra sails in the empty space."

Doug helped me on this final task, and we shook again, promising to stay in touch, and Doug started back to the parking lot. After a few feet he stopped, turned around, and came back.

"I just wanted to tell you something I never told you before." he said. "Remember when you met my son?"

I did. Doug's son was an Air Force captain temporarily stationed in the Bay Area, an academy graduate, a pilot, and a career man. Doug had introduced us a couple of months ago because his son had wanted to see the boat and meet the skipper he had heard so much about.

I had looked forward to meeting this man and assumed we would share an immediate rapport, as we were both pilots. How wrong I was. The captain was quite a sight in his impeccable uniform, every hair in place, much taller than Doug, and exhibiting the lean, strong physique of a long-distance runner. He saw me and he was aghast. I offered my hand and I do believe he hesitated to take it. We exchanged a dead fish shake and I could hardly get him to look in my general direction.

Doug told me that after they left his son counseled him to find another boat and another skipper.

"Obviously this person is incapable of planning for the future," Doug quoted his son.

"Wow. He said that?"

"Yeah. I asked him what made him think that. He said, well, take a look at him. He's a fat mess. He can't even plan his own health."

Doug paused for a moment.

"I told him you were one of the best planners I ever met, and we could have used you at NASA."

"Thanks, Doug."

We shook a third time. "Don't let anybody judge you based on your appearance. Congratulations on your departure. I have every confidence you will have a successful voyage."

On board, Joyce and Megan were in their sleeping bags chatting and giggling like two middle-school girls having a slumber party. I went to bed in my forward cabin without checking the weather report for the following day. I mean, why bother? We were leaving, no matter what.

Richard joined us at dawn, and my first impression was that he was certainly one amicable chap, given the early hour. He was a handsome, mustachioed fellow, reminding me of Burt Reynolds in his *Smokey and the Bandit* days. Like Joyce and Megan, he brought all his own foul weather gear in a seabag, along with his other clothes and a couple of books.

Within a few minutes I learned why Richard emitted such a chipper essence. He had a second seabag with him, larger than the first, this one stuffed with six-packs of Coors Lite. He was chain-drinking cans of beer, starting on a new can shortly after finishing the last.

I had seen this before with people I worked with, but fortunately, not in anyone I had lived with. The functional alcoholic. And he was quite open about it.

"Glenn, this is the way I choose to live my life," he told me, holding up a can of Coors. "Buzzed but fully capable of performing any act of seamanship you can imagine and some you cannot. A day, an hour spent unintoxicated is not worth living, as far as I am concerned."

"Richard is one of the most capable sailors I've ever met," Joyce added.

Normally I would have consulted Megan, asking whether she wished to crew with this man, but she was well within earshot and being informed as we spoke. I looked at her and exchanged glances. She shrugged.

Later, Joyce told me Richard was a highly successful commercial real estate investor, and a notorious playboy with the ladies.

"At least you brought your own beer," I said to Richard, looking him straight in the eye. "Stay the hell out of my Beck's and my Heineken."

I treated my crew to a final breakfast at Denny's.

* * *

I gave the order to cast off lines. At that point it became real. I had put my blue hand–bearing compass in the pocket of my bib overalls, and I fingered it as my crew coiled our dock lines and retrieved the fenders.

From shore we must have been a salty sight. It was a chilly, gray day, so we were all dressed in sea boots and our yellow overall bottoms with a sweater or sweatshirt on top. Our deck was stowed for sea and showed signs we were serious blue-water voyagers, such as the empty jerrycans lashed under Doug's Zodiac.

As I maneuvered across the marina, a couple watched us from the docks and called out, "You all headed south?"

"Yeah! Doing a Mexico cruise!"

I could see the envy in their eyes from fifty feet away.

Once we got out into the Alameda channel, I dug out my cell and began making some quick calls before we got out of cell range. I had to tell Alek, Kevin, Tara, Tweety and Paul we had just gotten underway. Everyone answered, as if they had been waiting. This could turn a person into a narcissist.

Last but not least, Peter Gibbons. The InfoData manager with the highly managed life, who told me bluntly I wouldn't do it. His was the only voice-mail I got, so I left a brief message to the effect of, "Yo, I'm outa here."

Serenity left the Alameda channel around 10:00 a.m. and we instantly faced the full power of the wind blasting from the sea beyond the Gate. The Bay was a deep greenish-gray and covered with whitecaps, uncommon so early in the day. The bridge itself was mostly obscured by mist—not the ethereal fog of spring and summer, but a drab miasma without motion or poetry.

"You wanted some heavy weather experience," Joyce said to me. "You're going to get some today."

"Mind taking the helm? I'm going to check the weather."

Richard was below, typing on his laptop, drinking a beer. I turned on the VHF radio and set it to WX1. A voice recording delivered the following words in a bloodless monotone:

. . . mixed swell southwest eight to ten feet and south at seven to ten feet. Patchy dense fog with visibility one nautical mile or less. Southwest winds at ten to twenty knots, local gusts to twenty-five knots, becoming twenty to twenty-five knots after midnight. There is a small craft warning for the waters from Point Reyes to Point Conception. A ridge of low pressure near shore will persist through Sunday. Today, combined seas to fifteen feet. Mixed swell southwest eight to ten feet . . .

I clicked off the radio. Richard cried out, "Heading into a little weather, are we?"

"We are indeed. Wouldn't want to get bored, would you?"

"Hell no. That's the spirit!" He took another swig from his can.

Topside, Joyce and Megan were peering ahead at the sea under the bridge. It was dark out there, downright foreboding.

"The wind is going to be more or less from the southwest, and strong, and we need to go southeast."

Joyce grimaced. "Ah-huh."

"So here's what I want to do. We motor out to Mile Rock, then raise sail, probably leave in one reef, and start beating west. We can come south as soon as the wind lets us."

"You want to beat through this?"

"Yeah. I don't think we have a lot of choice. They're calling for twenty-five knots tonight and it's coming from the wrong direction."

"Oh, those reports usually underestimate wind speed."

"That's great, then. We're in for it."

"Don't get your shorts all in a wad. Let's get out there and see what it's doing."

What it was doing was *blowing*. Hard. With all the gear we had added to the deck—*Ducky,* Doug's Zodiac, the jerrycans—we had picked up quite a bit of windage. Plus,

Serenity was riding a lot lower in the water than usual, weighed down by hundreds of pounds of food and water and new anchor chain, plus four people, their luggage, and a metric ton of Coors. Before we even passed under the bridge, the spray had wet the deck and we were all wearing woolen caps.

The GPS showed our speed just over four knots. I bent toward the steering column and tried to push the throttle forward a bit—and found we were *already* running at around ninety percent of our peak engine power. The sea and the wind were pushing us back, right on our nose, slowing our progress and burning more fuel. And we had just passed under the bridge.

"All right," I announced, "everyone make sure you're clipped to the jackline when you're topside."

Richard stuck his head out of the companionway hatch. "To hell with that!" He climbed out, went straight for the rail, dropped to his knees and began urinating overboard.

"Richard, we're going to raise sail in about twenty minutes," I told him. "I'm going to need you topside."

"Aye-aye!" he responded, went below, and quickly returned in full foulies.

It began to drizzle. Although it was near noon, the sky was growing darker by the minute.

I wanted to get into open water before we raised sail and cut the engine. There were no other vessels in sight at this minute, and certainly no other sailboats, but a large freighter could at any second emerge from the mist that covered the sea. *Radar,* I thought, and turned on the unit, which Doug and I had mounted in the overhead above the chart table. There were two contacts in the channel headed east toward us, but they were both more than fifteen miles away.

Joyce turned over the helm to me.

"One reef for now," I told her, and she nodded in agreement.

When we had cleared Mile Rock, the northwest tip of the San Francisco Peninsula, the crew took position to raise sail: Richard at the jib sheet, Megan at the furling line, Joyce at the main halyard which was at the base of the mast and in the most precarious location.

I decided to turn *Serenity* directly into the wind, but I saw we were *already* headed directly into the wind. I gave the signal to raise sail. Our yankee jib began to unroll from the forestay, and Joyce hauled the main straight up the mast, using the mast winch to get it up the final two feet.

Both sails flapped wildly. Right now they were serving as speed brakes, and the GPS showed that our speed had dropped below three knots, even with the engine at full power. We needed water motion across the rudder in order to steer. Worse, GPS speed is not the same as the speed of the boat relative to the water—GPS speed is our speed relative to the whole planet, the bottom of the sea. In a current, the speed of the water past the rudder could be quite different from the speed of the boat over the bottom. Because we had a slight ebb tide going in our direction, the relative motion of the water was not even three knots, as the GPS read. It was far less, and dropping.

When it hit zero, the boat was out of control.

The jib began to pull the bow to starboard. In two seconds both the main and the jib were bearing the full force of the twenty-five-knot-plus wind, and *Serenity* heeled to port like never before. The port gunwales went into the foaming water and a three-foot wave washed completely fore to aft, filling the cockpit well up to my knees. It went down into the tops of my seaboots, soaking my feet.

But that wasn't what really caught my attention. A swirl of seawater had the audacity to pour right down the companionway hatch and into my galley, soaking the quarterberth, the countertop, and the nav station. I could scarcely believe my eyes.

Richard said calmly, "We need to keep the hatch covered before we broach and sink."

Which was now a distinct possibility. The companionway hatch was huge, offering maybe sixteen square feet of open hole for the sea to invade.

Just then, the sails filled. With help from the engine, we gained a few knots' headway and the rudder became effective. We needed to come up close-hauled so we could sail north of the channel. All three crew were struggling to put a reef in the main. I held up two fingers and tried to shout, "Two reefs!" but that's exactly what they were doing. A "reef" in a sail means pulling down the sail partway and tying it in place to reduce the area exposed to the wind. This makes the sail temporarily smaller. It also reduces the ability of the sail to drive the boat forward. The skipper had to weigh that loss against the fact that full sails in a heavy wind could over-stress the rig or sweep the boat out of control.

Megan placed the companionway slats into place and closed the main hatch. I should have secured those slats to the boat, seeing now that if they went overboard, we'd have a sixteen square foot hole in the cabin with no way to close it. If we got knocked down, the sea could pour right into the interior, unimpeded.

I pulled the wheel so *Serenity* was pointed about fifty degrees off the wind. That was a mistake. The swells—more accurately two sets of swells coming from different directions—were pushing us backwards just like the wind. Pointed so close, the boat could not maintain headway. Our thirty-one horse diesel, even though properly sized for the boat, was no match against these conditions. I could feel the wheel begin to free-turn in my fingers, meaning the rudder was almost ineffective. We were stopping in the water.

Just before that happened, I put the wheel completely over and we fell off the wind twenty degrees or so. The sails filled. We heeled and picked up a bit of speed.

"Let the main out a bit!" I shouted to Joyce. "We need to fall off because there's no way we can move closer to the wind, not with these swells."

"No shit!" she screamed back.

I had hoped to be able to cut the engine. That was not possible. Without the extra thrust, the next large swell to hit us head-on would stop us in our tracks. Both the sea and the wind conspired against us, and they were almost overwhelming. But *Serenity* was emphatically motor-sailing now at a good clip, doing six knots over the bottom, and I began to calm down. But no one—including me—had noticed we were motor-sailing directly toward Point Bonita. We were moving toward land.

How could that be?

We were being driven backwards. Our bow faced the open water, creating a cruel illusion. In reality the swells and the wind were blowing us back and sideways toward the land a mile off our starboard side. In about twenty minutes we'd be wrecked on the rocks.

"All right," I said to Joyce. "Here's what we're gonna do. We're going to tack and try for a course of one-eight-zero. That's around seventy degrees off the wind. Because the coastline falls away to the east, that will take us further offshore.

Joyce twisted her mouth. Was she thinking of leeway blowing us east? Or turning back?

A wildly foaming wave the size of a Greyhound bus swallowed up the bowsprit and washed over the entire deck, triggering everyone to crouch lower and hold tighter.

I shouted, "Prepare to come about!"

Megan and Richard manned the port winch. These were not self-tailing winches, so they required two people to operate—one to crank, one to keep tension. Joyce took the main sheet.

"Ready about?" I screamed into the wind.

Everyone shouted back, "Ready!"

I pulled the wheel to port and the bow slowly swung over. There was little relative motion between the boat and the water, and the rudder felt loose in my hands.

Somehow we made the tack. I didn't want to go on autopilot just yet, so I turned over the helm to Joyce and went below to check the GPS and the radar. Every time someone came to or from deck they had two remove both companionway slats, which increased the chances of one of them eventually going over the side.

Below, I saw some shipping traffic approaching, but it was not a threat. Then I checked our speed over the bottom and my heart sank. Two-point-two knots? How could that be? Before my eyes it sank to two-point-one. Two-point-zero. Back to two-point-one.

Another wild wave shook the boat and I heard Richard cry, "Wheeeeee!"

Something made me examine the chartplotter a bit closer. I stopped breathing. Could this be real? Our heading was one-eight-zero. That was the direction our bow was pointed. But the two-point-one knots was almost *backwards*.

I mean, we expected a lot of leeway (being blown sideways) but this was absurd. The two-point-one knots was in a direction of one-one-zero. There was barely enough water motion to use the rudder, but our true motion was taking us back from whence we came.

If nothing changed, in about three hours we'd be on the beach.

I went topside. The wind seemed a bit stronger, and the rain was now coming down horizontally. I said to Joyce, "We need to come up as close as we can. We're being blown to shore."

"This *is* as close as we can!"

"Really? We can't come up just another ten or fifteen degrees?"

"Feel this!" Joyce put my hand on the wheel. It spun loose. "I can just maintain steerage."

"The swells are taking away our forward momentum."

"Ya think?"

"Then we need to lower sail and motor through until conditions change."

"Oh yeah? And when will that be?"

"I don't know. I didn't check the weather. Wait, they said something about Sunday."

Joyce shook her head.

Sails down, I turned the bow to course two-five-zero,

which was parallel to the main channel. We were south of it. The wind, the swells and the rain immediately joined forces to come at us from the *exact* direction I pointed the bow.

Richard took the helm and I stuck my head down into the companionway to check our GPS speed. Three-point-two knots.

The conditions had to change. We were running the diesel at close to full power. I knew we were burning around one-point-three gallons of fuel per hour. We could do this for another forty-eight hours, max, and that would be pushing it. After that, no power.

I made a mental decision to motor until noon tomorrow, and if conditions and our speed did not markedly improve, head back in. The trip back would be much faster, because the wind and swells would push us. Joyce would be furious because the Ha-Ha schedule was messed up. So what? Megan and I could wait out the storm and leave on our own. In fact, we probably should have done that to begin with.

We all took two-hour turns at the helm. I did not want to engage the autopilot because too many things had gone wrong already and I did not want to tempt fate. My emotions were clouding my thinking, and I suggested aloud we might try the autopilot after dark. Joyce said that was a bad idea.

Each hour the wind grew a bit stronger, the swells a bit higher. By late afternoon waves of foam routinely broke over the bow and washed across the entire deck.

Twilight came early and Joyce announced her determination to fix everyone some hot soup, at a minimum. I didn't realize how much the violent and varied motions of the boat had sapped my energy. I didn't feel sick, but as the sea was swallowed by darkness, the horizon vanished, and I began to get queasy.

I forced myself to crawl below to get my soup. Joyce said to me quietly, "Do you have any idea how wet it is down here?"

"Wet? What do you mean? Where is it wet?"

"Ah, everywhere."

I looked around the cabin. Spots were poorly illuminated but I could see a little wave of water swishing about the deck.

Yes, there were now waves *inside* the boat.

I wearily felt the cushions and opened some of the lockers. Everything was soaking wet. It wasn't all that different from that first morning after the storm when I found the cabin drenched. Only now it was with seawater instead of rainwater. Our cushions—our seats and bunks, the only places we had to sleep—were wet enough to wring out water. This time I could not run back to a dry apartment. None of us could.

I opened a tool locker. Everything soaked—there was even an inch of water on the bottom. I opened the locker where I had stowed dozens of extra AA and AAA batteries for our flashlights and other gear. The paper packages were mush, and the plastic around the batteries was not waterproof—they were corroding before my eyes.

We each got two or three hours of sleep that first night. Our speed over the bottom had crept down to two knots. We munched on yogurt and candy and crackers all night and I expressed my expectation that conditions would improve at daybreak and allow us to raise sail. At 3:00 I finished my hour at the helm and fell asleep sitting up at the nav table, my waterproof foulies protecting my ass from getting soaked by the wet quarterberth cushion. I must have been out for three hours, because Joyce woke me up and told me to go topside and look.

It had not gotten better. It had gotten worse. Every swell now washed across our deck. Our GPS speed was down to one-point-seven knots. All through the night we had come left in ten-degree increments, but each time the wind seemed to shift so it opposed us head-on. It was like an intelligent force, an *evil* force, that did not want us to venture any further.

I bent over the lifelines and retched a few loud, painful, dry heaves. Joyce put a bottle of water in my hand.

My head throbbed with caffeine deprivation. Almost twenty-four hours had passed since those two tepid cups at Denny's, and their coffee was weak anyhow. I decided I needed coffee before anything else. Fighting the motion of the boat every second, I filled the steel percolator with water and ground coffee and set it atop the stove to heat. I watched it with great anticipation, telling Megan at the helm she would have a steaming cup in a few minutes, after which I would relieve her. I had my insulated, covered cup ready, and visualized myself helming with one hand. I had done it before.

The coffee was ready. The deck dancing below my feet, I painstakingly positioned two spill-proof mugs in the sink, wedged between cookware so they would not fly off. I placed the percolator on the countertop for two seconds while I retrieved the half-and-half from the refrigerator.

Just then *Serenity* took a huge wave to the port side. The deck slid out from under me and I fell across the nav station. The percolator, now airborne, flew past my head and smashed against the salon table. Water and wet coffee grounds splattered everywhere.

I threw a bunch of paper towels on the mess and consoled myself that I had the foresight to get a stainless steel, unbreakable pot. Therefore, this mishap would only delay the coffee by fifteen minutes.

Which was wrong. I found that the glass top of the percolator, an essential piece, had shattered and was no more. We did not have another coffee pot aboard. Why buy a spare when the one we had was stainless steel and unbreakable?

I went topside, hooked my tether, and vomited over the side.

Geographic Flexibility

By daybreak we were twenty-five nautical miles offshore and facing the mouth of a bona fide storm. That storm would not let us go anywhere except where *it* wanted us to go.

Imagine you are on a bicycle with worn-out tires. You are on a steep hill covered in wet ice. You need to ride straight up the hill. When you do that, however, your wheels *spin spin spin* on the wet ice and you move forward maybe one foot per minute, no matter how hard you pedal. And you can't pedal forever. You try to ride sideways up the hill, maybe zigzag on up there. When you do that, your tires still *spin spin spin* on the wet ice, but you're making forward progress at a crawl. This seems like a reasonable strategy until you realize your whole bike is sliding sideways and nearly *backwards,* taking you slowly *down* the hill as you pedal furiously *up* the hill.

The instant you stop pedaling, you slide back down at a brisk clip.

Welcome to our nightmare.

It had stopped raining for the time being, but the dark gray swells kept rolling in from the southwest, taller and closer together than yesterday. *Serenity* was hobbyhorsing, pitching up and down far more than she should with every passing swell. Every time the bow buried itself in the water, we lost forward momentum and had to get it back until just before the next swell took it away again. That's why our speed was stuck at a couple of knots.

"You are big time bow-heavy, my friend," Richard said cheerfully as he drained another Coors.

He was right. Mostly this was because Doug and I had stowed three new anchors and hundreds of feet of 3/8-inch stainless steel chain rode, plus hundreds of feet of nylon rode, at the bottom of the forepeak below the Captain's Quarters. Much of this space had been occupied by the old plywood sewage tank and was therefore available. There was no other place we could stow all that ground tackle. It should have been relocated to the middle of the boat, but all that space was taken with food and two rubber fresh water bladders. Our bow was so heavy it was slowing us down *and* causing us to ship a lot more seawater across the deck and the forward hatch.

You may ask, Why didn't you just change direction?

That would have increased our speed, sure, but not in a direction we wanted to go. Plus, the sideways effect of the wind and swells pushed us in another direction we did not want—either directly at the shore, or directly away. The speed increase, therefore, was a cruel lie. It did not mean we would get to where we are going any sooner.

I needed to get an accurate reading of our fuel consumption. *Serenity* did not have a fuel tank gauge. Fortunately a kind soul had published a chart on the Downeast website that allowed me to use of a dipstick to estimate tank level. I knew we started twenty-one hours ago with the tank filled to half an inch from the extreme top, which meant seventy-four and a half gallons. I retrieved my dipstick (just a metal rod I got at Home

Depot), got on the deck and took three measurements so I could average them and decrease the effect of sloshing.

After making an adjustment for the fact we were running at sixty-percent power for the first two hours, I calculated a consumption of one-point-three-five gallons per hour at ninety-five-percent power, quite close to nominal. We had a bit more than forty-seven gallons remaining, say forty-four usable. If I didn't touch the throttle, it would last another thirty-two hours. We could motor like this until late tomorrow afternoon, and then that would be it.

We had plenty of electricity. The main bilge pump had done an excellent job pumping out all the seawater we had shipped aboard. No one was using the head because the forward section of the boat was pounding up and down too much. We were using buckets, except for Richard, who was doing his pissing straight overboard. I decided to try that, too—one of the last male privileges.

I checked the weather. More of the same: south-to-southwest swells, fifteen feet now at six seconds, wind southwest, twenty to twenty-five knots. Low pressure system expected to clear Sunday.

Sunday. Three days.

I studied the chart and tried to figure out a way we could sail out of this—use our sails to increase our speed in the right direction and at least get as far as Santa Barbara before having to refuel. We had not planned on stopping at all, but at least one stop before San Diego was growing increasingly likely.

"You do have a staysail?" asked Richard.

"Two of them, regular and storm-sized. You think it would be worth a shot?"

"Here's what I'm thinking. Yesterday we pulled out that yankee jib and it pretty much dominated the whole balance. There was no way the rudder could compensate for that much force." Which made sense. I remembered how the bow instantly took off and there was nothing I could do about it.

Richard thought about it. "Just the main would leave the rig unbalanced, too. So how about a double-reefed main and the storm staysail?"

"Would that drive us enough to shut down the engine, or at least throttle way back?"

"Hell, who knows?" Another swallow of Coors. "Wanna find out?"

I dug the storm staysail out of the forward bilge. The entire captain's quarters was also drenched because my carefully installed and bedded $1,000 Lexan hatch was leaking with every wave that broke over the bow. I positioned Joyce under the hatch so she could push the sail upward to the deck.

Megan was at the helm. Richard and I went topside and surveyed the situation.

He said, "Usually when I go forward of the mast in heavy weather, I work alone." He poked his index finger into my chest. "For you, I'll make an exception."

I am honored, I thought. I'm going forward in heavy weather with someone half-shitfaced on beer at eight o'clock in the morning. We clipped on, and crouching low and holding on for dear life, we moved forward. It was raining again, so we were both hooded and wearing gloves for an improved grip. On the bow, it was like riding a bucking bronco through a waterfall. Every time the deck plunged, we were weightless for a split second. This cut our traction to the deck, and if the boat was also rolling at the same time, we went sliding. We both had to hold on tightly with one hand and do whatever we had to do with the other. Even with the jackline, falling overboard in these conditions was a life-threatening event. Jacklines break. People go over the side tethered to the jackline and get beaten against the side of the boat by the seas—sort of like being run down by a truck over and over.

The less time we were here, the better.

I soon saw why Richard needed me. He didn't know much about the boat. Not his fault—mine, really. My first task was to retrieve the staysail sheet from the mast. Our staysail boom was fairly standard: a white metal pole turning about an inner forestay. I loosened the ties holding the boom in place and pounded on the Lexan hatch.

Joyce pushed the head of the sail to us and I clipped the leading edge to the inner forestay. As I expected, a wave washed over the deck and poured into the hatch. Joyce screamed—more in shock than fear—and let out a blue streak of sailor-ese, and slammed the hatch shut.

Richard stood and raised the staysail. It flapped wildly but it wouldn't give us a benefit until we fell off the wind and turned it into an airfoil. At the moment, it was bleeding our speed. We had no time to waste in getting the main up and reefed. That was the tricky part. Even though it was amidships, raising the main required both of us to stand on a wildly pitching and rolling deck.

Joyce didn't let me down—she came topside to assist. The three of us raised the main and then lowered it to put in two reefs, giving us a mini-main. I crawled from the cabin top into the cockpit and took the main sheet. I said to Megan, "Fall off to port a bit, ten degrees at a time. We want to see how close we can sail and make about four knots over the bottom."

Serenity didn't like what we were doing to her. Full keel, full displacement boats have their merits, but sailing close to the wind is not one of them. As our bow drifted to the left, the swells began pounding our starboard side. The main and staysails filled with air and I could almost feel their power pulling the boat forward. The crucial factor, however, was what sort of course we were being pulled forward along. I wasn't even sure exactly which way the wind was blowing, except "the wrong way." If we could make just four knots in the correct general direction, even within ninety degrees of the correct direction, and throttle down the engine and give it a rest, I would count it as a huge victory.

Megan did what I asked, kept falling off, and I kept letting out the main. Richard was adjusting the staysail. I stuck my head below and looked at the GPS: five knots! Five and a half!

"Holy shit! This is working!" I shouted. I backed off on the throttle to about seventy percent. The reduced engine noise was sweet to all our ears.

"Fall off just a bit more—we want four to five knots."

So far offshore, on an overcast and rainy day, we had no way of telling where the boat was pointed save for the compass. Megan was steering relative to the wind and not paying much attention to our magnetic heading—I hadn't specified a magnetic heading for her to follow. Our pedestal compass was reading two-five-zero, so at least we were moving somewhat south of due west. We were headed further offshore, but we could tack later and zigzag down the coast. And I had slashed our fuel consumption by half (RPM and fuel consumption are not linear) so we could motor like this for almost four days if we needed to. By then the storm would have passed.

Richard and I did a high five as I went below to take a closer look at the GPS. Still five knots. But our *direction* over the bottom was two-eight-zero degrees. We were going backwards. Sure, our *bow* was pointed just south of due west. But the leeway effect of the damned wind and swells combined to push us continuously sideways until our actual motion took us further north with every passing second.

I expected slow progress, but this was something else. We were burning fuel to move further and further from our destination.

Joyce and Richard came below and joined me at the nav station. I pointed to our actual course and shook my head.

"Last I checked," said Joyce, opening a yogurt. "San Diego was south of us."

"What's your next move, skip?"

"We can heave-to."

"For two and a half *days*?"

Heaving-to is an old heavy-weather sailing tactic. You shut down the engine and adjust the sails so they counter each other and hold the boat in place. The rudder is clamped down to port so when the boat tries to move the bow turns into the wind. Sounds crazy, but it's supposed to work. Allows the crew to rest and wait out the winds.

Richard shook his head. "With these waves, that's

taking a big chance. Usually a boat like this will heave-to just fine. But here you got contrary seas pushing you all over. Could jibe that boat."

Joyce said, "Could snap your boom and that's the end, brother."

"We drop sail, come to . . ." I checked the chart. "Come to one-five-zero. With leeway, that will take us gradually closer to shore. Then we see what it's doing . . . twelve hours from now. If it's the same-oh same-oh, we turn left and pull into Monterey. Should be able to make that by daybreak."

Joyce and Richard nodded their consent. We went topside to undo all we had done with the sails a few minutes ago.

Twelve hours later the conditions remained the same. We had been making two to three knots over the bottom all day, no more than forty-five nautical miles of straight line progress over the entire day. I ordered a course of one-one-zero degrees, which according to the GPS would put us at the mouth of Monterey Harbor at daybreak. Our speed shot up to six knots because we weren't fighting the wind head on—we were now taking it on the starboard side. The wild pitching had been replaced by a steady side-to-side roll.

I did figure out how to make coffee without the pot. I was wishing we had coffee filters and I suddenly remembered we *did:* the coffee filters we were supposed to poop into on the AirHead. Well, they could also be used to make *coffee.* I took a couple and put grounds in the middle and made a sort of tea bag I dunked in a pot of hot water.

But once caffeine deprivation sets in nothing short of a Starbucks venti can totally cure it.

That afternoon, about six hours before we made the turn toward Monterey, and over Joyce's stern protests, I activated the autopilot. She told me that autopilots were "useless" in these kinds of seas. I told her that our unit was no cheap plastic job ordered from the Waste Marine catalog. We had nothing less than a W-H commercial hydraulic autopilot, highly regarded for heavy seas—I read that on the Internet, so it must be true. Furthermore, it had been lovingly and painstakingly installed and calibrated by the team of Glenn Damato and Doug Chessman, and it could not fail.

I turned on the unit, set the course, engaged the clutch, and stood back. The bow wandered, so I adjusted the gain just as instructed by the manual. Not only did it work, but it held course far better than any of us could hope to do.

"But we still need a watch topside at all times," Joyce retorted.

"Of course. But this will take away a lot of the fatigue."

"If it works."

"Does it look like it's working to you?"

I stood the first "fully automatic automated autopilot" watch. Everyone else was below dozing or snacking with the companionway hatch shut. This was the first time I could think, alone, since we left. I had little to keep me occupied except to stay alert for any sort of unsafe conditions. The wind whistled through the standing rigging and all around me the greenish-gray sea churned and rolled, churned and rolled. A swell would pass over the bow and sometimes send a wall of water all the way back to where I was seated in the stern. Yesterday at this time, I would have at least moved my legs out of the way. Today I was far too exhausted. I let the surf run right over me, a sort of beached whale without the energy to react.

Fighting the constant motion of the boat was some of the hardest work I had done in a long, long time. Even while napping we had to brace ourselves against something solid, and we ended up exerting effort, at least subconsciously, to keep from flying out of place. The fatigue crept up on you.

Whenever I looked directly aft at a swell washing past the boat, I could see its top gracefully falling away and out of view as the wave receded. It was one of the most beautiful and elegant sights I had ever witnessed, and impossible to see from anywhere but the stern of a small sailboat at sea under heavy weather. The receding waves mesmerized me. The motion of the deck had picked up a steady rhythm and it was rocking me into a stupor aided by hunger, mild nausea, and a touch of caffeine deprivation.

Out of nowhere a freak wave rolled the deck to starboard. I felt my entire body flying through the air. The world had slipped into a strange, slow-motion cadence. I could see the deck on the far side of the boat slowly rising toward my face. There were all sorts of hard metal protrusions coming at me that could do me harm. I slowly raised my arms to break my fall. My hands struck the deck first, but with hardly any force at all. After flying at least eight feet, I landed as gently as a feather. My arms easily stopped my forward motion, and when my body came to a complete stop, my nose was about a quarter inch from smacking into the deck.

What the hell was *that?*

The companionway hatch opened and Joyce stuck her head out.

"You okay?"

"Oh yeah."

"Having fun?"

"Oh yeah."

Probably, the deck happened to be dropping rapidly *away* from me, the boat rolling to starboard again, just as my body landed. Or maybe the stern dropped into a wave trough. Whatever happened, I was on schedule to land in a rock hard place face-first, and for no apparent reason, it did not happen.

Guardian angel? Or King Neptune deciding he had screwed with me enough for one day?

After we set course toward Monterey I slept the sleep of the dead for over six hours. Someone must have taken my two-hour watch. I laid flat in the quarterberth, the engine pounding away just behind a thin bulkhead. Believe it or not, we were all still in our foulies. Every cushion and bunk was soaked, so stripping down to our clothes for sleeping would have been even more miserable.

The head was still unofficially off-limits. By this point each of us had used a bucket for at least one bowel movement. There wasn't much privacy, unless you wanted to shut yourself up in the forward compartment or the head, which no one did, so evidently everyone simply trusted their shipmates not to stare. I supposed this was no different from the days of the Vikings.

Joyce screamed into my ear, "We're *there!*"

I jerked awake. "What?"

"We're *there!*"

I swung out from the bunk and went topside. It was *just* starting to get light, and in the distance I could make out a buoy ahead of us. The air smelled wonderful, compared to below.

Megan said, "There's the channel marker," and pointed it out to me.

"Okay. Okay, thanks. Let's throttle back a bit and let me take care of business and get something to drink and then I'll relieve you."

I saw the water was calm, or relatively calm compared to what we had battled over the last two days. I didn't need to look at the chart to see the channel into Monterey Harbor was quite short and we'd be there just as the sky grew light enough to maneuver about the docks.

Once at the helm I asked, "Has anyone ever been to Monterey?"

"Sure."

"In a sailboat, I mean."

"No."

The very, very, very last thing I wanted to do right now was have to dock this boat in an unfamiliar marina—but there was no getting around it. I was sleepy, hungry, filthy, and needing coffee so badly I could hardly believe it. The only way I kept from weeping in despair was to remind myself there had to be a Starbucks somewhere in this town. My crew looked no better than I felt. I watched as they wearily set out the dock lines and fenders. I wondered how many would jump ship. Maybe when I left this place I'd be alone.

Monterey has a small but charming inner harbor and

marina. In a rising state of panic, I wondered if there would be any way to tell where we should tie up—but right away, we saw the fuel docks, clearly marked to differentiate commercial and pleasure boats.

We docked and tied up, a hundred and twenty nautical miles in forty-four wet and fun-filled hours from where we began.

It struck me that this was Sunday morning, the day the low pressure system was supposed to move away. The marina was deserted. Joyce and I went up to the office anyhow, following a primeval urge to get off the boat. To our surprise someone was there, a gray-bearded gentleman who looked thoroughly nautical and at home in Monterey, California. He took one look at the two of us and was probably overcome with pity. We must have been a sight, and I would guess that by comparison, we made the average crack addict look like a paragon of health and vitality.

I got out a few words about pulling in to wait out the weather and hoping to leave by nightfall. He nodded sympathetically and showed us a diagram.

"Take this slip here. We've had a lot of cruisers come in this weekend, so it's my last one."

"How much do we owe you?"

"If you're going to leave by tonight, it's on the house."

We thanked him and he gave us the keys to both the restrooms, which had hot showers, and the laundromat. And we didn't pay a dime.

Sheer luxury.

* * *

I treated everyone to a brunch at one of the restaurants in town. We all needed to get away from the boat. I got a newspaper and tried to act normal, attempting to slip back into my routine as a business traveler. The inescapable difference, however, was that no comfortable, dry hotel room was waiting for me anywhere.

We headed back to *Serenity* to clean up, dry up, and survey the damage. I was prepared for the worst, and I was not disappointed. Every locker contained between one and four inches of seawater. A lot of our packaged food was ruined. My AA and AAA batteries were destroyed. There wasn't a single cushion on the boat that wasn't soaking wet. Water had even gotten into the chart table, soaking several charts and all of our pencils. Even the logbook was a sodden mess.

To my surprise, the others seemed to take in the damage matter-of-factly, not as a happy event, but not a trigger for rage or rebellion, either. We methodically emptied out the solon and draped sleeping bags over the main boom. I bagged and trashed a ton of water-damaged goods. Joyce cleaned the galley and everyone got to wash and dry their clothes and take a hot shower.

No one said a word about leaving. Richard did mention that he needed to get back to the Bay Area by Friday evening, but we agreed that this was so far in the future it was not likely to become an issue. If for some reason we could not reach San Diego by Friday afternoon, I was comfortable diverting to Santa Barbara or Los Angeles so he could get back.

"We'd better make it down there by Friday," Joyce warned. "I have some networking events I can't miss."

We ate dinner aboard—chicken parmesan and spaghetti made by me.

"How do you cook so well?" Megan asked.

"Easy. Just don't care about caloric content."

At five o'clock Joyce and I went back to the office to return the keys and check the latest weather map. I knew a little about meteorology from my pilot training, but anyone could see that the low pressure area was pretty much stalled off the California coast.

"Oh, I heard she's moving north bit by bit, but there's still weather out there," the front desk fellow warned us. "So you folks be careful tonight and come back and see us soon."

We pulled out in the gathering dusk, Richard staying on the dock and walking the bowsprit to the extreme end, then adroitly leaping aboard at the last possible second.

As soon as we got into the channel it began to rain—heavy, soaking rain that came straight down. With darkness, visibility went down to a few hundred feet and I switched on the radar. We could not raise sail, this time because there was not *enough* wind. The good news was we had a topped-off fuel tank and we could point the damned boat any direction we pleased and motor on at six knots for three days if we wanted, almost all the way to San Diego.

I took the nine-to-midnight watch and everyone else immediately turned in, sleeping in their foulies to avoid the wet cushions. The night was pitch dark with no horizon, no stars, and no sky; just the boat droning southwest while rocking gently in three-foot swells. The rain would not let up. The autopilot was on and I sat with my back to the cabin bulkhead, watching the raindrops fall past our stern running light, which was the only object in the world I could see.

Maybe it was the rain, but my mind slipped into a melancholy I could not shake. Those three other people sleeping below, they each had dry apartments to go back to any time they really wanted. I did not. In fact, I used to live in a dry apartment that did not roll or pitch or shake, and contained a large refrigerator filled with tasty foods and beverages, plus a wide-screen, high-def television hooked up to cable. I had a job where I mostly stood around answering questions about software while sipping Diet Coke. All of that seemed like a fantasy life to me now, a fantasy life filled with amazing and impossible luxuries. Why did I give all that up?

And it was only day three.

Mutiny Postponed

Day four dawned warm, clear, sunny, and windless.

The sea was a flat sapphire prism. We had the choice of motoring south or floating in one place while praying for a breeze. We had a Ha-Ha to make, so we motored.

Ocean travel without wind, waves, or rain is easy—easier than flying, easier than driving. I set the throttle to sixty percent power and the autopilot to one-five-five degrees, and that was that. I created five waypoints on the GPS and all we needed to do was motor from one waypoint to the next. San Diego was four hundred nautical miles from Monterey and we had already covered sixty-three of them. If conditions did not change, we would arrive in sixty hours, Wednesday night, just about the same moment the fuel tank would be sucked dry.

But this was still the northern California coast. Conditions would change.

Meanwhile, my crew and I enjoyed a respite from the motion and the wet. Everyone had gotten at least six hours' sleep, and we guzzled about a gallon of java between us, made with our new $60 Monterey-bought stovetop coffee pot. Our refrigerator was working perfectly and we drank from an unending stream of cold water, Diet Coke, and Coors. We planned a barbecue feast for the evening meal.

We didn't stand formal watches that day, as is customary aboard small sailing craft during daylight hours under calm conditions. We each occasionally scanned the horizon for traffic and I kept track of our progress on the GPS chartplotter. Old habits formed in the Navy made me open the engine room hatch every hour or two to look at the engine, sniff for overheated metal or rubber, and listen to it. Fuel consumption was just under a gallon per hour.

Joyce suggested we take advantage of the warm sunshine to dry out the bunk cushions. We carried them topside one by one, stripped off the cotton covers, and rolled them to squeeze out the water. We then spread the covers across the lifelines and the two booms, and hoped we would have reasonably dry bunks by nightfall. The amount of water that had come aboard continued to amaze me.

Now that my crew and I didn't have to spend every second fighting for survival, we got to know each other better. Richard looked over my books, which were maybe ten percent of the total number of books I had in my apartment, and selected one of my favorites, *The Burden of Bad Ideas: How Modern Intellectuals Misshape Our Society*. One chapter is called, "Why Johnny's Teacher Can't Teach" and asks why many school systems attempt to improve the quality of teaching by spending a large chunk of their budgets on administrators instead of on, well, great teachers.

Richard sat down on the deck and began reading. About sixty seconds later he snapped the book shut, stood up, and returned it to the bookshelf.

"That's a really good book there, Richard." I told him. "I highly recommend it."

"Right-wing bullshit," he shot back.

"Really? In what way?"

He waved me off. "Pure right-wing bullshit."

"You should at least read the chapter about the declining quality of American public schools."

"Right. Wing. Bullshit." He pulled his hat over his eyes.

Joyce stuck her head through the companionway.

"I thought I told you I wanted all the right-wing literature off this boat before I came aboard."

"Is this what passes for liberalism these days? If you don't agree with something, 'Take it out of my sight?'"

"Sounds good to me," replied Richard from under his hat.

I tend to be libertarian in my views. Joyce had stumbled upon a couple of copies of *Reason* magazine in my bookcase the other day, nearly giving her a case of the vapors. You see, they contained articles advocating free market capitalism.

Joyce had gone to college in Berkeley.

"Please, no politics on this boat!" said Megan. "We should make that a rule right now."

"Isn't it a political decision not to allow political talk?" I asked.

Joyce's gnarled index finger pointed at me from out the companionway.

"I'm warning you one more time. I don't have to be exposed to any of your right wing beliefs."

I went below and dug three cans of Diet Coke out of the refrigerator. They were wonderfully cold, with ice crystals even. I would have to adjust the refrigerator before they all burst from freezing. Everyone got a can except Joyce, who never touched the stuff.

She reacted by throwing three bottles of water out the companionway onto the deck.

"For every Coke you drink," she told the three of us, "you get to drink one full bottle of water. I won't have anyone passing out due to dehydration."

I said to Megan, "She thinks that since caffeine is a mild diuretic, one or two Diet Cokes will dehydrate you."

Megan shook her head. "Only in really large amounts, like four cups of coffee at once." She said it low, so Joyce wouldn't hear.

"Told ya. Diet Coke *will not* dehydrate you."

"Yeah, it does."

I wasn't going to let this rest. I was right. "Imagine you're on a desert island. You have no water, only ten thousand cans of Diet Coke. Are you gonna tell me you would *not* drink the Diet Coke, because without water it would dehydrate you, and you'd pass out and die? You wouldn't drink any of it?"

She came topside with a large bottle of water for herself. "If I were on an island with ten thousand cans of Diet Coke, I'd drink coconut milk."

"You're missing the whole point. Say you have nothing to drink but Diet Coke. Are you saying it would be safer to drink nothing than to drink the Diet Coke?"

She didn't respond.

"Seriously, what's your answer?"

She took a swig of water and replied, "I'm beginning to understand why you're not married."

Megan giggled.

We would discover that Joyce was huge on hydration. With hydration comes urination. I was pleased to discover that our AirHead composting toilet system was functioning as advertised. Now that we had calm conditions, no one wanted to use a bucket for their bowel movements. Everyone was using the AirHead and following my meticulous instructions: poop into coffee filter, open the trap door and let it drop into lower compartment, turn crank two times. Richard and I were continuing to urinate over the side, but the ladies were using the AirHead for both number one and two. And it was working! The system was funneling their urine into the outside bottle. It was almost full already. I dumped it over the side and announced how much easier that was than using a holding tank. They looked back at me without any appreciation for the value of a well-functioning marine head.

We decided to have an early dinner so we could all eat together in the cockpit at dusk. The barbecue turned out perfectly. I had a small round grill unit that clipped onto the stern rail and could be stowed below when we were done. We had ribeye steaks and roasted red peppers, oven-roasted potatoes, corn on the cob with butter, and Kozy Shack rice pudding, all washed down with zinfandel served in plastic cups. We were certain that the first class passengers aboard the *Queen Mary II* could not possibly be enjoying better fare.

The breeze had been steadily building during the latter part of the afternoon, and just as we finished cleaning up for dinner, it turned into a genuine wind off our starboard beam. We four happy sailors raised the main and pulled out the jib. *Serenity* gratefully heeled to port and the rolling subsided a bit. Sails act as rolling stabilizers when they're up, so even with the three foot swells, our ride became smoother.

I cut the engine and we were swallowed by sweet, sweet silence. Our GPS speed held steady around five knots. I set the autopilot to one-six-five degrees magnetic, ten degrees to starboard, to offset the wind blowing us eastward. I went topside and helped Joyce trim our sails. We were on a beam reach, and I hoped the wind would stay constant through the night. At thirty miles off the California coast, we were near the boundary between shore weather and ocean weather, where winds tended to be more stable.

After running some calculations, I announced we would be in San Diego by sunset Wednesday, forty-eight hours. Secretly I told myself if our speed dropped below four and a half knots, I would start the engine. The last thing I wanted to do was try to enter San Diego harbor at night. All the sailing books agreed not to make a night entry, due to the surprising trickiness of navigating a marked channel in darkness, even with GPS. Still, as long as we had wind, I preferred to keep the engine off. We had almost forgotten that while sailing, you're not supposed to hear the *ker-bang ker-bang ker-bang* of the diesel twenty-four-seven—that's why they call it an *auxiliary* engine. A cruising vessel at sea normally runs the engine for an hour or two a day, if the solar cells and the wind turbine can't keep the batteries charged.

I had to consider the fact that our autopilot used a lot of electricity, so if we sailed for more than eight or nine hours without the engine, I would have to monitor the remaining battery charge carefully.

The full day of sunlight and fresh air had *almost* dried

our bunk cushions and covers. Once something gets wet with salt water, it never quite dries out because the salt crystals hold dampness. The covers would at some point need to be commercially cleaned before they were ever truly dry and comfortable again. But we would sleep on them tonight—and not in our foulies.

The sky went overcast, so I checked the weather. The recorded monotone said wind southwest ten to fifteen knots, seas west three to five feet at eleven seconds (meaning the crests of the swells would wash against our hull roughly eleven seconds apart). I told everyone we would hold our course.

I also posted the watch bill. It covered the hours from ten o'clock to eight o'clock the next morning, divided into five two-hour shifts. To be as fair as possible, I gave myself what I believed was the worst watch, the two-to-four. As I knew from my Navy days, a watch like that split the night in two. You didn't get enough sleep before the watch, and by the time you went back to bed, sunrise was only a couple of hours away. It was even worse if you drank coffee while you stood on watch. Everyone besides me would have at least six continuous hours flat on their backs in a bunk.

Joyce glanced at the watch bill and threw it at me. "This is bullshit. I can't stand the midwatch because I will never sleep a wink before midnight, which means I won't get to sleep at all until two and I won't be alert."

Megan and Richard solemnly inspected the piece of paper as if they were reading their own obituary.

"Richard, would you mind switching with Joyce?"

"No, because you got me down for the ten o'clock and six o'clock, and that's just perfect because those are the hours I naturally sleep."

"Joyce, how about switching with me?"

"Hell, no. The two to four cuts the night in half. You think I don't know that?"

"Megan? Mind switch —"

"Glenn, I would, except that I always get super, super sleepy at the stroke of midnight. I don't think I'd be able to stay awake."

"Well, we have a brand new coffee pot—"

"Then I'd never get back to sleep."

I grabbed the piece of paper and scratched my head. The three of them sat around in the gathering darkness of the main cabin. Now that the engine was off, the waves made a gentle *swosh-swosh-swosh* sound against the hull.

"I gave myself the two-to-four because I figured no one would want it. Megan, if you'd switch with me, you'll be able to sleep at midnight and everyone else will be satisfied, too."

She snatched the paper from my fingers.

"You want me to stand the two-to-four?"

"Right. This way—"

"No, thank you." She thrust the sheet back at me.

"Very well, then." I studied the watch bill. All three studied *me*. I told myself, this is not the military. No one is getting paid to do this, either. I should try to satisfy everyone's desires.

Which I thought I was doing.

They're all experienced sailors. They knew when they came aboard they were agreeing to follow the skipper's orders, even a lubberly neophyte like me.

Wait a minute. *Experienced sailors.* It hit me. They had *almost* gotten me.

"Since no one wants to make any accommodations for their shipmates, the watch bill stands as it is." I tacked it to the nav center, turned around and climbed the companionway ladder up to the deck.

No one said a word, but I heard someone giggle— probably Megan. The watch schedule I originally wrote was followed to the letter, without any change at all.

Never Make a Night Entry

With Richard taking the first watch, Joyce, Megan and I bedded down in the main cabin. We stowed our gear, knowing that no one would sleep in the only private cabin aboard, the forward captain's quarters. That was for in-port only. At sea, the bow moved up and down far too much.

I took the quarterberth by the nav station and the women occupied the two bunks port and starboard of the main salon table. For the first time, we had reasonably dry bunks.

That lasted a couple of hours.

Shortly before midnight, the rains came. This wasn't the drizzle of Storm One. The rain of Storm Two was the real deal, a no-fooling-around type of rain with great drops that pounded the deck like a hundred thousand little jackhammers.

The wind died, too.

I awoke with a start and saw from the chart table compass our heading was wandering . . . one-seven-zero, one-seven-five, then due south. And I could *feel* the boat turning under me and the sound of the waves changing their angle of attack.

Richard clambered down the ladder to wake me.

"Skip, we got no wind. Wanna start the motor?"

"Yeah. For now."

I told Richard it was okay to hit the starter. After a few seconds I motioned for him to advance the throttle; we needed to get some water moving past the rudder so the autopilot could point the boat. I donned my foulies and Richard and I lowered the mainsail and furled the jib. By that time Joyce was up to relieve Richard. She was boiling water for a thermos of tea. She wore a headband-mounted flashlight to avoid lighting up the cabin and waking Megan.

We all pretty much expected the water to come right inside, and we were not disappointed. I had spent thousands of dollars and hundreds of hours of labor to replace *Serenity's* old ports and big Plexiglas windows with ten, top-quality bronze opening ports, bedded with great care and gallons of 5200. And it paid off: The water was not coming in through any of the ports. It was coming in everywhere else.

I didn't know it at the time, but *Serenity's* foam deck core was saturated with water, so any additional leakage into that core resulted in water streaming into the boat from hundreds of hidden points. To this day I believe the main entry point was the hull–deck joint. To access this on a Downeaster 38 requires pulling every inch of the teak gunwales, an enormous job that I should have done first. But it hadn't been done at all. There were other spots, too, all throughout the deck. Water streamed in from hundreds of staple holes once used to hold the vinyl trim in place. It was sort of like being in a tent made of cheesecloth.

The quarterberth cushion was already soaked and it had only been raining for half an hour. I stayed in my foulies and put my head down on the chart table.

* * *

When Joyce woke me for my two o'clock watch the rain hadn't let up, and visibility was probably less than a hundred feet. I turned on the radar and saw only two contacts within twenty-four miles. There was no wind, but the swells had definitely picked up and changed direction. They were higher, closer together, and their new direction was directly against our desired heading.

Even with the throttle increased to around eighty percent, we were doing no more than three and a half knots over the bottom. So much for making San Diego by sunset tomorrow.

Richard needed to be put ashore by Friday. That was one constraint. We were down to about fifty gallons of fuel, and that was our second constraint. Sitting in the pouring rain around 2:30 a.m., thirty miles out in the ocean, I did a mental calculation and realized the only way we could continue to San Diego and be there on time for Richard was to experience near perfect sailing conditions commencing sometime tomorrow: about fifteen knots of breeze off our starboard side and small swells headed in our direction. That would give us seven knots over the bottom and help us make up lost time. I didn't expect it to happen. That meant another stop to put Richard ashore and refuel.

I heard Joyce still rummaging around below, even though she had been off watch for half an hour. She was slamming gear around and cursing, furious over the wetness encroaching on our home afloat. This is a situation that only a sailor or perhaps a homeless person experiences: you're tired, you crave a few hours of restful slumber, but there is no dry place to lie down.

The combination of wet and Joyce cussing woke up Megan and Richard. I felt like going below and apologizing, but I dared not. What baffled me was that it rained upon this boat many times over the past two years on the dock, at least this hard, with only a few odd drops making it below. I did not consider two crucial factors: Docked, the deck simply rests upon the motionless hull and the joint is pretty well sealed. The foam deck core is dry, so what moisture that does seep in is absorbed and eventually evaporates.

At sea, the vessel is a different beast entirely. The hull continuously flexes. Gaps and crevices open and close. After Storm One saturated the core, there was nowhere left for the new water to run except into our mattresses.

My crew bedded themselves down on the cabin sole, which in a house would be called the floor. There wasn't much of it, and the three of them ended up practically side-by-side in sleeping bags, buried in pillows and comforters. *Serenity* looked like an airport terminal during a massive blizzard.

Megan relieved me at four and I tried to say I was sorry for the wet. She shrugged it off. I fell asleep with my head down on the chart table, content in the knowledge that by daybreak the rain would let up.

Which was a total delusion.

In the morning there was no wind except for a thin breeze directly opposing us, no sea except for an infinite line of swells pounding us right on the nose. In the spirit of deja vu, the elements conspired to stop us from moving forward. Our engine was able to push us ahead at only about three and a half knots over the bottom. Assuming no change in the conditions, we didn't have enough fuel to motor to San Diego. There was no chance we would reach San Diego by Friday. Over coffee I told Richard I was putting him ashore in Santa Barbara the following morning.

Station WX1 on the VHF was just a recording giving wind and sea states and warnings. What I needed was a weather chart. It would be nice to know what this low pressure zone was expected to do over the next forty-eight hours. We did not have a dedicated weather fax machine, a device able to print weather faxes directly from radio signals. Instead, I had planned to do what a lot of cruisers did, and use our single sideband radio and a laptop as a weather map generator. I had purchased the software for this ($199) and a special single sideband USB modem ($1,199). None of it worked. Well, it worked, but instead of a weather fax, the software gave me a featureless black rectangle. I hadn't had the time to troubleshoot in port, so now, I plugged everything in and fired up the single sideband. My theory was that I hadn't received a signal, even though the software thought I had. So, my strategy was to let the set cycle through some likely frequencies, searching for weather maps in digital format.

Meanwhile, everyone was up for the day and munching on whatever they could find. The motion of the boat was gradually getting less comfortable as the seas increased. Visibility was just a couple hundred yards, so I turned on the radar as well—we were in a busy shipping and fishing channel, and traffic would increase as we approached Southern California.

I carefully stepped over the piles of blankets and sleeping bags on the cabin sole and made my way to the head. As I approached it, I smelled something I shouldn't have: crap.

It wasn't the barely noticeably earthy odor of the AirHead under normal operating conditions. This smelled more like a diaper. It was stronger when I opened the head door—definitely from our composting toilet.

Then I heard it: *sloshing.*

There shouldn't be anything sloshing in that composting toilet.

I opened the trap door and peered inside with my penlight (I had learned to always keep a small flashlight on my person). The AirHead was half full of thick brown liquid. The stink hit me in the face.

It must be urine. Female urine. Richard goes over the side. I go into the jug, always. I've been emptying the jug—not too often, maybe once a day. That couldn't be right, though. Joyce and Megan have been drinking thermos after thermos of hot tea. They must each drink a quart of the stuff hourly. The jug should have been filling up fast.

But it wasn't. Their urine was going somewhere else: down into the AirHead, soaking the peat moss and dried crap, which had been reconstituted with tea processed into lady piss.

I was feeling nauseated.

"Joyce, Megan, I got to talk to you guys."

Everyone had gone topside in their foulies, even in the heavy rain. They wanted to get out of the musky cabin and get some fresh air.

"The head is filled with piss."

"So why is that our fault?" Joyce shot back. "Why

single us out? You and Richard piss, do you not?"

"Yeah, but Richard goes over the side and I've been using my little wiener to direct it to the forward rim and into the jug, not the inside of the AirHead, where the peat is. We can't let liquid get down there. It destroys it. It's designed to work dry."

"So what the hell do you want us to do?"

"I think this happened yesterday when we were on a starboard tack. When the boat is flat, all urine flows right into the jug. When we were listing to port, the jug was higher than the trap door. I was still able to piss into the jug because I just pointed my pecker at it. But you guys... Well, I'm not going to draw you a picture, but I figure it kind of went more downward and straight through the trapdoor into the bottom."

Joyce sneered. "Why don't you draw us a picture, Glenn?"

I paused, letting the torrential downpour punctuate our exchange. Richard was just to my left, enjoying the conversation while chasing his coffee with a Coors.

"Look, I'm only saying we have to use it properly or it won't work and it's going to stink and eventually overflow."

"Who told you to get that damn thing anyhow?"

"Glenn, why didn't you install a standard marine head?" asked Megan.

"There are a couple of ways we can solve this. When we're on a starboard tack, maybe you ladies can sit further forward so your stream goes into the jug."

Both women chuckled at that, so I supposed there was something anatomically wrong with the idea. Never having been a woman, I really didn't want the details.

"Or, you can go into a bucket, and empty the bucket into the jug."

"How about if we empty the bucket on your head?" Megan asked, surprising me. She was joking, I hoped. Joyce and she high-fived.

I knew what I had to do now: empty the AirHead over the side. Fortunately it was only half full and weighed a mere forty pounds. It had a lid, and I carried it through the cabin and hefted it up the ladder and onto the afterdeck. Everyone skittered away as if it were radioactive. I donned my foulies and harness, tethered myself onto a jackline, climbed up on deck and heaved the mess over the leeward side. After rinsing it with salt water, I added more peat moss and it was ready again for use.

Then I smelled something just as bad as crap.

Smoke.

Something was burning. The blood drained from my head. Something was burning somewhere, and I'm not talking food-on-the-stove kind of burning, I'm talking electrical fire.

I looked around the cabin fruitlessly, wasting precious seconds. My Navy training kicked in and I dove for the master switch under the nav station. I threw it, cutting electricity from every circuit on the boat except the autopilot, which I knew was wired to the main bus with its own local breaker and fuse.

"Fire!" I shouted to everyone topside. I'll never forget their faces. It was technically correct to call away the fire in order to get everyone involved in fighting it—but I didn't know what was on fire.

Then I saw it: thin wisps of smoke coming from behind the nav station.

Joyce tumbled down the ladder just as I was opening the front panel. A big slab of gray smoke emerged. I didn't see any flames.

"Something must have shorted," she said. "Look at all that water. Sure as hell. Something must have shorted."

"The SSB. And the radar. All our communications and navigation power lines go through there and something must have gotten wet." There were two inches of water sloshing back and forth in the cubbyhole behind the panel.

I turned off all the gear and restored power to the rest of the boat. Without being asked, Megan plopped herself atop the quarterberth and sat there for an hour or so, watching the nav station with a glum expression, making sure the fire didn't reflash. Smart girl. A fire on a boat this small could kill us swiftly.

Later that afternoon I set the autopilot course for one-zero-zero degrees, turning the boat towards Santa Barbara, still fifty nautical miles away.

"We rounded Point Conception," I told Joyce.

Technically we were now in Southern California waters. The rain had slowed from a downpour to just heavy rain. I had told everyone we would arrive in Santa Barbara at dawn, but as soon as we changed course the swells were no longer hitting us on the nose and our speed rose to six knots.

Which meant we'd be entering the Santa Barbara channel about two in the morning.

Which, according to all the books, you're not supposed to do. I decided to do it anyway.

* * *

We enjoyed a hearty meal of Hamburger Helper with hot rolls I made from scratch, followed by a box of Oreos passed around until it was empty. I made a watch bill and omitted my own name, leaving instructions for whoever was on watch to wake me when we were five miles south of the channel entrance. Then I put in earplugs against the engine noise, donned foulies to keep the wetness of the quarterberth off me, and got my first horizontal sleep in forty hours.

I slept fitfully because the heat of the engine made the berth too hot. We were in warming climes now, and with the warmer air temperature and my foulies, I felt like I was like sleeping in a giant plastic sandwich bag atop a hot stove. It was almost a relief when Megan shook me awake.

The nav station chronometer said 2:07 a.m. I checked the GPS chartplotter and saw we were headed zero-two-zero, directly toward the Santa Barbara channel, which was short and marked with buoys on either side, three of them lighted. A notice on the chart read, *Mariners are warned that numerous vessels are anchored and moored east of Stern's Wharf. Caution should be exercised when transiting this area.*

I put a pair of binoculars over my neck and went topside and I discovered that the rain had stopped and the air smelled marvelous, some of the best air I've ever experienced. Even after only two days at sea, we could smell *the land* and all it meant—greenery, dirt, garbage—anything that didn't smell like boat was a guilty pleasure.

Visibility was excellent and the lights of Santa Barbara twinkled before us. The ocean itself was inky black, and looking port and starboard, I got the impression that a Tyrannosaurus Rex could be treading water alongside the boat and unless it actually roared I would have no idea.

Speaking of which, Joyce was awake. She busied herself in the galley and brought Megan tea, and a cup of coffee to me.

"Here's the plan," I said to them. "Just for safety, I'd like someone stationed below on the GPS at all times. I'm going to steer us down the channel by sight, but the GPS could be our backup. Who wants that job?"

"I'll do it," said Joyce, sipping tea, as usual.

As we got closer to shore the water grew flatter and I reduced throttle to make five knots, a conservative speed for this forbidden night entry. As we entered the channel, Joyce studied the chartplotter and called out, "Get over more to the right. You're on the edge of the channel."

"Okay, got it. Keep feeding me those directions."

It would have been ideal if the chartplotter were mounted in the cockpit, but I had decided to mount all electronics below, theoretically out of the elements. I sighted a range light at the far end of the channel that told me we were right where we should be.

"How are we doing?"

"Fine! You got a marker coming up on starboard. Three miles to the harbor."

I peered into the blackness and saw nothing. With the binoculars, it was relatively simple to keep on track using nothing but the range light on shore, which keeps you from straying too far to the left or right—a relic from the days before GPS.

Maybe it was the coffee, but I felt euphoric. I asked Megan, "Why do they say night entries are so tricky?"

"Stay on track!" called Joyce from below. "You're too far right again. Marker coming up on starboard."

I kept my eye on the range light, which assured me we were moving right down the center of the channel. I must have kept my eyes on it too long because I did not see the enormous metal buoy right smack in front of us. It materialized from the dark less than a boat length away, coming right at me at jogging speed. It must have been about fifteen feet high and bobbing merrily in the swell.

I cried out, "Shit!" and spun the wheel to port. *Serenity* heeled, and the buoy seemed like it was coming directly at me. I cut the wheel to starboard to port around it, the stern swung to the left, and the ugly monstrosity swept past me so close I could see its individual gobs of guano.

Megan glared at me. "That was close!"

Joyce called out, "Are we past the marker?"

"Yeah!"

Another few seconds and it would have cracked into our starboard bow. It would have been far worse than hitting the Oakland Bay Bridge, because there were no bumpers. Those things were solid metal and *heavy*. It could have caved in the side of the boat and sunk us.

Minutes later we entered the harbor and I saw that the "range light" was in truth a bright parking lot light at a Sambo's Restaurant—the original Sambo's, and I believe the only one that kept the original name.

Santa Barbara was asleep, nothing stirring in sight. I made a circle around the docks and the only place we could see to tie up was the fuel dock. All marinas and harbors have a strict rule, *Thou shalt not visit the fuel dock unless thou art purchasing fuel.* I figured if I bought several hundred dollars' worth of fuel in the morning, how could they complain?

It was so quiet that I planned to get some sleep topside, right on deck. Unfortunately, just as we secured the dock lines, it began to rain. We went below and Joyce and Megan joined Richard on the tangle of soggy sleeping bags and pillows that were spread out over the cabin sole. As for me, I decided it was more important to get out of my foulies. I spread out on the galley deck between the stove and the sink and fell asleep listening to the pitter-patter.

Half an hour later, a security guard woke me and told me I had to move the boat immediately as an overnight tie-up at the fuel dock was prohibited. I told him there was no place else to go, and in the morning I would buy some fuel and then we'd move—but not before. I bid him goodnight and shut the hatch.

Scavenger Hunt

We topped off *Serenity's* diesel tank for the third time in five days. All told, we'd motored three miles for every mile we sailed. This time of year, the charts said the wind and swells should have been steady and in our direction. What we found so far was either no wind, or a strong wind blowing directly against us.

But things were looking up. The day dawned bright and pristine, and the weather fax at the marina office showed no systems approaching Southern California, and promised clear conditions for the next several days.

"We had two powerful storms sweep up the coast over the last week," the woman behind the counter told us. "I've never seen this kind of weather so early. It's more like January or February."

"Tell us about it."

"You got caught out there?"

"We left Alameda Friday morning."

The woman offered us a sad smile. "Your luck may have just changed. I have exactly one slip available. What did you say your length was?"

"Forty-four overall including the bowsprit, thirty-eight on deck."

"There'll be some overhang but I think you'll be all right for one day."

We were fortunate to be able to dock at a slip instead of anchor off the beach. This would save us a lot of time drying out, washing clothes, topping off our fresh water tanks, and handling other miscellaneous tasks I wanted to get done between now and departure tomorrow afternoon.

After we tied up in our temporary slip, I gathered everyone in the cabin.

"I am so sorry it got so wet down here," I began.

Megan shrugged. "Hey, it's a boat."

"You have a lot of work to do before you go to the Marquesas," Richard told me. "It rains there year-round. You need a dry boat or you'll be up to your armpits in mildew."

"Yeah. Anyway, here's the plan. Looks like today and tomorrow are going to be gorgeous. We're going to bring everything topside and air it out in the sun. They got a great laundromat here, so we can clean a lot of our stuff later today. We're all going out to breakfast, my treat, and tonight we're all going to have dry beds—I'm going to get us rooms in the nearest hotel."

Joyce and Megan smiled at that.

Richard said, "And I'll be taking off very shortly for the airport. But if you want my advice, once you get down to Mexico, take this boat to a yard in Z-Town or Acapulco and have them re-bed your hull-to-deck joint and everything else, including that forward hatch. That's where your water's coming from. The ports are about the only thing that *didn't* leak."

"You're talking about pulling the whole deck off the hull?"

"You got it."

"That means taking the mast down, all the stays, the cap rails..."

"What choice do you have? Do as much of the job yourself as possible. Their hourly rates are cheaper down there but they work at a slower pace."

We hauled our bunk cushions and sleeping bags and pillows topside, took off the covers and draped everything over the deck and lifelines, exactly as we had done at sea two days earlier. The dark blue covers were stained with dry salt crystals from repeated soaking.

I saw that Megan was wearing a sweatshirt I had seen on someone else. "That's my shirt," I blurted out, taken by surprise. We were pretty much the same size and weight. Was this an error on her part? She smiled coyly and I added, "But go ahead and wear it."

The four of us hiked across the marina, headed toward Shoreline Drive and a hot breakfast cooked by someone else. We were all carrying knapsacks—Richard's with all his belongings, the rest of ours with just a change of clothes. Joyce and Richard walked together ahead of me, talking about their old sailing friends from the Neptune school.

Megan was now wearing my hat—a wide-brimmed, beige hat I had bought at a camping store to protect my head from the tropical sun. She began walking alongside me.

"So, Glenn. Where are you originally from?"

We bantered back and forth for a while: No, I had no family in the Bay Area. I moved there seven years ago to take a consulting job, then I was hired by the company I work for now... oops, used to work for until a couple of months ago.

"I work as an independent contractor," Megan told me. "I don't have to go back to work at a specific date. I'm a free agent."

"That's good to hear, because I need crew."

I was being pulled in two directions here. Richard was leaving today. Joyce had already told me she would probably leave *Serenity* shortly after we arrived at Cabo San Lucas, the southern cape of Baja Mexico and the finish line for the Ha-Ha. So that left Megan and me on the boat, just the two of us. I liked her as crew and maybe even as a friend. She was handy and pulled her weight and did not complain, and I had seen her helm and trim sails. She was top-notch—cool and competent, nearly perfect. As crew. But this wearing my stuff was unsettling. I hoped Megan saw me exactly as I saw her: a fellow sailor, reliable and of good temperament, but, well, too fat and ugly and unappealing to remotely consider for casual sex. She still reminded me of my old Navy buddy from Georgia. Did I remind her of one of her girlfriends? That would be fine by me.

Joyce hung up her cell and turned around to me. "I want four people on board when we do the Ha-Ha. There's usually a bunch of people looking for berths. I just talked to the Poobah, and he'll keep his eyes open and let us know if he finds any prospects."

"The Poo what?"

"The Poobah, the leader of the Ha-Ha."

"As in *The Grand Poobah*? The Big Cheese of our tribe?"

"Right. You'll see him at the skipper's meeting on Saturday."

225

"There's a meeting for skippers?"

"Supposed to be for skippers only, but everyone brings their first mate. So I'm coming along."

"Wait a minute. I don't remember appointing you first mate."

Megan giggled. Richard shook his head. Joyce glared.

We were seated in a booth at Sambo's surrounded by normal American life: people sipping coffee and reading the morning paper, waitresses carrying plates of omelets and hash browns. Yesterday's gray, wet, wave-tossed existence seemed a distant reality.

Richard and Megan excused themselves to use the restrooms. As soon as they were gone, Joyce put down her menu and looked me intensely in the eye.

"She's thirty-five, she's available, and she is definitely interested."

I put down my own menu. "Who are you talking about?"

"You know God-damned well who I'm talking about."

I could never put one over on Joyce. There was no way to avoid this conversation.

"Well, that's good to know. But I'm not interested in her. I want her as crew. She's great crew. I have nothing against her, in that sense. But I want her as a shipmate, absolutely nothing more. In fact, maybe you can offer some advice on that, because I sure don't want to—"

"Why?"

"Why am I not interested? Well . . . She's fat, enormously fat."

Joyce stared, trying to find the words. "Do you own

any mirrors? Surely you've seen yourself in a mirror at least once in your life."

"That doesn't matter to me. The part of my brain that likes women thinks I'm skinny and six feet tall."

Joyce threw me a smirk. "Are you sure you like women?"

"Quite sure. No anomalies in that area. It's just that I like my women feminine. I don't like the big, strong... butch type. Size and strength and, well, you know, *gruffness* are complete turnoffs for me."

"Beggars can't be choosy."

"I'm no beggar," I shot back. "I'm not desperate for a warm body. I know what I like in a woman, and if that's somehow unreasonable to other people, so be it. And who knows what's in store for the future? I expect to lose some weight on this trip. Maybe I'll meet a lovely, petite and attractive lady."

Joyce laughed out loud—not just a snicker, but a genuine laugh. Like most folks I've known, she seemed to have an intuitive sense that I would never wind up in a love affair with an attractive woman. People could not see it, could not imagine it.

"A beautiful and wealthy French woman," I added. "Who will take me to her mansion on a Tahiti mountaintop where we will make passionate love six times a day."

After breakfast Richard made a few phone calls and decided it was time for him to catch a cab to the airport. He hugged Joyce and Megan and firmly shook my hand, wished us luck, and reminded Joyce to call him as soon as we arrived in San Diego.

"When did you say you plan to arrive?"

"Saturday morning," I answered.

"And it had *better* be Saturday morning," Joyce warned. "I have things to do and people to see all weekend."

Now three, we walked down Shoreline and checked into the first decent motel we found. I threw my knapsack on the bed in my room. Everything about the motel was basic, but the sheer luxury of having this large, private, bone-dry room to myself made me almost giddy with joy. And the bathroom . . . a private toilet, a sink with little bars of soap, and a sparkling white shower with *hot running water.*

All this seemed too good to be true. After only five days at sea. What would it seem like after five months?

We went back to *Serenity* and embarked on a day-long frenzy of cleaning and stowing. We spoke with several curious onlookers throughout the day. Did you get caught in the storm? Headed south to Mexico? Doing the Ha-Ha?

I was surprised to find that my new batteries were ruined. Wrapping them up in *two* heavy duty trash bags did not keep them dry. I did not yet understand that the constant motion of a boat swiftly wears a hole in just about anything, and two layers of plastic were no match for the sea's persistence, or it's penchant for destroying anything I had paid good money for. We would have to stow everything that couldn't get wet outside certain lockers, maybe in the mesh bags Joyce had instructed me to buy for fruit and vegetables.

We cleaned our clothes in the coin laundry and discovered the powerful sun dried out our bedding faster than we expected. By sunset we had restored our clean, dry boat. Joyce made some inquiries and provided me with the address of a highly regarded Italian-American restaurant in downtown Santa Barbara.

"That's where I want to eat tonight," she said. The women were going to take full advantage of my willingness to buy us all some comfort and convenience during the time we were ashore. Most other skippers, they knew, would have anchored off the beach to save the $135 dock fee and simply fed the crew from the galley—anyone wishing to purchase meals or accommodations ashore was on her own. From a mathematical perspective, this spending pattern could not continue. When we got to Mexico we would have to get used to anchoring out and living and eating on the boat. I was no millionaire—I had a circumnavigation budget, no income, and I needed to have money left over to reestablish myself when the voyage was over.

For now I felt fortunate that both of my remaining crew had not said to me, "This sucks, I've had it, see ya," and caught a flight or a bus to San Diego to hook up with another skipper doing the Ha-Ha. Many of them owned yachts that put *Serenity* to shame. For one, they stayed dry.

After we each enjoyed a night's sleep of unspeakable luxury, we awoke refreshed and ready to embark. The weather promised to hold. We motored out of the harbor at mid-afternoon, and I plotted a course to San Diego. Due to the many islands off the Southern California shore, which were collectively called the Channel Islands, our path would make several changes in direction. We would proceed past Anacapa tonight, and then, to stay as far as possible from Los Angeles and Long Beach and the associated shipping traffic, we would pass between Santa Catalina Island and San Clemente Island. From there, we'd make a straight shot to San Diego.

"When?" asked Joyce.

"Friday night."

"That would be even better than Saturday morning. Yeah. Let's make it Friday night for sure, this way I wake up in San Diego. Oh, happy days!"

Before we got out of cell tower range, Joyce phoned Richard to tell him we were underway, and I phoned the San Diego West Marine to confirm that my life raft had arrived and I could pick it up at any time. I then called Hertz and reserved a car for Saturday and Sunday.

We found no significant wind several miles offshore, so we resigned to motor all night. As we passed the huge oil derricks that dotted the sea in these parts of California, our GPS and even our autopilot acted erratically, and I had to turn them off and take the helm. This was bad news: With only three of us aboard, we would each have only four hours' rest before standing watch again, and now it looked like we would be hand-steering. We'd each have to spend a third of our hours stuck behind a wheel.

Fortunately, we had an old-fashioned magnetic compass in our steering pedestal that only required a small bit of electricity at night; in the form of a penlight so we could read it. Yet I was desperate for the autopilot, and waited until we'd passed the oil derrick to try the autopilot and then the GPS once more. They both worked normally —a major relief. It must have been some freaky electromagnetic interference coming from the derrick.

The following morning we found some wind—and it was blowing in our direction. We decided to test the new spinnaker I had purchased and *Serenity's* spinnaker pole. Setting this tricky sail took about twenty minutes. I pretty much left it up to the women while I hand-steered to be sure we kept the wind coming from one direction.

"From now on it's going to be light winds," Joyce assured me. "We're going to get a lot of use out of that sail over the next couple of weeks."

A spinnaker is a downwind sail, and it must have been invented because it is virtually impossible to sail downwind with an ordinary mainsail and jib, which are perfect for when the wind is off the beam or from slightly ahead of the boat. In reality, full keel, heavy displacement boats were not good matches for spinnakers when the wind was light and coming from behind at the same time. There wasn't much power to drive the boat, and when I cut the engine our speed sank to three and a half knots.

"Unless it picks up," I informed my crew, "We're gonna pull into San Diego Saturday afternoon instead of Friday night."

"Take it down!" bellowed Joyce.

It was Friday night after all, really just after midnight Saturday morning, when *Serenity* cleared the first channel marker. Yes, we were going to make another night entry, second one in three days. This time Megan manned the GPS chartplotter while Joyce and I, binoculars ready, guided the boat down the channel's centerline.

Once inside the harbor we had no specific destination. All we knew for sure was we didn't want to have to anchor off the beach, which would waste a lot of time rowing back and forth to shore, and there would be a huge demand for slips based on the time of year and the fact that the Ha-Ha was set to begin in two days.

According to my cruising guide, there were about a dozen large and mid-sized marinas scattered about the Bay, some of them on the southern end at least sixteen water miles away. Fortunately, the largest marina by far, with the most slips and facilities, was less than a mile from the harbor mouth: Shelter Island. We would try there first. It was my earnest hope to find some reasonable place to tie up and get a good night's rest.

As I entered the marina I reduced our speed to the minimum possible to steer the boat, around two knots. The parking lots and docks were well lit, but the water was another matter. It was blacker than black, and I imagined smacking into some obstruction and wreaking havoc on my hull.

The place was vast, far larger than any marina I had ever seen in the San Francisco Bay Area. We crept up and down the narrow waterways searching for an empty spot of dock. It seemed like every boat on the West Coast had exactly the same idea—earlier today. Every available spot was filled. That included the police dock at the entrance to Shelter Island Inlet, where overnight tie-ups were technically forbidden but evidently tolerated.

Finally we spotted an empty slip. I turned the boat, and my crew stationed themselves port and starboard ready to jump ashore with dock lines.

Trouble was, the slip in front of us was *too* dark.

I idled the engine and slipped it into reverse.

"What the hell are you doing?" Joyce whispered back. As far as we knew, this was an "owned" slip that just happened not to have a boat in it. If there was someone around, we didn't want to attract attention.

"Turning around," I answered. "I need to see what's in that slip."

"There's *nothing* in that slip!"

"You're probably right. But it's so dark there could be something there and we won't see it until it's too late."

Even when crawling, a twenty-thousand-pound vessel has a lot of inertia. As I knew from experience, it can do a lot of damage in the blink of an eye. I maneuvered our bow around for another pass and told Megan where she could find a spotlight below. I should have thought of this sooner.

We approached the same slip and Megan shined the light ahead of us.

She cried, "Stop!"

I idled and looked: Occupying almost the full length and breadth of the slip was a beautiful old double-ender with a teak deck and hull painted navy blue. We would have smashed directly into it.

We backed away and Megan doused the light. Incredibly, Joyce held this against *me*.

"Nice going, almost wrecking that boat."

I announced we were going to try for the next marina, Harbor Island, a mile or so farther up the Bay. If there were no space there, we would do just as well to anchor for the night.

But on the way out of Shelter Island we spotted

another empty-looking slip, and an inspection with the spotlight proved it was indeed empty. Ominously, someone had left lines neatly coiled on the dock. This slip clearly belonged to someone—and they were paying rent for it. But whoever they were, they were not here now. And it was only a couple of hundred feet from the marina office. This wouldn't do my karma any good, I decided, but we tied up.

We bedded down in our dry bunks, and no one disturbed us. As soon as the gray morning dawned, I ran to the marina office, hoping they were open early so we could beg a slip and get out from where we were. Those coiled lines looked like someone was expecting to come back soon.

"How big is your boat?" the young man behind the counter asked. That he asked at all was good news, because it meant they were not completely full.

"Thirty-eight on deck . . ."

"What's the beam?"

"Twelve feet."

"Hmmm. You may be all right, but it'll be close. Really close. You ever docked med style?"

This guy who held our fate looked no older than high school, but he'd probably been sailing for ten years, which was several times my own experience.

"You mean bow to the pier? Side-by-side?"

"Right. Let me show you the spot and I'll let you decide. And I'm going to need some ID and your insurance."

Once I inspected the spot I knew why he needed to see my insurance document. It looked *exactly* twelve feet wide, not an inch more. I would have to maneuver *Serenity* down a narrow waterway between parked boats and then turn her ninety degrees, somehow, and then *somehow* get the entire hull between two other yachts, both ocean sailing vessels much larger and better equipped than mine, and probably worth a million dollars each. No kidding.

"I'll take it."

I dashed back to *Serenity* and instructed the ladies to get on the lines and get ready to shove off. We backed out of the slip, Joyce guiding the bowsprit from the dock and pulling herself up and aboard at the last possible moment, something I couldn't do with my big, fat belly. I got fixated on her for a moment and didn't see that I was about to back into a powerboat. It must have been just coming back from a fishing expedition, and was waiting just off our stern. We waved to them—a tall, gray-haired man at the wheel and another man and a woman, but they did not wave back. Just scowled at us with pissed-off expressions.

"Rude people," said Megan. "No patience."

"Yeah. I guess they didn't catch any fish last night."

I put our bow over and put the engine into forward gear, heading toward our first stop—the fuel dock. Two seconds later it dawned on me. I looked over my shoulder and sure enough, the powerboat was turning into the dock where we had just spent the night.

The fuel dock was enormous, and quite busy for this early hour. We filled our diesel tank and cast off. Just when the lines were on board, Joyce's cell buzzed and she jumped up and down with excitement.

"Go back to the fuel dock!" she commanded. "My good

friends Steve and Donna Markham are right there and I haven't seen them in ages! Go back, go back, go back!"

"Joyce, come on. I need your help getting into our slip. You can see them later."

A middle-aged couple were waving from the foot of the fuel dock. Joyce let out a scream of ecstasy and pointed a trembling finger in my direction.

"Turn this damn thing around right now and bring us back to that dock! Or so help me God, I will crew another boat on the Ha-Ha and you know I will!"

I sighed. Technically Megan and I could do the Ha-Ha by ourselves, but I'd rather have Joyce on board. And I didn't doubt that if she were given a good enough reason, she would leave. We pulled up to the dock again and she leaped off and sprinted toward the waiting couple. I looked over my left shoulder and saw, to my horror, a huge trawler slipping into the end of the fuel dock crosswise, right behind us. Our path of retreat was now blocked.

It wasn't feasible to wait them out, because already there was another boat waiting for us to leave. Trouble was, the only way we could get out of this and get to our slip was to motor backwards for at least a hundred yards.

Which I happened to know how to do, thanks to Leslie's day of special handling instruction.

I faced directly aft and gripped the top of the wheel. Then I slipped the clutch from neutral to reverse and we were off. I had to be *ultra* careful to move the top of the wheel left or right in micro-increments. The rudder had a strange effect when the water was moving the other way, and too much movement left or right would send our stern out of control. I kept *Serenity*'s speed at two knots. It felt like a balancing act, teetering on the edge of a precipice.

We cleared the fuel dock bottleneck into more open water. Engine back in neutral, I turned around and prepared to switch over to forward driving. I half-expected to see Megan watching in awe, but she was industriously coiling dock lines.

"Megan, a word real quick . . . This slip is going to be a super-tight fit. It's a med moor, just about as wide as we are, and there's two boats on either side. We need fenders on both sides, and I'm going to need you to somehow help keep us from rubbing either of our neighbors. We can't so much as smudge their hulls or they'll be up in arms."

"So you want me to kick them off if we come too close?"

"Yeah, but gently, because there won't be any clearance on the other side either." I left unsaid that it might be too narrow for us altogether, something I did not want to tell the marina guy lest he change his mind and rent the space to a narrower boat. This was going to take every bit of whatever boat handling skill I had developed in the two years since the Great Loch Lomond Smashup. I kept our speed low, but not too low. The timing had to be perfect. Megan had wisely positioned herself at the bow.

I spotted the slip and eased back on the throttle ever so slightly. I cut the wheel.

Megan remarked, "That *is* narrow."

She went out on the sprit and pushed against the starboard boat's gunwale with her right foot, which avoided contact and pointed us straight in. I idled the engine. We were now too far to port. Megan dashed port to starboard and back again to prevent contact as we slid forward at less than a foot a second. I realized I couldn't do anything else at the helm, so I took the port side and she took the starboard. The bow was creeping counter-clockwise like a watch's second hand. The instant it came within a couple of feet from the dock, we both grabbed the lifelines on our neighbors' boats and grappled *Serenity* to a complete stop.

There had been no boat-to-boat contact whatsoever. On both sides there was less than two inches of clearance.

We high-fived and collapsed on the cabin top to relax.

San Diego was all about last-minute preparations for leaving the United States. Some of it I should have gotten done a month ago, but I simply ran out of time. Some of it was related to the Ha-Ha. Joyce had warned me I needed to attend a mandatory skipper's meeting this afternoon, and then there was a costume party–barbecue going on tomorrow, where she hoped to network and recruit at least one other person to crew with us as far as Cabo, or farther.

First on my long list of to-dos was return Doug's Zodiac, *Minnow*. Megan and I deflated it on the dock and rolled it into a tight package secured with twine... Twine. Must buy some more twine, too. It was vital to buy as much as possible today and tomorrow because in Mexico anything American yachtsmen are likely to need sells at inflated prices in the stores near shore.

I took a cab to the airport and picket up the rental car. Then it was off to the nearest UPS Store to send *Minnow* on her way back to her owner. As I discovered, I wasn't the only one with that idea; there was a long line of other cruisers shipping items home at the last minute.

Next stop was West Marine. I picked up our hard case emergency life raft, six thousand dollars' worth of survival gear that I prayed to God we would never use. It was small and light enough for one person to carry to my trunk.

While at West, I picked up a Topclimber solo mast climbing device. Every ocean cruising yacht needs a means for someone to reach the top of the mast, in *Serenity's* case fifty feet above the water. The traditional way of climbing was with metal steps screwed into the mast at intervals of roughly two feet. We could have done this at the shipyard, but I didn't like the idea. The task would have taken more time, and there was no guarantee the screws wouldn't come out, especially while supporting over two hundred pounds of weight. Besides that, the solution would have required a second crew member to hold a safety line— which was the same problem we'd face had I opted for a bosun's chair. It's just a piece of wood you sit in while someone else winches you aloft. And likewise, I didn't trust either of those twenty-five-year-old mast winches to hold two hundred pounds.

So it was to be the Topclimber, a clever gadget that clipped onto a halyard and theoretically allowed any sailor to "walk" up the line using only leg muscles. Each foot was encased in a strap attached to a ratchet that clipped to the line. You simply alternated the ratchets so one leg, then the other, could be pulled higher. You could climb to the top of the mast alone.

Sounded simple.

Next stop was Home Depot, where I loaded up on still more AA and AAA batteries to replace the second batch that had been ruined. This time I also bought a few waterproof storage boxes to forestall a second round of flood damage. I also picked up two dozen rubber and nylon bungee cords at Joyce's request (i.e., demand).

While headed back to the car my cell buzzed.

"Where the hell are you?"

"Picking up all the stuff we need, what do you think?"

"You have a car?"

"Of course."

"Terrific! We need to be at the skipper's meeting five-thirty today. Pick me up at five. Do not be late. This is important, Glenn. The Poobah says he may have found us crew. But she wants to meet us tomorrow."

"She?"

"Got a problem with that?"

"I'll be outnumbered three to one."

"Sounds perfect."

The last two items on my list would be a more challenging to find. Both were related to the diesel engine. First, I had decided to buy what is known as a Baja fuel filter, a large aluminum funnel-like device that allows the sailor to filter diesel fuel as it pumped onto the boat, before it even gets to the tank. Diesel engines are rugged but extremely sensitive to fuel contamination, much more so than gasoline engines. If just a microscopic amount of water, algae, or other debris reaches the expensive fuel injectors, the entire engine could require a costly and time-consuming rebuild. Worse yet, the loss of the engine at a bad time could wreck the boat.

I had installed a $400 RACOR filter system when Jon and I re-powered *Serenity,* but that filter was just a last line of defense—the fuel in the tank itself needed to be kept perfectly clean and dry. If it wasn't, dirt and scum would accumulate at the bottom and then, during extreme weather when the engine would be most needed, the debris would get stirred up and clog the RACOR, shutting the engine down.

The fuel sold in Mexico these days was known to be a lot cleaner and drier than in years past, but a dirty batch still snuck through occasionally, and it would be sold to *gringo* yachtsmen, *no problemo*. I tracked down a filter in a store about twenty miles up the coast and gave my MasterCard number over the phone so they would hold it until I got there. Hundreds of cruisers were swarming the San Diego area this time of year, getting ready to head off to Mexico and Polynesia, and I was taking no chances.

My final item posed a challenge. Like all marine diesels, *Serenity's* engine was water-cooled, and there was an engine-driven pump to drive seawater from a through-hull strainer to a heat exchanger where the seawater cooled freshwater that in turn cooled the engine. Lose that pump, the flow of seawater stops, the freshwater overheats, the engine overheats, and then an alarm sounds. If the engine is kept running, it will overheat and seize, which means it will become a five-hundred-pound paperweight.

The system was quite reliable, except for one small component: the little rubber paddlewheel impeller inside the seawater pump. Sometimes they lasted for years, but they also had a reputation for burning out if *anything* interrupted the flow of seawater for just a few seconds. By "burning out" I mean disintegrating, at which point you have no pump and no engine.

The $11,000 engine, did not come with a spare.

A prudent yachtsman always carries spares. If I had a brain I would have gotten some over the web a long time ago. But it's not as simple as it seems. The engine manufacturer, Yanmar, doesn't seem to like owners ordering any parts on their own. They want everything done by one of their authorized repair personnel. But they do not make house calls to Polynesia.

Jon got me the parts manual (he had to order it himself—I could not buy one) so I knew the exact serial number for the impeller my engine model required. All engine makes and models took different impellers. I had the phone numbers of a couple of marine diesel supply centers but they both told me they did not carry the part.

I had to get those impellers *now*. They would be next to impossible to get overseas, requiring a long wait if I could get them at all.

Google provided me with the numbers of four diesel shops. I began calling them in order of proximity. First two, no dice. The third took almost twenty minutes to tell me they did not carry the part. Finally, on the fourth and final shop, success. It was in Escondido, thirty-four miles away.

I waited at the front counter as a woman checked for the impellers. She came back empty-handed and said she couldn't find them but she knew they had to be there someplace, as they were in the system. She enlisted the help of a guy who looked like a mechanic, and who understood why I was so intent on scoring some of these little black rubber doodads. He nodded and returned with an opened cardboard box with the correct serial number. The impeller was no more than three inches wide.

"Perfect. Thanks a lot, man. How much?"

"Thirty-five dollars."

"I'll take six."

Victory. I had nailed every item on my long list of to-do's. I headed back to Shelter Island, confident that we were prepared for the worst situation Fate could throw our way.

Part III

Breaking Free

Churn Churn Churn

The big news at the skipper's meeting was the weather report. It wasn't good.

I wasn't surprised.

There were one hundred and sixty-seven boats registered in the Baja Ha-Ha rally. Judging from the appearance of the other people crammed into West Marine, virtually all of them were couples, some married and some not, of every age from just barely out of their teens to a handful of octogenarians. Everyone was fit and tanned and looked the part. Megan and I were the rally's token fat people.

Joyce introduced me to the famed Poobah, a handsome and genial man in his mid-sixties whose real name when not Ha-Ha-ing was Dennis. I learned that Poo was publisher and owner of a popular sailing magazine, one I had frequently read, but the magazine had no "official" connection with the Ha-Ha, so it was considered a faux pas to mention it. The Ha-Ha was a separate legal entity, so if anyone's boat sank or people were placed in jeopardy, the magazine stayed completely out of the liability loop. Smart guy, this Poobah. He would do his Ha-Ha-ing in a sixty-five-foot luxury catamaran.

Our Poobah called the meeting to order. Despite the horseplay and a general adult fraternity mood, the man had some serious information to put out. First was our route. There would be two stops along the Baja peninsula, Bahia Tortugas (Turtle Bay) and Bahia Santa Maria. He reminded everyone that provisioning items such as groceries *were not* available at these stops. Bahia Tortugas was just a tiny fishing village with one dirt road leading out to the distant main highway. We would be anchored in the bay, which had plenty of room to allow space between boats at anchor. Bahia Santa Maria—well, that was just a *bahia*, no village at all.

He told us that roll call would begin at eight o'clock each morning, and everyone wrote down the frequency. Boats that did not have a single sideband radio were advised to make an arrangement with a boat that did, and contact them by VHF.

Next came the weather.

After officiating fourteen consecutive Ha-Has and enjoying near-ideal sailing conditions in each, the Poobah explained that inevitably, an early season system was bound to move in from the Pacific to make the rally a bit more . . . fun.

Nervous chuckles all around.

This was not a true storm in any sense of the word— just a low pressure zone that promised unseasonal winds and sea conditions. This time of year usually offered sailors a lull between hurricane season and the winter storms, and northwest winds that pushed the boats south on an easy beam reach, congruent with the current, which was flowing in the same direction. This year we could expect "opposing" swells and winds, so we'd have to be prepared for churning seas.

"A washing machine," I said to Joyce. She nodded, lips

drawn tight.

The main event going down Sunday was the barbecue, and as far as I was concerned the principal reason for going was to meet our prospective crew member, and to share our travel plans with the other skippers. The three of us drove together to a waterside park on Shelter Island. We found the Poobah dressed in his pirate costume, and he introduced us to Loukia and her fiancé, Bruce, both from the Bay Area and in their early thirties.

She was quite fit, and as she shook our hands, she struck me as friendly, pleasant, and highly intelligent—before she had said scarcely a word.

"So what do you do up in San Jose when you're not sailing?" I asked her.

"Do you mean as an occupation? Bruce and I are both research biologists at GeneFab in Los Gatos."

"Wow."

"A biologist," Joyce repeated. "You're going to love our head."

Loukia laughed. "Oh oh. Dirty, huh?"

"No, no, no," I countered. "It's a composting head." I tried to summon up some chemistry. "It works by allowing aerobic bacteria to compost our poop. No holding tank, no water. With a holding tank, anaerobic bacteria generate noxious odors—sulfur dioxide, for example. None of that on board *Serenity*."

It turned out that Bruce was an experienced racing sailor and had a berth on a lightweight boat built for speed. There were no berths available for Loukia, so she needed to hitch a ride as far as Cabo, where she and Bruce would hang out for a few days in a hotel and then fly back to San Jose to conclude their vacation.

I let Joyce and Megan chat Loukia up while I worked the rest of the crowd, meeting other skippers and letting them know I was recruiting additional crew for a season in Mexico and a ride to the South Seas. I had spoken to maybe a dozen people when I realized I had scarcely ever been this gregarious before. Normally I hated crowds, loathed parties. I always felt that my plump physique put me at a disadvantage, as well as my being single. Here, I didn't care. I was on a mission, and I felt welcomed as a member of this small fraternity of crazy people who sailed the ocean in small plastic boats for no good reason at all.

I told everyone we had come down from the Bay Area and several people asked if we had caught any of the bad weather. "Oh sure," I told them. "We were on a double-reefed main and storm jib part of the way, had one good day reaching, then motored the rest of the way to make sure we got here in time. No big deal."

The barbecue was winding down and we had yet to show Loukia the boat. Joyce whispered to me, "She's sailing with us."

"But she hasn't even seen the boat."

"I just told you, she's sailing with us."

I drove the three women back to the dock and they never quit their happy jabbering. It seemed like we found our fourth, which was great news because it meant each of us could sleep six uninterrupted hours at night instead of four—more people, less time on watch.

Loukia said she loved the boat. I introduced her to the

AirHead, and demonstrated placing a coffee filter on the bottom and then opening the trap door and turning the crank. As I expected, the coffee filter elicited a big laugh from all three. "They're also good for making coffee," I added.

I took advantage of the gathering to carefully explain to everyone the importance of letting no urine get into the main "poo chamber." It all had to go into the outside jug. Under normal conditions, this was no problem regardless of the urinator's gender. But under certain conditions of heel, I warned them, a certain gender that shall remain unspecified can, due to biological limitations—"

"Hey now!"

"Due to biological limitations and deficiencies, be unable to direct said urine toward the outer rim that leads to the jug. Therefore—" I produced a small bucket from under the cabinet—"please tinkle in this, and pour it into the jug."

It was almost dark and we still hadn't provisioned. We decided I would stay aboard and complete some last-minute maintenance while Joyce and Megan drove Loukia to her hotel for her belongings. They would also go food shopping at Trader Joe's with my MasterCard.

"Absolutely no seafood," I reminded them.

"Are you allergic?" asked Loukia.

"No. I loathe the sight of it and the smell of it and I just hate it."

Ha-Ha departure day finally dawned, overcast and nearly windless. I ran out to the marina office to return our restroom keys. We had to be at the "starting line" (the harbor entrance) at eight o'clock sharp.

As I hurried back to the dock I suddenly became aware this was the last time I would be standing on US soil for quite some time, possibly three years or more depending on whether I had the inclination and the funds to fly back home during the circumnavigation. I stopped, came to attention, and saluted the flag flying at the tip of Shelter Island. Then I turned around, jumped onto the dock, and ran toward the boat. Beneath my feet was nothing but boards and water. How long would it be before I felt US soil under me again?

We left our slip and motored out of the harbor to join the Ha-Ha fleet, which now consisted of scores of sailboats spread out nearly to the horizon. Most people were motoring in tight circles, some with sails already flying. There were colored signal flags, air horns, and even a few fireworks. There was a festive spirit in the air, but it was from a distant and simpler time, when people took joy in doing things together that didn't involve making money or advancing their careers or acquiring a bigger house.

Joyce began pointing out all the boats and people she knew. A beautiful Tartan 48 with a teak deck passed fifty feet off our port side and I recognized Pete and Jen Babcock from Portland, Oregon, whom I had just met and spoken to yesterday. They were sailing with their two daughters, around ten and seven years old. We waved and the whole family waved back at us.

Before eight, Joyce was at our single sideband confirming our position at the starting line. A red rocket zipped into the air, and a mighty cry of air horns and human voices spread out over the water. On this rather dreary Monday morning, while millions of Southern

Californians commuted to their workplaces, oblivious to our plans, the Baja Ha-Ha had officially begun.

The day went well. We found wind right away, and before noon we were making five knots on a close reach over low swells. I had secured the engines and we watched the Coronado Islands pass several miles to our east, which meant we were in Mexican waters.

Regardless of the system passing through our area over the next two days, I expected to sail as much as possible and leave the engine silent for twenty-three hours a day. That meant the alternator would not be charging our battery bank, which meant it would be continuously drained. We had two major power loads: the autopilot and the refrigerator. We had two means of keeping the batteries trickle-charged without the engine: the solar panel Doug had installed across our stern davits, and our wind turbine. The turbine was spinning, but even using a battery monitor, it was hard to tell whether the cells were net charging or net discharging. I decided it was probably close to breaking even, and we would have to watch the battery level carefully to keep them from being totally discharged.

Joyce continuously prepared a thermos of hot tea for herself and her female shipmates. I don't think any of them ever stopped drinking tea that first day, ever. I was given water and Gatorade and instructed to keep drinking.

"For every Diet Coke, sixteen ounces of water," Joyce admonished. I didn't think that was necessary, but I was on this boat with someone who almost had a captain's license, a registered nurse, and a professional biologist. I didn't feel I had room to argue.

The system hit around midnight. No rain, just rapid changes in wind direction and speed. We lowered sail and I started the engine, making the battery issue moot. I stood watch around two o'clock and kept track of about a dozen sets of running lights that dotted the horizon—our fellow Ha-Ha participants. After spreading out, each boat was on average about a mile from the closest other boat.

After an hour sea and sky blended into a single black sphere at the center of which were my drowsy eyes. Few people have the opportunity to be outdoors, on a cloudless night, for a long enough period of time to *feel* the stars turning around them—no, the whole universe. There was no difference between the distant sparks strung along the horizon and the stars rising on my left. I would spot a green and red bow light off our stern and it would grow brighter as whoever it was gained on us, then they would pass us and the light would become solid white. I was getting good at recognizing which way a boat was headed at night based on the appearance of the running lights.

I awoke to a gray, wave-churning world. Joyce was at the single sideband and the Poobah was conducting roll call. I listened to each vessel's name and response, and when *Serenity's* name was called, Joyce reported that all was well.

There was a terrible stink and I sat up to find out where it was coming from. Megan was three feet away, pants down, crouched over a bucket, halfway through a major bowel movement. I put the blanket over my face. What was wrong with the AirHead?

Minutes later I swung out of the bunk but I could not stand upright. *Serenity* was *dancing*, quite energetically, back and forth, up and down, jerking this way and that, in a sort of random Brownian motion. I put on my harness and went topside. It was as I expected: The sea was covered with foam as far as I could see, a great expanse of churning and bubbling wavelets crashing into each other at all angles. The sea was churning like the water in a gargantuan washing machine. This happens when the current or tide is going one way, and another current is going another way, and the wind is in direct opposition to whatever the water wants to do. It happens on a smaller and less turbulent scale under the Gate when the tide is ebbing but the wind is blowing in from the sea.

I felt sick immediately and regretted not saturating myself with Dramamine starting yesterday morning. Joyce was on watch.

"You got a problem with the head," she told me.

Those were words I didn't want to hear.

"What's wrong?"

"Go see for yourself. You got a problem. Fix it."

I already had a pretty good idea what she was talking about. I made my way forward and that baby diaper stench confirmed it. Only this time the container was *full*—really, more than full. With three women processing about a gallon of tea each per hour I knew this had to happen; I had just been too much in denial to check it. With the sideways jerking of the boat, a thick brown sludge had oozed over the rim of the AirHead, down the sides, and spread out over the deck, under the head door and into the main salon. A comforter and two pillows were laying in the filth and soaking it up.

I had to get topside for some fresh air.

At the tea drinkers I shouted, "Didn't I tell you guys not to piss into the AirHead?"

Joyce gave me her look. This time it wasn't much of a match for the environmental conditions.

"We did our best and you *will not* blame us. *You* picked that head, now *you* live with the consequences."

The fact that she was *telling* me to do it, rather than asking, ticked me off. Nevertheless, the longer I waited the worse it would be. I went below thinking about the best way to tackle this. It would be heavy, maybe seventy pounds. I could heft it up the ladder myself but the way the boat was moving . . . I dashed topside, hooked my tether and just made it to the life line before I threw up the digestive remnants of last night's chicken cacciatore.

Below, both Megan and Loukia were asleep or at least pretending to be. Thinking about a nice pot of hot coffee, I uncovered the AirHead and fastened the top as firmly as I could. Then I unbolted the bottom, freeing the entire unit.

"Please, God, let me get this dumped over the side." I could not imagine the results if what I was about to do did not go well. I began to move the filled container across the deck. I had to hold my head down to see what I was doing, which made the nausea worse. It wasn't that hard to scoot it aft up to the ladder. I put both arms around it and put it on the second step, maybe eighteen inches from the cabin sole.

The boat continued to dance almost at random. I should have checked my footing. I moved the container to the third step. So far so good. Three more steps and I could lift it over the transom and onto the deck, and from there it would be a cakewalk.

Fourth step. Doing good.

Off the fourth step, the boat *jerked*, and my left leg flew out from under my body. In an instant the entire weight of the container and its contents was resting on my right side, but there was no chance I could bring my right leg under me fast enough to support myself and the AirHead at the same time. I felt myself going down, and the container coming with me.

I struck the sole and the container contents exploded everywhere. It was a thin brown gruel, more urine than anything else, but with plenty of peat and crap and toilet paper and coffee filters suspended in it. Half the cabin was immediately covered with filth, and it spread rapidly across the sole with each jerk and roll of the boat. I had gotten plenty of it on my person, including my face and hair, which was not good news knowing that the next opportunity for a hot shower was at least nine days away.

I retched, spitting out gritty particles and my own sour vomit.

Joyce looked down from the companionway hatch and said nothing.

A Modicum of Shame

I had done it. I had created a mess that was physically impossible to clean up.

And make no mistake: it was my mess, and my shipmates made that abundantly clear by failing to offer even token assistance toward eliminating the biohazard, or at least stopping the spread. Joyce remained topside; Megan and Loukia stayed in their bunks. In their eyes, I suppose, I had failed to provide them with a valid means of eliminating their wastes, so this was a catastrophe entirely of my making.

Serenity carried a limited supply of paper towels and I could have used up every roll. I thought of using a flat piece of cardboard to scoop most of the mess back into the container, but we banished cardboard boxes because they tend to harbor roach eggs. I ended up using our dustpan and my bare hands.

Did you know that female urine is more concentrated than male? I assure you, it's true.

Some of it was dribbling into the bilge and there was nothing I could do about that. I got as much as possible back into the AirHead—maybe about half—and hefted that topside and over the life lines. Since the wind was more or less blowing off our bow, there was no leeward side, and a lot of the slop blew back against the hull, anointing us for all to see.

I kept a few spare comforters for crew, and because everyone had brought their own sleeping bags, I retrieved three of them and used the first to mop up as much of the slop as possible from the sole and the ladder and galley cabinets. Then I took it topside and pitched it overboard. Joyce, normally hypersensitive about aluminum cans going overboard, said nothing. The second blanket I wetted with seawater from a bucket hauled up on a rope, then squeezed out the excess and used the now damp blanket to wipe up more sewage. Blanket over the side. Repeat with the third blanket.

Then I took one roll of paper towels and began going over everything with a spray bottle of organic, green, eco-safe, hippie household cleanser. All the used paper towels, over the side.

I said to Joyce, "I need your help for a minute." I hauled a few buckets of seawater to the deck and she poured them over my foulies, washing the remaining brown grit into the cockpit drain. Then I used saltwater soap and cold water to clean off my head, face, arms and hands as best I could.

I went below and announced to the crew, "The head is secured. Use buckets."

My new order did not include me. I put more peat into the now empty AirHead and christened it with my morning dump. When I was done I turned the crank and taped the cover shut with a sign: SECURED. *They* would use buckets.

* * *

The wind became steady from the southwest. We were fortunate that it didn't rain a drop, and our bunks stayed dry.

Technically the Ha-Ha was a rally, a sort of sailing race, even though the rally committee stressed fun over competition. Nevertheless, each entry boat was required to record the time of departure and arrival from each port and the total number of minutes they spent running the engine, which I suppose would be used to handicap us. At any given time we could see five or six other cruisers around us. Everyone was sailing, and moving faster than us. They would appear on the aft horizon, gradually approach, and within an hour, sail right past us.

Joyce said to me, "I'm not going to be the last one in. I don't care if we're the second-to-last or the third-to-last, but I will not be the last boat."

"Sounds good," I answered. "Let's raise some sail."

When changing sails at sea on a short-handed boat (and four is considered short-handed by most) it's a good idea to get everyone on deck and involved. Joyce and I could have done it ourselves. We could have used the autopilot to head directly into the wind and raised the main and the jib in that order, and then fallen off the wind and trimmed the sails. Instead, I stationed Loukia at the jib sheet and Megan as her assistant, ready with the winch handle. Joyce took position on the cabin top at the mainsail boom, and I headed the boat into the wind and left the wheel under automatic control.

That was a mistake. I should have had Joyce and Loukia raise the main, and then called everyone back in the cockpit to deal with the jib, while I hand-steered the boat to accommodate sudden changes in wind direction.

The autopilot, remember, has no idea what the wind is doing. It steers by magnetic direction only.

The main went up no problem. It luffed violently, requiring me to really bear down on the halyard in order to winch the top of the sail right up to the extreme tip of the mast. This was necessary for us to control the shape of the main and get the most power out of it. In view of all the boats passing us, that's what other people were doing.

I called for Loukia to pull the jib out. With a roller-furling system, the jib is stored wrapped around the forestay. We pull it out—unroll it really—using a sheet attached to the foot of the sail. Loukia pulled and pulled, and swiftly ran out of steam. Physically she was on the pudgy side, but it was a dainty sort of female pudgy as opposed to Megan's rough-and-tumble Rosie O'Donnell biker-chick heftiness. I assisted her while Megan made sure the furling line was paying out smoothly and going into the drum. There was a flat metal spool at the bottom of the forestay that held a line we would pull to reverse the process and roll the jib back on the stay.

The main stopped luffing.

I should have immediately grabbed the wheel, pulled the autopilot lever, and steered the boat back into the wind. But I didn't.

I'm not sure what happened next, but it was quick and it was baffling. While the autopilot was faithfully keeping us pointed in the same direction, the wind was doing its own thing and blowing on us from the port side. The twenty-foot mainsail boom was still held firmly in place by the mainsheets, thank God, but the jib was another matter. The jib was "held" to the boat only by the sheet held by Loukia's small, soft, research-scientist hands.

259

The jib filled with wind and took off. Loukia wisely let go of the sheet, and it took off as well. In an instant the enormous jib was flapping like crazy at a ninety-degree angle to the boat. The combined power of the engine and the autopilot-guided rudder kept us pointed in the same direction, now perpendicular to the wind.

The end of the jib sheet was snapping in the air like a huge horsewhip. There were probably hundreds of pounds of pressure on the forestay, and for that reason, we couldn't furl it up again until we headed up into the wind. I finally took control of the wheel.

My crew waited for orders. I'm pretty sure Joyce was lost, or she would have suggested our next step.

"I'm heading up!" I shouted. "Be ready to furl it back in!"

Furling a jib is a simple matter, but it takes two people: one to furl, the other to keep tension on the sheet so the sail furls evenly and correctly. Our sheet was free and snapping wildly over the turbulent waves of the Pacific. We tried anyhow. Under orders from me, Joyce and Megan hauled the furling line and began bringing in the jib.

Something went wrong. The wind may have shifted again, or the end of the sheet may have been blown over the mast, but somehow the whole jib got twisted and knotted up. We were able to furl it, more or less. When we ran out of furling line there was a big ugly bulge of sail about two-thirds up the forestay. The sheet had wrapped several times around the top of the stay, almost fifty feet above the water.

The jib was no longer usable. Worse, it looked really bad—like something had gone hideously wrong. Well, something had. We raised the staysail, and along with a single-reefed main, the boat was balanced enough to make seven knots through the foam-specked sea.

Bahia Tortugas was an amazing landfall. We made the bay entrance at dawn, and found the Ha-Ha fleet already at anchor. We were probably last. No matter, as the bay was two-by-three miles of pristine blue water, and there was plenty of room for everyone.

We anchored in about twenty feet of water over a sandy bottom. The practice I had with Doug came in handy, and we ended up equidistant from three other boats. Joyce was on the VHF announcing our arrival to the Poobah and her friends.

The Ha-Ha scheduled a beach party this afternoon, and I wanted to fix the jib before the festivities began. Joyce found the fouled jib embarrassing, and experienced sailors took this sort of thing sternly. Worse, if I acquired a reputation as a klutz, I would have difficulty recruiting an experienced crew for points south.

As I broke out the Topclimber gear, a flat-bottomed fishing boat pulled alongside us. There were two suntanned, hard-muscled fishermen aboard, accompanied by four or five little boys and girls. They were offering live lobster for sale or trade.

"No thank you, *amigo!*" I waved them off.

The children gleefully pointed to the big brown smear on *Serenity's* hull, held their noses and laughed, "*Caca, caca!*"

"*Sí, el caca,*" I sighed, and wished I knew more Spanish.

They had been told no, but the fishing boat (called a *panga* in Mexico, Central America, and much of the rest of the world) had no intention of giving up. Joyce tossed some candy to the kids and Megan and Loukia began chatting up the fishermen in halting Spanish. I began setting up the Topclimber gear, figuring I would make the ascent when the ladies were good and ready to help me.

I read the instruction manual and inspected the equipment, which was mainly a modified harness with two leg ratchets. It needed to use a static line, for which a halyard with a secured bottom end would do. I also readied a second harness for use as a safety line.

I wasn't paying attention to what was happening with the fishermen.

The *panga* motored off to cheerful waves and goodbyes. Megan and Loukia were triumphantly holding up *live lobsters* while Joyce snapped pictures with her cell. They had bucketfuls of lobsters.

I was beyond furious.

"Damn it, I said no seafood!" I yelled, the first time I raised my voice in anger since we left Alameda. The first time aboard *Serenity*, in fact. But I had had enough.

"You don't have to eat it!" Joyce giggled.

"It's going to stink up my whole boat, stink up my pots and dishes, make everything smell like lobster, which is disgusting!"

"Like the boat doesn't stink already," Megan pointed out.

I thought I was ticked off then, but that was nothing compared to finding a nearly empty spare battery box sitting on the chart table. They had traded almost all of our AA and AAA batteries for a couple of buckets of lobsters.

"I can't believe it!" I screamed. "You traded our spare batteries, *my* spare batteries, without even asking me? I can't believe my eyes! You have some nerve!"

"Relax," consoled Joyce. "You can afford it."

So that was it: rich-guy syndrome. I had tried to be nice with the restaurant meals, the hotel room, and giving them my MasterCard to go food shopping. They concluded I had an infinite supply of money—and that I probably "owed" them for making them crew such a boat as *Serenity*.

I don't think I was ever more enraged in my life after seeing those batteries gone. There were three packages left out of maybe thirty economy-sized ones that I expected to last a year.

I prepared to climb the mast with Megan acting as my safety helper. I sure as hell didn't want to, but there was no choice. There was no chance of freeing the jib otherwise. I imagined something would go wrong and I would drop twenty or thirty feet and end up on the deck with a shattered ribcage, compound fractures of my leg or arm, maybe a dislocated shoulder, or worse. And there were no emergency facilities at Bahia Tortugas—not even a clinic. We were over a hundred miles from the nearest medical facility.

Call me a wimp, but that's what was going through my mind as I donned the Topclimbers.

It didn't matter how I felt, because I couldn't do it. It was harder than it looked, much harder. I just didn't have the strength to haul my fat carcass up the rope in a controlled fashion. I got maybe ten feet up and it was obvious I was struggling, twisting and turning, gasping for breath. It was manifestly unsafe to continue, and I knew it.

"Get your ass down," ordered Joyce. "I found someone who will fix this for us."

"I want to try it first," said Megan.

Feeling humiliated, I handed over the Topclimbers and offered some suggestions. She didn't fare much better. If anyone had a chance of reaching the top it was Joyce, and she wasn't stepping forward as a volunteer.

Instead she was back on the VHF.

"My friend and former student Karl is going to bail your ass out. He's on his way now. Thank me later."

A top-of-the-line black Zodiac hailed *Serenity* and pulled up alongside. The man on board must have been over six-foot-two, lean and muscular, with chiseled features. He looked like a German Adonis or Olympic track star: Hans Gruber's son, only not so terroristic. He was about thirty and wearing nothing but a red Speedo. They embraced and Joyce introduced each member of the crew.

"You are skipper, *ja*?" Karl asked as he weakly shook my hand. I could tell he was skeptical and wanted me to know it. Obviously, Joyce should be the skipper.

Karl and Joyce had a little powwow about the jib and Karl seemed to shrug it off as no big deal. He was familiar with the Topclimbers and once he had them on, he scaled the mast in approximately five seconds. After taking in the view, Karl unwrapped the jib sheet from the stay.

"Get ready to unfurl it," Joyce told me. Megan and I went to the cockpit and got ready. Karl dropped the end of the sheet down to Joyce and she brought it aft to us. We pulled the jib off the stay and furled it back perfectly.

I just happened to have a few bottles of Beck's in the refrigerator for special occasions, and I handed one to Karl. I expected him to be just a bit pleased that this pasty-faced American fellow at least had the chops to hand him a chilled bottle of authentic German beer on a hot sunny morning on the desolate Baja Peninsula, but he accepted it nonchalantly and drained it as quickly as he had climbed the mast.

"Be a little bit more careful with your sails, skipper man, *ja*?" he told me.

"Good advice, thank you very much. And I should learn how to go aloft, too."

His expression communicated he really didn't see a chance of that happening in his lifetime, so it wasn't worth a verbal response. Karl handed me the empty bottle —I half expected him to crush it in his fingers. He accepted the humble thanks of everyone before riding off in his Zodiac.

Joyce waved her finger at me. "Count your lucky stars I knew Karl and he was willing to help us."

It's Not You, It's Me

Joyce also had friends who gave us all a lift to the beach
for the afternoon party, which meant we did not need to
put Ducky in the water and row nearly two miles. I noted
that just about everyone was using an inflatable dink with
a small gasoline outboard. Again, Joyce reminded me I was
fortunate she knew so many sailors who could lend us a
hand.

I wondered if I should consider getting an outboard for
Ducky and keeping it and the fuel stowed on the afterdeck.
If I could get one in Mexico, it would cost me.

Except for several hundred partiers on the beach and a
few tents set up by the Mexican beer company Tecate, the
beach at Bahia Tortugas was the most remote piece of real
estate I had ever trod upon. The bay itself was surrounded
on three sides by rocky hills that could have been on Mars.
We drank Tecate, networked with our fellow cruisers, and
beachcombed for whale bones and teeth. Word was the
weather would be terrific from this point forward.

In order to induce me to focus on crew recruitment,
Joyce told me she had found out in San Diego she would
need to fly home a day or two after we reached Cabo. That
was always my assumption, but my hope was that she
would end up staying aboard until Acapulco. I relied on her
to tell it like it is; my goal was to avoid a yes-crew who

wouldn't contradict unsafe or unwise orders.

I mentioned this to Megan and asked for her help finding at least one more crew member who wished to spend the season in Mexico.

She looked at me, gave a coy smile, and said, "Sure, Glenn, but you know I'm with you all the way to Vallarta, Z-Town, Acapulco . . . Wherever we want to go is fine."

And she was wearing my hat, which I needed.

"I appreciate that, I really do. But I honestly think it would be safer and easier on us both if we had three or four."

"Boat's too crowded with four," she responded. "We can get along fine with two."

"What about night watches?"

"What about 'em? We do, say, three and three, take naps during the day whenever we feel like it. Most cruisers only have two people, you know."

I *almost* answered back, "Yeah, but they're married or they're lovers."

We scanned the beach for teeth. Nearly all of the adults had coupled off in sets of two or four or six, the even number per clique due to the natural social unit of one man and one woman. (I hadn't noticed any gay cruisers yet.) How many times had I been in a similar situation, with the roles reversed? Especially in my late twenties and early thirties, when there were still a sizable portion of my peers not coupled off, I used to meet the women of my dreams at work or while taking a night class or even as a library patron. I would talk to them and ask open-ended questions, be interested in them, and all the other Dale Carnegie pointers. But something was usually missing. They would never *look* at me as they did other men—taller men, men with more of a male presence. For me there was the glass wall: conversations were civil but never comfortable. If I did ask them out for coffee, I saw a phantom flicker across their faces; that mix of surprise and a touch of annoyance, then, "That's very sweet, but I'm seeing someone."

I did not want to be on that boat alone with Megan. In fact, I had a bad feeling about this whole thing. Should I directly discuss the subject openly with her, here and now? I had a feeling that if I did, she would say the thought never crossed her mind, and it wasn't a problem, and in fact she hoped to hook up with an old boyfriend in Z-Town for Christmas. In fact, she would *have* to say that. Then, surprise surprise, two days after we're in Cabo she's on another boat or flying back to the Bay Area, and I'm single-handed.

But if I ignored the matter, what would happen once Joyce and Loukia were gone?

The Ha-Ha fleet spent a refreshing and idyllic two days in Bahia Tortugas. It was nearly perfect, marred only when my crew did cook their lobsters, and it did make the boat stink like a fish house. I stayed on deck and finished the last of our bread making sandwiches. I demanded they do a thorough job scouring every pot and dish and fork and cup they used, but it didn't matter. Everything had a lobstery smell to it, even the plastic cups, which they had washed in the same water as everything else. I sequestered a few plastic cups for my own use and wrote my name on them with waterproof marker.

On the second day a tough looking *hombre* named

Hector came around with a *panga* selling diesel fuel from a five thousand liter tank. With his black goatee, shaved head, scary tattoos, and do-not-screw-with-me face, Hector could have gotten a job with Hollywood central casting playing the stereotypical lethal Mexican prison gangbanger. Here he was just a man trying to make a living selling fuel.

The following day we prepared to get underway after a dawn roll call. The next rest stop was Bahia Santa Maria, a bit over two hundred nautical miles south, and the leg was expected to take two days. The voice of the Poobah over the VHF cautioned everyone not to try to leave the bay all at once, and to report the time they cleared Cabo Tortola.

We could scarcely believe it, but it was a perfect day for sailing. The sea was a gorgeous, unearthly shade of blue and there wasn't a cloud in sight. Both the gentle breeze and the small, widely space swells were headed in our direction. It was warm enough to be on deck in a T-shirt or light sweatshirt.

For the first time we were surrounded by an abundance of visible marine life. On the way down we spied an occasional flash of gray—a porpoise or seal watching us pass—but today it was like being inside a public aquarium—but instead of us watching them from our own natural environment, it was the other way around. I saw my first whale at sea—a California gray most likely. As if on cue, the whale lifted its tail fins out of the water and fanned them at us before it disappeared. In an instant, I forgot all about the AirHead, about Karl, about the batteries, about the boat that couldn't stop leaking.

* * *

The wind gradually clocked northward until it was blowing almost directly opposite our intended heading. To the uninitiated, this may seem like an ideal circumstance, because the boat can "be pushed" by the wind directly. That may have been more or less true in the days of the square rigger (picture the *HMS Bounty*) but today's sloops and cutters are designed to sail upwind, with the wind blowing off their beam and a little aft. When the wind is blowing *directly* from astern, we could put our main boom straight out perpendicular to the hull, but it could not go all the way to ninety degrees because it was blocked by the mast stays. About seventy-five degrees was the furthest out we could put it.

When a sailboat is running downwind there should be some means of preventing the mainsail from accidentally swinging the boom to the other side of the boat—*hard and fast*. This is known as an unintentional jibe, and it can break the boom, pull down the mast, and kill people standing on deck. It happens when the relative angle between the boat and the wind changes so that the wind "gets in front of" the mainsail and without much warning swings it violently to the opposite side of the vessel. It's easier for this to happen than it sounds.

Serenity had no built-in preventers, or lines intended to hold the boom in place and prevent unintentional jibes. I had purchased long lengths of three-eighths inch nylon lines just for this purpose, and we rigged them on both sides to serve as temporary preventers.

The breeze was never strong enough to consider using our spinnaker, a sail specially designed for downwind travel. Our yankee jib hung slack so we furled it to avoid a sudden gust playing havoc with the boat.

The night was moonlit, but even so, the stars were brilliant and awe-inspiring. I looked forward to seeing the night sky on passages when the moon was wasn't up and the full glory of the Milky Way was apparent. Stars to our east seemed to emerge directly from the horizon almost as bright and steady as the ones directly overhead. To our west, constellations seemed to be sinking directly into the sea, the effect appearing so beautiful it was artificial, and if this were a planetarium I'd be thinking, "That looks pretty obviously like computer generated special effects."

I had given everyone a safety tour as they came on board, including Joyce. Harnesses hooked to the jacklines after sunset, no exceptions. No sleeping on watch. Wake me if you have any questions or doubts whatsoever. If you're not sure about waking me, wake me.

Just as dawn began on day two of this perfect passage, I awoke to distant shouting. I sat up and listened. Joyce and Loukia were yelling at each other in the cockpit. It was still quite dark so I put on my harness before going topside. The two women were seated, not looking at each other.

"What's all the hubbub about?"

"Oh, nothing!" Joyce shouted back. "She just tried to outrun a cruise ship, that's all."

I looked at Loukia, who had been on watch. "What happened?"

She held up both hands. "We passed a ship. That's about it."

"Well, how close was the ship?"

"About from me to you," Joyce answered. "The engine

noise woke me up."

I was stunned. "You're kidding."

Loukia snarled, "We were safe at all times."

From Joyce: "Bull. Shit."

I scanned around us and saw what looked like a cruise ship about five miles away, the hull already below the horizon. It was headed south, so it must have come up behind us. We saw four or five cruise ships each night, lit up like Manhattan Island, six hundred to nine hundred feet long and close to two hundred feet tall—moving skyscrapers. And they *did* move, around twenty-four knots, which may not seem like much until you've seen something that big moving that fast, throwing up a huge foaming wake that disturbed the sea for a mile on each side.

An average of one sailboat per year is lost on the West Coast to mysterious circumstances—no distress call. The cause is probably a direct hit from cruise ships or freighters hauling ass to the next port. Small boats appear on their radars, but usually, the big boat doesn't alter its course. When struck with sudden overwhelming force, fiberglass shatters like glass (well, it *is* glass) and the boat goes down in seconds, the emergency radio beacon with it. The cruise line might notice some scratches in the paint job.

Loukia had probably fallen asleep. She was wakened by the noise of the ship, suddenly upon her, the sight of the bow spray inducing panic. Forgetting about the engine, she attempted to sail *Serenity* out of the ships' path and barely made it.

* * *

273

The excellent conditions continued, and contributed to our gradually rising complacency. I caught everyone at least once, walking around topside without being hooked on. I reminded them: "Look at me, I'm clipping on whenever I'm topside, even in broad daylight."

"That's smart," said Joyce. "Because if you fall overboard, we ain't going back to fish you out."

At eight o'clock the Poobah took roll and asked for the names of the boats that had sailed all night, without touching their engines even once. He sounded like he didn't expect there would be many, because winds were mostly light. A handful of yacht names sounded from the speaker.

"*Serenity!*" Joyce shouted into the mic.

"*Serenity?*" came Poo's skeptical voice.

"That's ten-four, *Serenity,* Glenn Damato, first mate Joyce Zimmerman!"

"That's a bravo zulu for *Serenity,*" responded the Poobah. "I believe you are the only full displacement boat who didn't motor last night."

Megan had brought her guitar and strummed some tunes throughout the afternoon. I ate a big lunch and decide to take a nap. I woke to the sound of female laughter. It sounded like everyone had patched up their squabbles and there was some sort of horseplay going on around the cockpit. I was still half asleep, and the brilliant tropical sky made it temporarily difficult to look out the companionway hatch.

But what I saw confused the hell out of me. For a moment I thought I was hallucinating. I saw a *giant baby* standing on my afterdeck.

Or what looked exactly like a giant baby, an infant,

naked, with its butt facing my direction. How can there be a giant baby on my boat? Then I saw two others. One of the other "babies" faced me frontally and the illusion evaporated. It wasn't a baby. It was just Megan. All three women were taking a group cockpit shower, a sailing tradition during pleasant conditions. They were all completely naked and didn't seem to care I had awoken from my nap and would see them.

I was not in any way excited by this event. At the beach party the other day, I had seen dozens of young women who, had they been wet and naked a few feet away, would have perked up my interest. Yet I was finicky about women in a way only a girlfriend-less geek can be. It was a physical and permanent characteristic of mine, a part of my psyche I could not turn off—or on. And to prove it, I sat at the nav station and checked our position on the chartplotter.

We were making six knots over the bottom with hardly any motion to the boat. I didn't know it at that moment, but Joyce and Megan had set the spinnaker and we were being pulled along by that sail alone.

We barbecued the last of our San Diego steaks at dusk. At first we found it impossible to light the rail-mounted charcoal grill with a steady breeze blowing directly from behind us. Matches and grill lighters and even rolled up pieces of paper blew out. Then Loukia came up with a solution: a tampon, rubbed with a little bit of diesel fuel. Worked so well they should probably sell them at West Marine. We decided from now on we would only light the grill with a tampon, our unique *Serenity* tradition.

* * *

As we settled into our night watch routine, I told everyone if we headed directly toward the entrance to Bahia Santa Maria we would arrive around two o'clock in the morning. I had decided against making a night entry. The cruising guide chart showed a large bay with a wide entrance, but there were no lighted buoys and lots of boats already at anchor.

We had in our favor radar, the GPS, the bright moonlight, and the fact that the bay entrance was seven miles wide. But that was *too* wide. Where was the fleet? What if we ended up dropping the hook three miles from where we should be? I also knew it was harder than it sounded to determine your position based on radar returns from mountains, and I didn't know exactly how accurate the Garmin GPS charts were in Mexico. Bottom line: in every case where I optimistically "pushed the envelope," we had a close call and only luck saved us from disaster. On the theory that our luck would run out eventually, I decided to play it ultra-safe until I acquired more experience.

"So if we're not entering at night, what are we gonna do?" asked Joyce.

I indicated a waypoint I had saved on the chartplotter. "See that spot? That's five miles due west of the anchorage. We're headed for that spot. When we get there, which will be there between one and two tonight, we come to a beam reach headed west. If the wind is coming from where it is now, that will be a heading of about two-five-zero. We keep reaching for two hours. Then we tack and take a reciprocal heading back to the initial point, say zero-seven-zero degrees. We'll arrive back at the point at dawn, drop sail, motor in."

"I want to sail in for once," said Joyce. "Looks better."

Should we have mounted the Collision Avoidance Radar Detector I had purchased a couple of months ago? I decided against it. It was made for single-handed sailing, when the only person aboard would have to be asleep at least five or six hours a day. But with four, it struck me as permission to sleep on watch. I didn't like that idea, especially after the cruise ship incident. Visibility was perfect—there was no excuse for not seeing every ship within ten miles.

I made sure I was on watch when we reached the point. There was no wind at all, so Joyce and I dropped sail and we set an autopilot course of two-seven-zero, due west. I turned over the watch at two o'clock to Megan with instructions to come about at four o'clock to heading zero-nine-zero, and have Loukia wake me at half past five.

It didn't quite work out like that. I woke on my own. The sun was not up but the sky was bright enough to see. A gorgeous full moon was suspended two inches above the western horizon, pale yellow and surreal. I was enjoying the sight when it dawned on me: why is that moon off our bow?

We had never turned around. We motored west all night and we were now over twenty nautical miles from Bahia Santa Maria when we should be five.

I calmly asked Megan and Loukia what part of my instructions did they not understand.

Joyce could not stand to hear a man interrogating women, which to her was backwards from the natural and proper order of the universe.

She growled, "Shut the hell up! Will you please shut your damn mouth for once? First you say two-seven-zero.

Then you don't want two-seven-zero. Make up your mind!"

I realized I should have written everything down.

"And now, thanks to you," Joyce continued, "We're going to be the very last boat to drop our hook."

Bahia Santa Maria was five times the size of Tortugas, and located in a more remote area. Here, there was no village at all. We were over six hundred miles south of San Diego, in true tropical waters. We did have to backtrack twenty miles, but it was a glorious twenty miles. Maybe because we were on the only boat around, we were trailed by a crowd of seals, sea turtles, porpoises, and—I could have sworn—a great white shark.

We would be anchored here with the rest of the Ha-Ha fleet for two days. Today was on the schedule as a "lazy" day, the only thing on the schedule an informal skipper's happy hour at four o'clock on the Poobah's massive luxury catamaran—"Skippers only, now. Sorry, no first mates, and I mean that," came the Poo's satiny voice over the VHF.

Most cruisers took the day to visit with friends, and there were Zodiacs zipping constantly between the scores of anchored yachts like minivans delivering kids to soccer practice. We had almost recreated American suburbia inside a pristine Baja inlet.

I took a sun shower on deck, in my bathing suit.

"I got you a ride to the skipper's happy hour," Joyce told me. "Be ready at four and Bart will come by and pick you up and take you back, too."

"Thanks."

"Listen to me," she said, a more serious note entering

her voice. "Loukia and I are going to a dinner party aboard *Wind Chimes*. We're going to be gone by the time you get back from the happy hour, and we will be gone all night long."

She was annunciating each word clearly. All of a sudden, I got it.

"Yeah, we will be gone, Loukia and I, *all night loooong*. We will see you and Megan in the morning, okay?"

There were about a hundred skippers crammed aboard the *Profligate*, the Poobah's personal Ha-Ha flagship. Happy hour consisted of standing in a long line and requesting either a mass-produced margarita, lime daiquiri, or gin and tonic. The other skippers were gregarious or taciturn, not too much between, and as expected, I was the only fatty out of over a hundred men. I mingled for an hour, and Bart's wife swung by right on time to pick us up.

I prayed they would invite me over to their boat for dinner. No such luck. I arrived back at *Serenity* and scaled the boarding ladder. They roared off.

My next hope was that Megan would not be on board. But she was. I began to understand that all this was deliberate. *Play it cool*, I told myself. Keep it platonic. Usually I am all for directness and openness, but my instincts cried out against it here. Maybe I was just getting my shorts in a knot over nothing. We were going to be alone for a while. So what?

Megan was softly strumming her guitar belowdecks when I arrived. I wondered if she'd just started a minute ago, as the Zodiac approached. She was dressed in a flowery blouse as if she were going somewhere, and for an

279

instant I expected her to tell me she had been invited to dinner on another boat. Instead she said, "I'm making chicken cacciatore tonight, just like you showed us how. Would you rather have it with rice or noodles?"

"Oh, that sounds great. Whatever you prefer. Rice sounds good. Unless you'd rather have noodles."

We puttered around the galley as the sun neared the horizon. Here in the tropics, celestial bodies tend to set more "straight down" than they do farther north, so twilight is much shorter. I knew from the last week that at six it would get dark quickly, and by twenty after, it would be like midnight.

While the final cooking was going on I read a history magazine and Megan went into the head for a while. I set two places on the cockpit table. My mind was racing. I just wanted to eat, clean up, read a little, and turn in. Alone.

Megan came back aft and she was wearing nothing but a skimpy, sheer nightie. She avoided my gaze and busied herself in the galley.

It was clear: There was no chance whatsoever at ducking this issue any longer.

Based on her appearance in the nightie, I had no qualms whatsoever about taking my cup, plate, and silverware back from the cockpit table and setting them on the chart table at the nav center. That was where I usually ate, anyway, and she knew it. I was trying to send a nonthreatening, nonverbal message that she had overstepped the bounds. Maybe she would get the message and we would both eat dinner and clean up together and talk about sailing and just decide to be friends. I mean, hasn't this been done to *me* about a million times?

Once again, it didn't quite work out like that.

I woke behind the closed door of the forward captain's quarters, where I usually slept while not a sea. I could hear someone rummaging about the cabin, knocking pans around. Voices, muffled curses. Joyce and Loukia. It was nine thirty already. I took a chance that it was safe to open the door.

Neither of them said a word to me. The congealed remains of the chicken cacciatore was on the stove. Pot lids, dishes, and cups were scattered about. Most of my books had been knocked from the shelves and littered the cabin sole. The glass face of the chronometer was smashed, which must have been what I heard breaking, but the real equipment like the chartplotter, single sideband, and radar were okay.

I stepped over the mess and began to pick up books.

"Clean this shit up," Joyce growled.

I used the head, and when I emerged Joyce said, not at all angrily, "Megan's gone."

I swung my head to the port bunk. Her knapsack and green sleeping bag, gone. Her guitar, gone. That meant she was really *gone*.

"Found another boat?" I asked.

"Yup."

There was no reason to say anything more. Joyce had found her that boat, no doubt, and that was fine by me. Just as with Doug, Megan had her strong points, but a fundamental flaw prevented her from crewing on *Serenity*.

Or was it me?

Maybe someone with terrific people skills could have

handled it better. In the end she'd still be on board and we'd be friends and shipmates. Or maybe that was just not possible with a woman. I couldn't figure it out. I tried to be honest, but not insulting or cruel. Many women hadn't been so considerate to me: "You're a little pipsqueak," or, "You're nothing to me," or, "I feel nothing for you."

I took it like a man, was instructed never to dwell on it, and not to get angry. Yet a completely different standard existed for *them*.

We put the matter behind us and neither Joyce nor Loukia nor I spoke of the subject again.

We had one more full day in Santa Maria. Like any American neighborhood filled with couples and families, there was a tremendous amount of socializing going on. Couples, families, and women, singly or in pairs or trios, rode back and forth visiting between the boats for drinks, coffee, lunch, dinner, or just to chat. As usual, single men were left alone. We were the wildcards in any society, as if no one was quite sure what we'd say or do, but assumed we preferred to be left alone anyhow. After all, if that were not true, wouldn't we be coupled off like normal people?

I stayed on board, did maintenance, and caught up on my reading.

Our departure instructions for the next day had the fleet leaving the bay at six o'clock, the crack of dawn. This was the last leg, the final one hundred and seventy-two nautical miles to Cabo San Lucas, and the Poobah wanted to allow as much daylight as possible to make sure the slower boats could reach Cabo by nightfall of the second day.

We rose in darkness, drank our tea and coffee, and readied our boat for sea. There was a surprising chill in the air, and the three of us were in jackets.

When the time came to pull the hook, I started the engine and asked Joyce to take Megan's usual place on the bowsprit, which meant manhandling the Danforth in place when the windlass pulled it out of the water. I judged Joyce much stronger than Loukia.

But she didn't like that idea.

"Let me take the wheel," she said. "You handle the anchor."

I *was* stronger than her, so she had a point. Even so, operating the engine and steering the boat in close quarters—an anchorage with almost two hundred boats qualifies as such—was traditionally the skipper's or owner's privilege. A tremendous amount of damage could be done in a short time, to my boat and someone else's boat, from a simple error in judgment.

"I want you on the sprit."

"*Why?*"

"I'm used to handling this boat," I told her.

"You're shitting me, right? I was a sailing instructor for nine years, for pete's sake! Get out there, because I am not going to grapple with your filthy damn anchor at six o'clock in the morning!"

I didn't want to fight with her all day. We went back to the cockpit and I grabbed the throttle. "This one is the throttle," I said. "And this one is the clutch, forward for forward, back for back, straight up for neutral."

She glowered at me in rage. "Do you think I'm stupid?"

"Come forward until I give the signal. We'll use the winch to pull it up and then I'll take over."

"Do you think I've never done this before?" Her nostrils flared and she was hissing her words. I was playing with fire.

Joyce took us forward until I saw the chain go vertical which meant we were over the anchor. Loukia activated the windlass and then jumped through the forward hatch so she could stick her arms into the chain locker and make sure the chain didn't kink as it came aboard.

As I secured the anchor, *Serenity* drifted aft with the tide, and in seconds we were dangerously close to a beautiful yacht off our port quarter that was still at anchor.

I called out, "Watch it behind us! Pull us forward!"

Joyce glanced over her shoulder. She was alarmed and maybe a bit embarrassed at the proximity of the other boat, which she hadn't seen.

I heard the engine engage and she gunned it a bit.

Except it wasn't in forward gear. *It was in reverse.*

We were accelerating directly toward the other boat.

Oh my freakin' God Almighty. "Forward!" I screamed. "*FORWARD!*"

She pushed a lever *forward,* but it wasn't the gear shift. It was the throttle.

She looked at me, panic-stricken.

I began sprinting aft. I saw nothing but the wheel, thought of nothing but the engine controls. I leaped from the cabin top to the cockpit with such adrenaline-fueled grace I could have been cast to play the next Batman.

Clutch neutral.

Throttle back a bit.

Clutch forward.

Throttle FULL POWER!

I looked over my shoulder and could see the faces of an entire family of five. *Serenity's* stern missed their stern by mere feet.

I throttled back and we swung past them within easy speaking distance. "I am so sorry!" I called out. "First mate's gonna be keelhauled tonight!"

Joyce stomped away, humiliated.

We swung out to sea and I called out into the companionway, "From now on, you are the anchor-handler!"

She didn't answer. Instead, to my dismay, Loukia calmly informed me she had heard the entire exchange and it would not have happened if I had simply avoided yelling. So please, in the future, could I please refrain from the yelling? Thank you. And an apology to Joyce would be in order.

Once we got away from Bahia Santa Maria the last leg of the Ha-Ha was wonderful. Maybe the place was bad karma for us all.

As soon as the sun was above the yardarm, the tropics welcomed us with open arms. It was *hot*—beach weather, suntan lotion weather, peace and love and relaxation weather. Joyce was on the VHF and the single sideband radios for a good part of the day, making plans with friends and just gossiping. The radios were like her cell phone at sea.

That night was our last night together as a crew. Finally we had some ideal night sailing under the stars. The moon didn't come up until about ten, so we were treated to a few hours of complete darkness. The Milky

Way stretched overhead, and it was so clear and bright I would have sworn it was three-dimensional—and then I realized that it *was* three dimensional, only on a scale of tens of thousands of light years instead of feet and inches.

Loukia and I had a great conversation about exobiology and the origins of life and interstellar travel and the Drake Equation and Fermi's Paradox . . . all the nerdy ideas that I've ever loved, made a hundred times more real with the universe hanging over our heads.

Cabo Day dawned perfect, and Joyce did our final roll call with the Poo. I announced we would sail into the harbor shortly after noon, and the ladies were ecstatic. Everything bad was forgotten, and a good omen arrived, in the form of a tiny brown bird that alighted on our deck and would not leave. We fed her cracker crumbs and sesame seeds, and she was with us the entire last three hours of the voyage, strutting back and forth and issuing an occasional tweet. If you haven't been on a small boat for ten days without cable television or Internet, the entertainment value and sheer excitement of something like this is probably easy to miss.

As promised, we rounded Cabo Falso at noon and turned sharply left into the bay. The rugged brown rocks slipped to port and revealed a bustling resort town with hotels, a mall, chain restaurants, and jam-packed bars that I planned to steer well clear of. Two cruise ships were already moored about three quarters of a mile off the beach.

"Checking in" to Mexico was a formal process, and our Poobah had sternly advised everyone to play it by the book. Technically, only the skipper was allowed ashore until the Mexican customs and immigration authorities cleared the vessel. However, there were gray areas in Cabo, and it was universal practice for arriving yachts to stop at the fuel dock to take on diesel and potable water, and then be gone. This was not counted as being ashore, but the rule was you had to get your fuel and water and *vamoose*—absolutely no socializing or grocery shopping or people switching boats.

We were lucky to get the last of five spots on the fuel dock. Joyce assured me the Baja filter, which slowed down the fueling process, was not necessary here, as this was a top-notch source that supplied the charter fishing fleet. Loukia handled the fuel line topside and I went below to monitor the fill. This required opening the fuel tank vent cover so I could physically see how close we were to the top, and that in turn required removing the bottom two steps from the companionway ladder, leaving only the top three in place. We also filled our water tanks from a potable water hose.

While fueling we were boarded by a young woman in the blue uniform of Mexican Immigration. She asked Loukia to take her to the captain. I was asked to take out all of our fresh meat and fruits and vegetables, which the young woman and I dropped into a trash bag for disposal. We probably lost about fifty bucks' worth of food.

Clever *hombres*, those Mexican Immigration authorities. The fuel dock was just a decoy, allowing them to efficiently board arriving yachts and seize all their fresh food.

Now that *Serenity* was topped off, our next goal was to anchor off the beach. It was a gorgeous spot, a bit rolly because the beach, being a beach, was fully exposed to the Pacific without much of a breakwater barrier. We dropped the hook in about thirty feet of crystal clear water, so clear we could *visually confirm* how the anchor dug in from the deck of the boat. We were maybe four hundred feet beyond the breakers, and spread before us was a solid mile and a half of ritzy hotels and condos and all-night beach parties.

I had the urge to don my bathing suit and jump overboard, but Joyce would have none of it. The law required that I check us into Mexico *pronto,* and no one but I could leave the vessel until this was done. Both Joyce and Loukia were in an *extreme* hurry to leave. They gazed toward the beach with the hungry look of the incarcerated, eying the forbidden fruit made all the more delicious because they were stuck on a small craft.

Whoever waxes in prose about the "freedom" of ocean sailing has either never done it, or they are deliberately telling their armchair sailor readers what they want to hear. Rest assured: it is a myth.

Joyce had already filled out the paperwork. I had completed our equipment list showing the make, model, and serial number of every significant piece of electronic gear aboard. I also needed copies of everyone's passport and *Serenity*'s US Coast Guard registration document. Joyce triple-checked that all our materials were in order, and hailed a *panga* to take me ashore.

"And you head *straight* back here the instant we are cleared in, got that?" she told me. "Loukia and I are marooned until you come back."

By one o'clock there were already at least fifty yachts anchored off the beach, most of them associated with the Ha-Ha. A marina slip was expensive (around $900 per week, I heard) and few were available here without prior reservation. Anchoring off the beach was free.

But anchored out, you needed to provide your own transportation to and from the marina docks, over a mile round trip. Many people used their powered Zodiacs, but there was always a cluster of four or five *pangas* waiting a few hundred yards away, like taxis at a stand. We only had to wave our arms at them until they noticed. One-way fare was negotiable, but five bucks was the standard for one or two people without heavy luggage.

The *panga* operators in Mexico were invariably helpful and good-natured. I sorely regretted I knew only a few words of Spanish. I would have to fix that.

Deposited on the dock with my knapsack containing our papers, I strode toward the block where the map showed the customs and immigration office was located. I could see right away that Cabo was about rich people and gigantic charter deep-sea fishing boats. All the trim, neatly attired Americans looked like doctors or lawyers or executives on a three-day jaunt with the mistress. There were also plenty of couples and families from the cruise ships, mostly wandering about, unsure of which knickknack shop to hit next.

It was quite hot, at least eighty degrees, but Joyce made sure I was wearing khakis and a button-down shirt. You did *not* conduct official business in Mexico in shorts and t-shirt, she warned me. Show some respect. I found the office and there were around fifty Ha-Ha skippers queued in the atrium, over half of them in shorts and t-shirts.

If you knew Spanish you could choose to conduct the entire transaction directly with a Mexican customs official, paying only the basic vessel entrance and visa fees.

Otherwise, you didn't have much choice but to hire an agent to conduct the transaction on your behalf, for $375. Everyone thought in terms of dollars, and MasterCard would handle the currency conversions. It was a highly efficient machine to collect as much cash as possible as quickly as possible, without upsetting the *gringos* too much, and without any delay in cutting us loose to hit the bars and clubs. I was surprised to be done in an hour, less time than it took to get a driver's license renewal at any American DMV.

Back on board, my female overseers still would not permit me to swim.

"Loukia needs to go meet up with Bruce right now. They have a hotel room."

I gave them their entry paperwork and hailed another *panga*. Once at the marina I tipped the driver and helped Loukia carry her heavy luggage to the end of the pier. There was Bruce and the couple was reunited. Loukia hugged me goodbye and said she had a wonderful time and wished me "following seas."

Joyce had one more pressing demand. It was necessary that she check her e-mail *immediately*. Fortunately she had her laptop with her and there were plenty of Internet cafes all over Cabo. However, she told me, her computer was infected with viruses. Every time she launched her browser, the virus would take over and bury her in popup windows with animations that brought the whole system to a stop. It was clearly my moral obligation to help her fix this, being that I worked for a computer company and all.

I agreed, my only request being to let me check my e-mail too. I even refrained from requiring her to say "please."

We found a cafe and ordered a couple of lattes while I booted up her system. It turned out that Internet Explorer was infected all right, but not with viruses—just a couple of aggressive Trojan horses that launched dozens of popup ads every chance they got. I was able to eliminate them by uninstalling two "free toolbars" and scrubbing Internet Explorer with a freeware utility I trusted.

"Hurry it up, will you?" Joyce admonished over her latte. Which I had paid for.

I got an idea.

I changed her Internet Explorer home page to the home page of the Republican Party.

I checked my e-mail and decided to send an arrival notice from my own laptop later, maybe *mañana*. I gave the laptop back to Joyce saying, "I believe I got just about all of the viruses. You should be able to use your browser now." She snatched it and launched Internet Explorer. I sipped my latte, barely able to control my expression. I would have to make a hasty retreat, but not quite yet.

I watched her face. Eyebrows knitted. Lips twisted. Her body jumped back from the laptop as if it were a demon spawn from Hell.

"What the—"

"What's the matter?"

"What is *this*?"

She turned the screen so I could see it. Something or other about Karl Rove.

"Huh. Try closing and restarting the browser."

She did. I drained the latte and got ready to take off.

"Oh, *no*." Joyce murmured. "It's still happening. This

can't be. This just can't be."

"You may have to contact Microsoft support. I'll see you back on the boat."

Joyce would not be leaving *Serenity* for a couple of days, unsure of whether to fly back to the Bay Area or to Arizona. She was certain her family situation required her immediate departure. I had asked her a few days ago whether she could help me take *Serenity* on a two-day motor sail across three hundred miles of calm blue sea to Puerto Vallarta, and the answer was "Sorry, no-can-do."

I went for a long, meandering walk through the harbor area of Cabo that first afternoon. It was essentially an American shopping strip transplanted to Mexico, and a high-end shopping strip at that. There was a ritzy enclosed mall with stores that would be at home on Rodeo Drive in Beverly Hills. There were a dozen chain eateries and scores of bars large and small for vacationers who simply wanted to *drink*, an activity that seemed to be the most popular of all.

It felt terrific to be free from the boat, able to choose my own path, and simply *walk* to different places and see different things on leg power alone. I had no desire to try any Mexican food, so I had dinner at Johnny Rockets: cheeseburger, french fries, chocolate shake, with plenty of Heinz ketchup. There was no way anyone could convince me that any Mexican food could be as delicious as that I had just eaten.

I was back on board at dusk relaxing with a book. Joyce got off her *panga* shortly after ten, just about the time I was ready to turn in. She was not a happy camper.

"Do not speak to me!"

"What? What did I do?"

"My good friend Larry Wilcox was able to fix your stupid little stunt. He said it was very childish, not even a good prank, and morally wrong."

"Sounds like Larry might be a Democrat."

"You ever do anything that stupid again and I won't . . . I won't help you get crew. How's that?"

"Okay, deal."

"An apology would be appropriate at this point."

"Okay. I'm sorry my little joke made you so upset."

"Try again."

"I apologize for setting your home page to the GOP. I won't do it again, and when I did it I did not understand it would cause you such emotional and spiritual trauma."

She did not pick up on the sarcasm, which was probably just as well.

"And I found you crew, maybe."

"Really? From the Ha-Ha?"

"She wants to meet you first."

She?

The Baja Ha-Ha rally contained one more event, and it was a major brouhaha: the awards presentation, hosted by the Poobah decked out in full pirate regalia.

Like third grade, everyone got an award. Each skipper was called to the stage individually and presented with the traditional green wooden fish that signified finishing the Baja Ha-Ha, an achievement it was claimed, tongue in cheek, can never be taken away from you once earned. The event was loud and boisterous and fueled by free Tecate.

Imagine over three hundred sailors in a marina parking lot, liberated after almost two weeks at sea.

I planned to leave as early as possible, but not before I met my prospective crew member. But something seemed to have gone wrong. On the *panga* ride ashore, Joyce told me her name was Erica and she was an experienced sailor looking for a berth all the way to Polynesia and maybe New Zealand. Now, as the ceremony was winding down, I still had not been introduced to Erica, and Joyce seemed to be ducking the issue.

"Well, do you see her?"

"No, I do not, and quit asking."

"This is important. I want to make sure she doesn't end up on some other boat."

Joyce had been carefully avoiding my gaze. "If you don't meet her, you don't meet her, and that's that. It's not like she's the only damn person looking for a boat."

That was mysterious. I figured I should go chat with Poo and let him know I was still looking for crew, any crew, interested in sailing Mexico and maybe elsewhere.

When he saw me he asked, "We found you a very eager crew member. Have you met Erica?"

"Well, no. Is she around?"

"She's right over there," the Poobah indicated by pointing. "See those folks?"

"Yes sir! Which one?"

"The blonde in the dark blue tank top."

My knees went weak.

I approached the circle of friends and extended my hand toward the woman the Poo had pointed out. She appeared to be in her thirties and was fit and quite pretty. I loved the way she was wearing her hair, tied back in a knot. Loved it.

"Are you Erica? I'm Glenn."

"I am *not* Erica!" she shot back.

"Okay," I pulled my hand back, quickly scanned the small circle of women. "Sorry. I'm looking for Erica. Has anyone seen her?"

"We have *not* seen Erica," the woman who was not Erica told me, a bit too pointedly.

"But you do know her?"

"We do *not* know anyone by that name."

Intuitively I glanced sideways at one of the other women. She cast her eyes to the ground.

"Okay, thanks anyway," I said meekly and walked away, face burning.

I met Joyce back at the boat and recounted the story. It turned out Erica had declined to meet face-to-face until Joyce pointed *me* out from a "safe" distance. When she saw me the deal was dead. She would not crew.

"I wouldn't worry about it. There are people who want to head south who do not have a boat, let me assure you. But they don't stay in Cabo. In fact, nobody stays in Cabo. This anchorage is too rolly and everything's too expensive. Real cruisers head to Puerto or Z-Town right away. That's what you should do."

Now that the Ha-Ha was over, I was finally free. In an instant, I had been released of all responsibilities, of all deadlines, of all need to do *anything* right here and right now. Everything could wait for *mañana*, a word that can mean, contrary to popular opinion, not just "tomorrow" but also "sometime."

And on the next morning, I had no idea what to do.

Without encumbrances, without any form of ticking clock, every minute and every hour was just like any other. I rose at dawn but it didn't really matter. I went ashore toting a bag of kitchen trash and my knapsack, but it didn't really matter. All the *freedom* felt constraining, annoying—something I could not escape if I wanted.

I was cruising, living the dream, and the amazing thing was I felt like I was in jail.

Tourist Attraction

Joyce was catching an afternoon flight back to San Francisco today. I loaded her luggage into the *panga* and jumped aboard. As soon as we docked I turned to her and launched into one of those final goodbye speeches.

"Oh, no," she cut me off. "You're buying me lunch. You owe me."

One last time I played Mister Deep Pockets and we enjoyed a leisurely and margarita-enhanced meal at the most expensive-looking place she could see. I think that was the first and only time I saw Joyce drink, and after just two, she became a different person.

"You did exceptionally well. I want you to know that."

"Really?"

"Hell, yeah. I wouldn't be saying it if it weren't the honest truth."

"I did make plenty of mistakes—"

"Everyone does, Glenn. Everyone. But do you know the biggest problem with people being skipper for the first time? Even people who have been sailing for years? They can't make a decision. Really and truly, you give them all the information they need, they couldn't make a decision if their lives depended on it. Which it might one day. They just can't do it. They want someone else to make the decision, and they just agree to it, and that's that. But the

297

skipper, any good skipper, will be able to make a decision on their own. It may not be the best decision. Conditions change. Then the skipper has to . . . change the decision, too, sometimes. But you'd be surprised at all the yahoos out there who can't decide whether to put their right shoe on first or second unless someone else tells 'em."

I told her I wasn't sure if I was cut out for long distance cruising.

"Whatever. But you should spend one season in Mexico, regardless. I mean, you're here!"

"Yeah."

"You're here, the boat's here, just relax for a while. You got plenty of time."

And that was the problem.

We hugged our goodbyes and promised to keep in touch and then she was off to the airport. She would be back in her own apartment in a matter of hours, I thought. The very idea made my head swim with envy. My own "apartment" was floating at anchor, ready to move at a moment's notice.

I settled into a routine. I could choose any bunk on board, but I stayed in the forward cabin because it had an opening deck hatch, and I was able to sleep with the stars overhead yet avoid the heavy morning dew that would soak everything if I slept on deck.

Being anchored off a tropical beach may strike you as idyllic, but in reality it was not. There were two main problems: noise and rolling swells. The sound of the music and the DJs from the hotels and nightclubs that lined the beach continued unabated until four a.m. every night. As I tried to fall asleep, I was serenaded by an endless stream of DJ-led *rumbas* and conga lines and who knows what else. And no one would ever grow tired of it, because every two or three days the flock of tourists was replaced by another flock of *different* tourists.

Cabo was what seasoned cruisers called a *rolly* anchorage. Your boat never stopped rolling. Sometimes it rolled a little, sometimes a lot, but it never stopped, not for a minute, not ever. The beach anchorage at Cabo was exposed to the Pacific, and as I understood it, most anchorages in Mexico were like that—little or no breakwater—Cabo being one of the worst. I noticed a distinct pattern: after four to seven smaller rolls, an especially large roll would occur. Because of the big rolls, you had to think about what you were about to put down and ask yourself if it okay for that object to go flying. I lost some food and drink that way, and had to be prudent when boiling water, always wearing my foulies to do so.

I rose every day just before dawn and urinated over the side. I did this sometimes at night, too, so I left my aluminum boarding ladder always down in case I flipped over the lifeline and overboard during a drowsy nocturnal piss.

Then came the cravings. A morning newspaper. Internet. *Something* besides the rocking of the boat and the constant buzz of jet skis over the water. I found I really didn't want to make coffee on the boat and drink it while staring into space or reading a book or a magazine I had already read ten times, or looking at the same scenery outside the boat. I needed to drink my morning coffee while reading a *newspaper,* damn it.

So I would pack some necessities in my knapsack, bag

yesterday's trash, and stand on my cabin top waving for a *panga*. I should have been using *Ducky*, just for the exercise and the practice, but I didn't. On reaching the dock I would get rid of the trash and swing by the American-style market to pick up a newspaper. They usually had a few California newspapers and something printed for the Americans in Cabo, but nothing showing today's news—just yesterday or the day before. That was fine by me; it was a newspaper, and yesterday's news was today's new to me.

Next stop was a cafe in the ritzy mall, a Starbucks knockoff that made passable coffee. I would have some kind of pastry or croissant, too. All of this, the cafe fare and the newspaper and the *panga*, were not cheap, but I did not care. I was duplicating my natural habitat, that of the business traveler. I knew it was wrong. But I did it anyhow.

Once caffeinated, I was ready for the Internet. I had my choice of Internet cafes and restaurants and each one had a good Wi-Fi signal and plenty of open tables in the morning. The day after arrival I broadcast an e-mail to all my sailing and InfoData friends to brag about *Serenity*'s safe arrival in Cabo: Alek, Kevin, Tara, Tweety, Jon, Doug, Paul, and even Peter Gibbons. Especially Peter, who told me I wouldn't do it. I described the ridiculously clear water and my first snorkel dives around the boat. Schools of multicolored tropical fish swam right past me, and I could see stingrays and larger fish that may have been barracudas.

And when I was done with the Internet, I was out of things to do.

Sure, I should have been back on board doing boat

work. Waterproofing, for one. Or installing the reverse osmosis water maker. But you know what? I was damned sick of boat work. I *wanted* to run out of things to do. It felt great, even though it was a lie.

When Forrest Gump felt distraught over Jenny and he didn't know what to do, he ran. And ran and ran and ran. Well, I was fat, so I couldn't run for long. I decided to walk and walk and walk.

It worked for me.

I saw every inch of the tourist zone of Cabo, several times each day. I recognized the armed guards standing outside of the jewelry stores. I knew which sewer holes to avoid because they emitted noxious odors when approached from downwind. I found the hardware stores, the chandleries, the ATMs. Each day I personally inspected the hordes of tourists swarming from the cruise ships, and became something of an expert on the demographics of the various lines:

Carnival: Young families, young couples, kind of rough around the edges.

Royal Caribbean: Yuppie ladder-climber types.

Princess: Urbane and diverse, like the crowd at an LA Dodgers game.

Holland America: Old folks.

Norwegian: Wealthy. "My dear, next time we shall take our own ship."

Every few days I bagged my laundry and had a dry cleaner do it for a reasonable price. It made no sense for me to attempt the same aboard, especially since it would use up a lot of fresh water and the suds would end up in the sea near the beach.

I knew every aisle of the American-style supermarket. I bought some produce and pasta and cheese there, but I wasn't thrilled with it. It wasn't much of a supermarket, really. It reminded me of those small neighborhood markets that were common until the 1990s, when they were replaced in most parts of America with full-blown super-duper markets, the ones with twenty-five aisles and six kinds of organic arugula. So what would a genuine Mexican supermarket be like? The cruising guide said there was a market less than half a mile away if I just followed one of the streets *away* from the touristy sections into the *real* Cabo San Lucas, the actual Mexican town that surrounded the American Disneyland–Mexico against the waterside. So I headed northwest, and after a few blocks there was nothing touristy about the landscape.

The neighborhoods were run down, or seemed that way to me. Few windows had insect screens. I was on a main commercial street, and the most popular small business was secondhand stores, sort of like garage sales with other people's stuff. Clothing and furniture and electronics abounded.

It was depressing.

Finally, the food market. First stop: produce.

I stopped dead. I could not believe my eyes. The produce, all of it, swarmed with insects. I don't mean an occasional ant or spider: I mean all of it *swarmed with insects*. Not your wimpy American insects, either. These were the real deal. I saw a head of lettuce that was alive with enormous skittering cockroaches. It was downright Kafkaesque. Other produce was covered with flies and there were plenty of spiders and ants all around. Shaken, I headed for the door.

All that walking gave me time to think.

Every day I became a bit angrier about the Erica incident. I could not forget about it. What was her problem? All right, I get it, I'm no Brad Pitt. But so what? She couldn't talk to me like a normal human being, inspect the boat, phone the women who had already served as crew, and help me sail to the next town? *Right now* we could be provisioning for sea and getting ready to leave. We could have enjoyed an easy and pleasant sail to Acapulco, where there are better facilities and more cruisers. Why could she not do that?

It was, of course, that magical effect I had on women, the instant they laid eyes on me. Like the charismatic qualities of the true Ladies' Man, it could not be explained through appearance alone. It was the negative charisma shared by all nerds.

My brother Paul wasn't significantly taller than me, yet he was not a nerd and had no problems in the girlfriend department. As my face was pudgy, his had the lean, hungry look of the jackal—not quite feral, but someone who could use a good home-cooked meal and some tender loving care.

This had always been true. In the summer I was twelve and my brother ten, we were sent to stay for a week with an aunt and uncle who lived in suburban Old Bridge, New Jersey. Aunt Julie was ecstatic about the visit because there happened to be two girls visiting for the summer with her next-door neighbor, and these girls also happened to be twelve and ten.

"You're going to have a girlfriend, Glennie." Aunt Julie purred to me over the phone. "Mark my words. You and Paulie both. We got Susan next door and her cousin Shelley is staying with them and they're the same ages as you boys. You're going to have a little girlfriend as soon as you get here, you just wait and see!"

She was a lovely optimist, my Aunt Julie, and her words sent a thrill up my spine. I was twelve. I knew what girls were. Hardly talked to them, yet, but I knew about girls, about what you can do with girls. Kiss. Make out. What would that be like? My heart pounded.

Was she right? Would I have a girlfriend? She sure seemed to think so. What about my younger brother? He was ten, a baby, and I doubted he could handle something like that, so I guess it would be Susan and I sneaking away to make out, while Paulie and Shelley could, I dunno, watch Scooby Doo on TV.

It didn't quite work out that way.

The girls took one look at Paul and could not tear their eyes from him for one second. They fired questions at him, and he answered, embarrassed at all the sudden attention. I tried to talk to Susan, but her brain was focused on Paul one hundred percent. I noticed she smiled when speaking to Paul, but not to me.

The next morning Paul and I were in the kitchen finishing our Cheerios when the doorbell rang. Aunt Julie opened the front door and I could hear her greet Susan and Shelley.

Susan's voice sang, "Can Paulie come out?"

Aunt Julie carefully responded, "There are two boys staying here, Susan. Glenn and Paulie. Two boys. They'll both come out as soon as they're finished breakfast."

The disappointment and pure *confusion* over their powerful infatuation with my younger brother turned to bile in my throat. How could this be? All Paulie does, really, is watch television. At least I read books and make electrical things, on my own. Why the powerful fascination with him, and the complete lack of interest in *me*?

Even at age twelve, I was emitting "nerd rays," some sort of invisible energy field that revolted females yet could not be explained by science or reason. Paul, in contrast, was emitting his "jock rays," which had an equally enigmatic positive effect that went beyond all logic.

This was the world I may not have chosen, but it was the only world I had. And one thing was becoming apparent: I could not escape it in a boat, and probably a spacecraft wouldn't be helpful either. Paradoxically, the rejection effect seemed to be intensified by this voyage, even while alone in Cabo. There was no escaping the narrative, not as long as I drew breath.

Were there ever moments, however brief, when I was free from my Albatross of Rejection? Yes. Those moments that I would normally consider the worst, the low points, those times when I was overwhelmed by fatigue or rage or simple fear for my life. Those were times of sweet escape. Those, too, were times of incremental change, although I didn't fully grasp that fact yet.

My nine-hour walks made a daily shower a necessity, not a luxury. *Serenity* did not have an inside shower so I hung my black rubber sunshower bag from the boom each morning and when I got back to the boat, the three gallons were nice and warm.

I took my showers right there in the cockpit. At first I waited until about ten minutes after sunset so the darkness would give me some privacy, but then I realized none of the boats anchored around me took notice. So I began my shower the instant the last ray of sun vanished, which was six p.m. on the nose this time of year.

Technically, public nudity was illegal in Mexico but it was never enforced if it occurred on vessels well offshore and no one raised a fuss about it. As soon as I had myself all lathered up head to toe, a large and well-populated tour boat motored by. It was one of those ever popular sunset dinner cruises. The first time, the boat passed maybe three hundred feet off and a portion of the guests saw me and waved.

The second time the boat came closer. There were more people at the rail. More people shouted and waved and snapped pictures and took video. I waved back.

The third day the tour boat came closer still. Just about every soul on board was lining the port rails. Men, women, and children laughed and cheered and documented the experience with plenty of still and video footage: *Naked Fat Man Taking a Shower.*

It's funny because he's fat.

By the fourth day I knew this was no fluke. It seemed like they were announcing it over the loudspeaker in advance, and passing as close to *Serenity* as was safe. All sudsed up, I waved, turned around, gave them some butt. A cheer went up and the photoflashes popped all over. As far as I knew, this was the highlight of the tour. I imagined that People were posting all over the Internet and bragging to their friends that the Naked Fat Man of Cabo had actually waved to them personally.

I had become a tourist attraction.

At that point I figured it was probably time to leave.

My chart showed three ports on the west coast of Mexico: Puerto Vallarta, Z-Town (Mazatlan) and Acapulco. Each had an anchorage, as well as marinas, boatyards, and generally more facilities than Cabo, and it was more economical, too. The first two ports would be reached in a couple of days, Acapulco in seven or eight days.

I took it as a forgone conclusion that my next leg should be one of the three, the question being, which one? Or maybe spend a couple of months at each, and then head to Hawaii or French Polynesia in May?

No matter what, it looked like I would be leaving Cabo alone. After the first week, just about all of the Ha-Ha fleet had moved on, most of them heading north back to California for the infamous *Baja Bash,* a reputedly difficult eight-hundred-mile trip against the prevailing winds and swells. I had tried everything I could think of to recruit at least one more crew member, even an inexperienced person to at least stand watch. There was an informal bulletin board for cruisers outside the Mexican customs office, and I scanned it daily. I also tried Craigslist. Finally, at eight each morning, there was a casual roll call for cruisers in the greater Cabo area and I began making short, verbal pleas for crew. Wasn't there anyone out there sick of their boat, and needing to get sick of a different boat?

Apparently not.

What bothered me about the Mexican destinations was that all three were further from California than where I am now. I would be traveling farther away from home. So why did that bother me? Wasn't that the general idea?

I needed some confirmation that heading to one of those other Mexican ports was a good idea, something to spur me on. The ranks of ordinary cruisers were growing thin in Cabo. I noticed more smaller, simpler vessels anchored off the beach, tiny sloops around twenty-four to thirty feet, appearing cheaply constructed—coastal cruisers, really, intended for weekend sailing—but people used them for long-distance cruising, too. Almost always, they belonged to men single-handing.

I wanted to talk to these guys, get the straight skinny on Mexico. I thought of taking *Ducky* around with a six pack of Beck's, but the trouble was my binoculars never showed anyone on deck of one of these boats. Eventually I understood that these single-handers had two modes: drinking ashore or sleeping on the boat. They didn't hang at the tourist bars. They sure didn't hang at Johnny Rockets or The Hard Rock Cafe either.

Wandering around Cabo, I was able to find a few single-handers eating at inexpensive tourist cantinas. These men did not look or sound healthy to me. They were emaciated and peered at me through bloodshot eyes. They were always squinting, yet had no sunglasses. Without exception, their hair was a bird nest and their clothing threadbare.

"I don't think it matters much what you do," one middle-aged single-hander told me. "It doesn't matter much what I do, either. It's all the same everywhere, and let me tell you something else. In this country, in Mexico, right now, you can't buy land in Mexico. I mean, you can, you can't, but if you do, it has to be in a certain part with a minimum of so many Mexican nationals. So, no."

Finally I understood: These were the homeless of the sea lanes. They were poor, painfully so, and they lived in their own isolated worlds. Like me, they may have started with a "nut" of money saved from a great job or a stock market rally, but eventually it was all gone and a hand-to-mouth existence took over. These men were what I usually called "transients," and I did not wish to join their ranks.

I climbed off the *panga* onto my deck. I still hadn't moved *Ducky* from her tie-down on the cabin top. I closed the hatches up whenever I left for the day, and when I opened them, the boat smelled like a food pantry. It was not a pleasant smell. I could still detect the lobster from Bahia Tortugas.

In the warmth and humidity, anything edible not placed in the refrigerator spoiled after two days, tops. The refrigerator was tiny by normal standards, less than two cubic feet. It was working fine, though, running on the charging power of the solar panels and the wind turbine.

I sat down at the nav station and put my head in my hands. I had to come to grips with the fact that I was not enjoying the cruising lifestyle. I couldn't deny it any longer.

A voice in my head told me, *It takes time to adjust!*

That may be true, but everything that was contributing to my growing, gnawing homesickness would become *worse* as I sailed south, not better. Cabo San Lucas was widely considered to be virtually identical to the United States. It was one big shopping strip, for goodness sake. I could buy virtually anything except books and magazines. They had Internet. The climate was mild, and the insects few and far between. It wasn't raining, and everything inside *Serenity* was dry. My gear was in good shape—near perfect, in fact.

And yet.

I wasn't having fun, and I was lonely. With a job, I had regular human contact. Here I had none. Everyone was coupled off. With limited Internet (even in Cabo) and limited reading matter and entertainment, I felt the pangs of information starvation. I checked my e-mail twice a day, and that was not nearly enough.

My mind raced. I didn't have a job. I could fly back to California tonight if I really wanted, but I could not abandon this boat in Mexico, not legally. The Mexican government would track me down through the vessel registration number and charge me for disposal. Plus, *Serenity* was valuable and held tons of expensive equipment.

Suppose I did make it back to the States? What then? Get a job as a manual laborer, transform myself into a fit and tanned piece of beefcake, hook up with a cute honey, and come back to Mexico next year?

Forces were pulling me south, too. I had spent so much time, effort, and money to get this far. Why throw that all away?

Why was I here to begin with?

I paced the salon. It was nearing sunset and my admirers on the dinner cruise would be by soon. There were powerful arguments for heading both north and south. I felt like Buridan's Ass, the hypothetical donkey placed exactly between two exactly equal bales of hay. Buridan hypothesized the ass would starve because if the bales were exactly equal there was no reason to choose one over the other and the animal would be immobile.

I needed a tie-breaker, something to give an unexpected benefit to one course or the other. I couldn't think of anything. It was maddening: For five minutes, I would accept that I could not go back, and then I would change my mind, and for another five minutes I would accept that if each day I grew more homesick and bored, there was no reason to move farther from home.

Back and forth, back and forth.

For an instant I truly considered flipping a coin and accepting the outcome as binding.

Then I thought of a tie-breaker. It was a long shot, but suppose I explained the situation to Peter Gibbons and asked to come back to work for InfoData?

Suppose I had my job back?

Tired as I was from my daily hiking, I spent a restless night. It was the excitement of knowing that tomorrow I would find out my destiny.

I composed the email in my head as I waited for the *panga* to pick me up. I would explain my dilemma and ask directly for a yes or no decision as soon as possible. Whatever the response, I needed to prepare *Serenity* for sea. No matter if the destination were north or south, this voyage would be made single-handed.

I connected my laptop and began to write my message,

a presentation really. I knew I was a good instructor. As I wrote, I realized it hinged on whether InfoData was hiring. And the answer was probably not. Like any public corporation, they had to do everything by the book, and the book said that former employees re-applying had to be treated *exactly* the same as any other candidate, held to the same standards, and re-hired only if an open position already existed.

My message sent, I decided to hang out at the beach for the rest of the day. I promised myself I would not check my e-mail again until five o'clock.

That did not happen. I checked it shortly after noon.

No response.

I was piqued, and worried. Peter liked me because I made him lots of money, kept my expenses reasonable, and consistently got good customer evaluations. He probably didn't think much of me personally because I was a few years older than he, I was not a manager, and I did not have a family of my own. To hell with that. Let him get over his prejudices.

I explained to myself he had to check on things, and then I went hiking.

Five o'clock, no response at all. Not even a "got your message, sit tight" answer.

That was disheartening. I spent another restless night. I was getting used to the perky DJ's voice blasting over me from the beach every night, but now it was just grating.

In the morning I headed back ashore with my stomach aflutter. I had a feeling there would be an answer one way or the other. Regardless, I vowed that after coffee I would top off my fuel and water tanks in preparation for the coming voyage, be it north or south.

There was a response from Peter.

It began, *Don't get your hopes up.*

Not good.

I was angry and disappointed, and that told me that deep down I wanted the job back and I wanted to return to my old life. That was something. Did that mean that whatever I had come out here for was achieved? No. But the adventure wasn't over yet.

Peter explained in his e-mail that the company had been *considering* opening up a position in the second or third quarter of next year; in other words, four to seven months from now, a position might exist. However, they had seen a definite uptick in demand, maybe not enough to justify opening up the position right now, but the company knew that by hiring a recent employee they would save a lot of time and money on training. Our software was extraordinarily specialized and quite complex, so even ideal candidates often needed months to reach a solid level of production.

He wanted me to call him as soon as I got the chance.

I made a beeline to the nearest pay phone and got him on the first ring.

"¡Hola!" I cried into the line. "I am a *gringo* in Mexico. I bring you lots of tequila if you kindly give me job in exchange. *Muchos gracias, mi amigo.*"

Peter told me this phone call was my job interview, and I had already blown it because the job requires fluency in English.

He was doing something he didn't do too often: joking.

The next day there was another e-mail asking if I could

teach a week-long course at a federal agency in Washington, DC starting December seventeenth.

I answered yes, absolutely.

I called and we sealed the deal, the paperwork to be handled after I arrived back in California.

"Just don't forget your green card, *gringo*," he warned. I'm not sure he knew what the term meant.

There was plenty of work left to do. I acquired a few more plastic jerrycans at a local chandlery, filled them with extra diesel and lashed them to *Serenity's* deck—*not* to the lifeline stanchions, which I think is really dumb, but to eye rings on the cabin top. I had witnessed people getting ready for the Baja Bash loading extra jerrycans of fuel. There was but one reliable place to refuel for the next seven hundred miles up to Ensenada, fifty miles south of the US border, and that was Bahia Tortugas. I was toting close to a hundred gallons, so I hoped I would not need to refuel at all. I would sail as much as possible, but that depended on what the wind and waves were doing.

I set my departure date and called my brother Paul. I explained what I was doing and why.

"It's a good thing you didn't ask me to come, because I'll tell you the answer right now. No way!"

I explained what I needed. I estimated it would take five to ten days to reach San Diego, maybe as long as two weeks. If the conditions were extremely adverse, I would pull into a *bahia* and wait it out. There might not be any village or phones—probably would not be. So, give it two weeks. If he did not hear from me in two weeks, I instructed him to call the US Coast Guard and give them the particulars of the voyage. I had him write down a description of *Serenity*, my route, departure date, and my

EPIRB serial number, which would be transmitted in the event of an emergency.

What I didn't say is that I didn't expect any of that to be much help if something went wrong. I expected that if the worst happened, it would be swift and sure. No drifting around in a life raft dying of thirst and starvation. It would be a broken bone, a cracked rib, a really bad cut, any one of which would likely result in shock and without first aid, death.

Joyce e-mailed me back and said this was a bad idea and I should go out to Puerto or Z-Town and find some crew there.

I went to the market and bought as much food as I could carry, most of it simple to prepare and eat. I didn't expect to do any real cooking, just heating. Lots of canned soup and stew. Bread, fruit, pasta, plenty of cookies and yogurt. I hated the Mexican formula for Diet Coke, so I loaded up on powered drinks and various off-brand sodas.

My final stop was Mexican Immigration, where I needed to clear out of the country officially. A couple of hundred dollars later I had my paperwork in hand, showing San Diego as my destination and myself as *El Capitano* and the sole person on board.

I was stocked, stowed, and stoked. Another day in Cabo would be time wasted.

Karma Houdini

First challenge: weigh anchor by myself. That was impossible. It took at least two people, and preferably a third to ensure the chain did not kink as it entered the locker. I decided to get a little cocky and do the impossible before breakfast.

It was hard, but not impossible. I ran back and forth from the cockpit to the windlass like a madman. She was coming up, and I idled the throttle and leaped through the forward hatch to unkink the chain. I fastened the Danforth to the bowsprit with a couple of bungees and dashed back to the cockpit because the boat was adrift. Clutch in forward, throttle forward, and I was off.

I steered between the other boats anchored off the beach. It was still quite early and practically no one was on deck. I saw a little girl and waved to her, experiencing the macabre thought that perhaps she was the last human being I would ever see in my life.

The first morning and afternoon were uneventful. There was a slight breeze from the northwest but not nearly enough to sail upwind. The swells were modest, and *Serenity* and I were making five knots over the bottom at seventy percent power. I took advantage of the pleasant conditions to install and test the Collision Avoidance Radar Detector I had bought months ago. It worked: The passage of a small fishing trawler elicited a loud and annoying *beeep* with every sweep of its radar.

I hadn't figured out my sleeping strategy yet. It's against international maritime law to operate a vessel in international waters without a continuous and alert watch posted. So to be legal, I *couldn't* sleep.

If the autopilot quit, I was really screwed.

I cooked myself an early dinner in anticipation of the winds picking up around sunset, and I wasn't disappointed. We were seeing a nice ten to twelve knots from west-northwest. It was time to raise sail, alone, for the first time.

This was when the pedal hit the metal. Personally, I would have just motored to San Diego if that were possible. But it wasn't. Even with the extra jerrycans of fuel, *Serenity*'s maximum range under ideal conditions was maybe four hundred nautical miles. That would not take me to the nearest source of fuel, Hector the Tough Guy in Bahia Tortugas. In order to get home, I had to sail.

The boat was now bobbing and pitching, and it was rapidly turning pitch dark, and my tummy flutters had returned in earnest. I headed the autopilot into the wind and raised the main, then the jib, again frantically doing the work of two or three people but doing it adequately. It reminded me of the first few times I soloed an airplane: I had to be hyper-vigilant for errors, because they could be unforgiving.

Before it got truly dark I made sure I had several penlights in my pockets and there were extra batteries in the chart table where I could find them by feel. I knew that in a few moments the boat would be shrouded in a blackness hard to imagine on land, and I wanted to make sure all the small jobs were taken care of first.

Serenity came to a close reach and we were sailing along so well I was able to cut the engine. *Six knots over the bottom!* I was delighted—all that speed, no fuel required. This was because the swells were still modest and not directly opposing me.

Around ten o'clock in the evening I grew drowsy and decided to take a cat nap on deck, given that the CARD would wake me up if a ship approached. I stretched out on deck with my head on the windward side. I rested, I was still too wound up to sleep.

After midnight the wind died and I took the sails down and motored the rest of the night. The stars were astonishing. The inky blackness, the repetitive nature of the engine vibration, and the slosh of water against the hull acted as natural sedatives—hypnotics, really—and that's why Joyce favored two-hour night watches and not three or four. After two hours of it, you were mentally on another planet. By four, I was convinced I was only an *observer*, witnessing myself single-hand a sailboat through the dark Pacific night, for surely such a thing could not be really happening.

I got through that first night by taking several catnaps. I kept them short by putting my legs up on the chart table. After about fifteen minutes, the lack of circulation would wake me up. I did not entirely trust the CARD. There were cruising boats out here *not* using radar and *not* keeping a safe watch. My plan was to scan the horizon every fifteen to twenty minutes.

Many single-handers advised sleeping soundly during the day, when people could see you, and staying up all night. That made sense, but for now, I preferred not to do it.

The evening of the second day was shaping up to be similar to the first. I raised sail and we traveled on a close reach. The wind was stronger than yesterday and I was delighted to make seven knots over the bottom. This was because I was carrying a lot of jib: Before she left, Joyce helped me change our yankee jib with a lighter but much larger 150-percent genoa. She explained I could partially unfurl it to adjust to changing conditions. When partially unfurled, the furling line would keep the drum from turning and letting the remainder of the genny loose.

The wind was a little closer than yesterday, and the boat already had a lot of sideways heel, making it more difficult to do simple things. In fact it seemed the wind was steadily growing *stronger* instead of waning like yesterday, so I would have to keep a watch on it.

I had a sudden urge to watch a DVD on my laptop. Just as *Naked Gun 33 1/3* was starting up, I felt and heard a loud *THWANG!* coming from up forward. Then the sound of the furler. The deck heeled even more.

Not good.

I went topside, clipped on, and saw that the entire genny was now free and pulling the boat strongly to starboard. That was way, way too much sail to fly in this wind. I needed to furl half of it right now.

But why had it unfurled just now? And what the hell was that *THWANG* noise?

I grabbed the furling line and it was slack in my hands.

I pulled it. It was totally free. That could not be. It was connected to the furling drum. I kept pulling on the line and reached the end and I understood what happened: Over the past five hours, the furling line had chafed through and broke. Now there was no way to furl up the genoa.

All right then. I needed to *drop* the genoa. Pronto. That was simple enough: just release the halyard and it would drop down the forestay. To do that I had to turn the boat into the wind and release the tension on the genny. It would still require that I pull it down the forestay, as the wind tension would hold it in place. I turned on the engine and brought us up into the strengthening wind. The genny and the main began luffing furiously. I made my way forward and released the halyard. Then I pulled downward on the genoa.

It was stuck.

Something was holding that sail in place. I studied the situation as the deck beneath my feet pitched wildly. Then I saw it. The genoa did not completely unfurl from the forestay. There was still some of it, maybe two or three turns, wrapped around the stay. In that condition there was no chance of dropping the sail.

Yet the wind was picking up. It was clear there would be Santa Ana–type winds, which could build to fifty knots or more as the night wore on. That sail was *huge*. The engine was barely making headway because the force of the wind against the sails. I could not lower the main until the genoa was down, because then the boat would be unbalanced and out of control. If the wind got any stronger, it would be out of control anyway.

I tried to understand why the furling drum would not

turn anymore. I had seen this before, mostly on Kevin's boat because his genny needed a lot of furling line. The line was tangled up in the drum, "overwrapped" was the word. When that happens, you could still turn the drum the other way. If you had a furling line. Which I did not.

I could turn the drum *by hand.*

That was the only way out. Go out on the bowsprit, right now, and furl the genoa by turning the drum by hand. Just grab it and turn the damn thing.

The bowsprit was lost in darkness. It plunged up and down with each passing swell. Go out on the bowsprit on a pitching boat? Was that better or worse than letting the boat go out of control in a fifty knot wind?

I was tempted to make a deal with the Lord: my complete faith for the rest of my life (or some other offering) in exchange for safe passage. But I made no such deal. God would just have to wait for some other opportunity to claim me, because tonight, I would go out there and fix the sail by myself.

I don't think God looks upon "deals" favorably. I mean, if it were possible for the person to do whatever it is they promise to do, if it had been within their power, and if they knew it was the right thing to do, why not just do it? And how could anybody convince themselves that a promise to carry out a common-sense action would induce God to intervene with the physical universe?

In the theological sense, I believe there is a Supreme Intelligence who really can and does intervene—but rarely and through quantum probability, to avoid violating conservation of energy. God can but does not violate the laws of physics. Humanity must be confident that those laws will *always* hold.

In short, God does not horse trade. I was on my own.

Before me lay a clear choice between the bowsprit and a high likelihood of an out-of-control boat. The bowsprit struck me as the better choice. Yes, absolutely, it scared me. Petrified me. I could think of lots of things that could go wrong. The sprit was jerking around violently and I could be pitched over the top and off the boat. Harness and tether? Sure, but so what? That meant I would still be attached to the boat by an inch-wide nylon strap. That did not mean I could haul myself back on board while being thrown against the hull, not a fatty like me.

It was a matter of just doing it. Acting as if there was no fear. Behaving, at least on the outside, fearlessly.

I had one advantage: I had witness fearlessness once. I knew there wasn't much difference between fearlessness and stupidity. But even if they were one in the same, I had once witnessed fearlessness with my own eyes. The question for tonight was, Do I remember it vividly enough to use it as an example and duplicate the effect?

My father was in the Marines, and they say the Marines are fearless.

I didn't like my father, and he didn't like me. He was a tenth-grade dropout. He was lazy, had no respect for education, and never achieved anything in life besides odd jobs such as bouncer and general gopher at the local strip joint. He couldn't understand why I preferred books to sports, and wanted none of it.

When I was fifteen and my brother thirteen, we shared an efficiency apartment with Dad in a bad neighborhood in New Jersey. Mom had disappeared with her boyfriend a couple of years earlier. Paul and I were walking home one night and it must have been winter, because it was dark.

We were robbed at knifepoint by two older teens, losing what small amounts of cash we had. We were both petrified by the bare blades they waved in front of our faces.

"I will cut you," one of the muggers said.

We made the mistake of telling Dad. How do you think he reacted? Rage? No. I knew his anger, and he wasn't angry. He just listened to the story and told us to get in the car.

"But Dad, where are we going?"

"Shut up and get in the car."

He was calm, determined, and had a distant look in his eye. He knew what he was going to do. Why be emotional about it?

We drove around looking for the muggers. They had knives? So what? Our father had no weapon, not even a tire iron. We drove around for twenty minutes, looking silently. Dad wanted to find them *bad*. Paul and I exchanged glances. What would happen if we did find them?

We turned down another street and there they were, standing outside a liquor store laughing and joking.

"That them? You sure? You sure?"

Dad parked the car not ten feet from where they were standing.

He stepped out and we saw his legs scissor across the sidewalk as he made a beeline toward the muggers.

They saw him coming, and in one second *they knew*.

I will never forget the looks on their faces. I believe I have never seen any person more shocked and panicked that those two teenagers. And I have never seen anyone run faster. They were off in a flash, arms pumping furiously with the kind of unconstrained terror of a man being chased by a hungry tiger.

Dad sprinted after them. They knew their time had come. They could deal with a vengeful man. They could deal with a raging man—after all, they had switchblades. But they could not deal with a fearless man.

I saw one of them pull the crumpled dollar bills they had stolen from us out of his pocket and drop them on the sidewalk. The other did the same.

My old man. Fearless? Or just stupid? He was probably lucky he couldn't catch them.

You don't see much of this nowadays. People are smarter. They would contact the police. They would avoid going out at night. They would move to a safer neighborhood. They would do the intelligent things. Acting fearlessly, stupidly, usually got you sued. Or killed.

Tonight might be the one time in my life when I had a chance to act fearlessly. Not *be* fearless, mind you. I was scared shitless because there was no one else around. Whatever happened would happen, and there would be no help, and no witnesses. But my goal, my need, was only to act with *that look,* as if I had no fear. To act as a fearless man. There would probably never be another opportunity.

I went below and put a four-inch stainless bolt in my pocket. There was a hole in the furling drum that I could use to secure it once the genny was furled—all I had to do was put the bolt through the hole and put a nut on it. I put some extra nuts in my pocket in case I dropped one. Then I went forward and out on the sprit.

Calmly.

It was like riding a bucking bronco. I wrapped my right leg around the starboard rail in case a freakishly large pitch tried to throw me right off the boat. I grabbed the drum with both hands and turned. With that big sail it was almost impossible to move, but I completed the first turn. *It was working.* It got easier as more of the sail was on the forestay. I stopped and rested several times, but I couldn't take forever because the effort of holding myself on the sprit was exhausting me.

A few more turns, and the sail was on. Two more turns to wrap the sheets around the sail. Bolt in, nut on. I had to back off now, careful not to get complacent and fall at the last minute.

Done. The genoa was furled.

I would have to do that again if I wanted to use the sail again, and I probably would—but not until daylight. I dropped the main and adjusted the autopilot heading so we were back on course, wind abeam.

By the time *Serenity* was back in shape and motoring with all sail down it was close to eleven o'clock and I was completely spent. There was no chance at staying awake for long. Between the fatigue I already felt from missing sleep last night and the exertion tonight and the hypnotic effects of the engine vibration, I was a goner.

But you know what? I felt I had earned a little karma. I mean, after the furling line breaking, what else could happen in one night? I looked over the sea. The water was rough and the wind strong and there were no lights anywhere—not a vessel in sight. With the karmic goodwill I had earned tonight, I deserved the reward of a serious slumber. I turned up the volume on the CARD and went below.

*   *   *

I awoke some time later and felt a little reckless over having slept for a few hours. I stood on the companionway ladder and hooked my tether to the jackline. Looking straight aft, I could see several fairly bright white lights, but I didn't know if they were stars or the lights of ships on the horizon. Topside, the wind was still howling and I could *feel* the sea but not see it—it was that dark. I scanned the horizon. The air smelled marvelous, incredibly clean and fresh, almost intoxicating.

I was almost ready to go back below when I noticed a star off my port bow. This was a peculiar star because it was moving *back and forth*.

I was looking upwards at it at maybe a thirty degree angle. The arc the star made was quickly growing larger. It also seemed to be moving upwards in the sky. It had to be some sort of aircraft. A UFO? A few more seconds and the star's arc got *really* big. Something in the back of my mind told me I was looking at something close.

I dropped my gaze and saw the white hull of a sailboat, less than fifty feet away, barreling through the waves straight at me.

It was going to crash into my port side in about five seconds.

I lunged at the autopilot disconnect lever then spun the wheel to starboard as fast as I could. The other boat slid right past my port quarter, missing by a few feet. It was gorgeous and larger than *Serenity,* with a teak deck and neat coils of rope. The skipper was flying a backed staysail and a heavily reefed main. And I am one hundred percent certain there was no one on deck.

This was someone's idea of heaving to. Okay, fine, but the idiots showed no running lights. The single white light I saw atop the mast was an anchor light, to be used while at anchor. It was the only light they were showing, which was why their hull did not appear until it was right on top of me. If they had turned on their running lights I would have seen them coming from miles away.

Or maybe not. I had been asleep.

I watched the other boat recede off to the horizon, white anchor light arcing merrily back and forth. They were making excellent headway, driven by the winds coming off my port bow. Our relative speed was probably ten knots or more.

Fiberglass does not do well when struck with a strong, sudden force. I believe if we had collided, both yachts would have been lost. Could I have gotten the life raft out of the aft lazarette in time, the painter line cut in time, and then boarded it?

Now I was really beat. I asked myself: what are the odds of something like that happening *again,* on the same night? Millions to one, at least. I didn't have to worry about it.

I went below and fell asleep.

After four days, the accumulated sleep deprivation left me feeling and acting dumb. That was dangerous, but I didn't know what to do about it. When the sun was up I didn't feel like sleeping—I was bone-tired but I could not sleep. I fashioned a sleep mask out of some dark cloth, but I still couldn't rest peacefully during the day. I think I was afraid the mask would be *too* effective and I would be dead to the world for hours.

The upper west coast of Baja, especially the area around Isle de Guadeloupe, is sometimes known as the great white shark capital of the world. On the fifth morning all the sharks for miles around decided to make sure I understood I was treading on their territory. For no apparent reason scores of great whites, large, small and in between, surrounded *Serenity* on all sides and kept up with the boat for hours. Why the sudden interest? Were they trying to tell me something? I checked the bilges for water —no, I wasn't sinking. I stood on the after deck safely tethered to a jackline and watched them circle.

Despite the constant mental fog and schools of sharks, I began to believe I would make it. My fuel was low and there was a good chance I would have to stop at Bahia Tortugas and see Hector in a couple of days, but I would make it. I had left the United States just a few weeks ago, prepared for and expecting a world cruise. Here I was coming back, never having gone farther than Cabo San Lucas, a voyage of a bit more than two thousand miles.

Wasn't that a bad thing? A wasteful thing? A shameful thing?

Did I come out here just to watch the man-eating wildlife?

I thought back to my original need to become something more than a software instructor. How much voyaging did I think it would take to reach that point? If I couldn't define exactly what it was I expected to become, how could I hope to answer that question? And if I couldn't define the scope of the voyage it would require to metamorphose me into a butterfly or whatever, how did I know it did not happen or that it could not happen?

I didn't become a transient, and that was a genuinely worthy thing. I could support myself and I had a useful and productive job. I wasn't a drunk on a dilapidated vessel without the ability to earn enough money to properly maintain it. I had made some friends.

Was it enough? I did not yet know.

I fell into a daily routine of using the genny during the daylight and hand-furling it well before dark. I would have loved to switch it with the yankee, but the fouled drum would not let me completely unwrap the last couple of feel from the forestay. The wind was steady from the northwest and that meant the foot of the genny had to come way, way back aft—I had it cranked back to within three feet of the main starboard winch. This put a lot of heel on the boat but I could avoid using my engine.

Since I couldn't sleep during the day, I thought about exactly what I would do once I got back to San Diego. I wanted to put *Serenity* up for sale, but I didn't know if a broker would want to list and actively sell her. There was no true market for sailboats. Unlike houses and cars, no one really needed to buy a boat. They were purchases of emotion and passion, and no one could predict whether a particular boat would sell. Brokers did not like to spend time on yachts priced much less than six figures—the commission was too low. Yet because I wasn't going to live in San Diego, I needed someone who would actively sell the boat for me—and that was a lot to ask.

Boats deteriorated rapidly at the dock. And dock fees for a slip that would hold *Serenity* went for about $1,300 a month in San Diego.

Whatever. I would worry about it later.

On the fourth night out, the fatigue had accumulated to the point I could dream while wide awake, but only at night. I had a few conversations with my deceased grandparents, which is not as scary as it sounds because I was fully aware it was a dream while it was going on.

In order to stay safe at night and avoid long periods of slumber, I tried to catnap on my knees while resting my upper torso on the cabin top. After fifteen minutes, the pain in my knees would wake me up and I would stand and scan the horizon.

The sun came up and my thoughts became worldly. In order to do this cruising thing, I told myself, I would need multiple streams of income that could continue while I was at sea. Part of the pressure had been knowing I had no income, yet I was spending money every day on equipment I did not anticipate having to purchase, a lot of it mandated by Joyce. It did not take a lot of imagination to visualize the day I would be broke and need to sell the boat, or take any menial labor job in order to survive, as many cruisers have been known to do. I owned no real estate to fall back on.

Or would that make a difference? Suppose I suddenly came into a million dollars and I could cruise without money worries. Would it make sense to spend it getting seasick, wet, lonely and scared? Couldn't I be a girlfriendless geek on dry land, where at least I'd have some new Internet porn every once in a while and a real pizza any time the urge struck?

Damn it, I'd earned some closure on this thing, hadn't I? Where was it? What had I become? I was almost two thirds of the way back to San Diego and my time to figure things out was running low. The voyage was essentially over. Maybe there was nothing to figure out, and that was the answer to my inquiry: I hadn't become anything I hadn't been before.

What a surprise.

I looked over my left shoulder and witnessed two gray whales swimming side by side in flawless synchronization. They were no more than seventy feet away, close enough to see the individual barnacles growing on their skin. They dove together, two great tail fins arcing above the water, then slipping elegantly below with hardly a splash or a sound. Two minutes later they surfaced, and we made eye contact—we saw each other, the three of us, I know we did. After accompanying me for about a mile, both creatures turned directly toward *Serenity* and made another deep dive. They were going under the boat. I fingered the latch to the lazarette containing the life raft just in case, but the whales didn't strike or graze my hull. They passed well under and went back to whatever they had been doing before I invaded their turf.

The fifth day brought *Serenity* just south of Isla de Cedros. By that point I was more at peace with the world and my decision to come back. I was a confirmed consumer at heart, and I prized my creature comforts. I treasured an unbroken flow of printed and electronic information. I wouldn't take those things for granted again, and I wouldn't forget how it was to be without them.

Apotheosis

I kicked the useless impellers aside and tried to *think*.

All I needed was seawater flowing through the diesel engine's heat exchanger. It was that simple. A heavy flow of seawater would cool the freshwater, which would cool the engine. I could get my power back and avoid being wrecked. But if I was to solve this, it had to be solved *now*.

I held the seawater pump inlet hose in my hands. It was standard inch-and-a-half hosing. What could I use to force seawater through it? Hand pumping was out, as I would need this to work for hours. The solution had to be able to function without human intervention for at least the three or four days' journey to San Diego.

How about the main bilge pump?

I needed to deal with the pump *discharge*. Because it was a standard hull penetration line, it was the same inside diameter as the engine seawater pump inlet. Only problem was, the bilge pump was in the bilge and the discharge hose ran up the side of the engine room to an outlet about three feet above the waterline. It would take a while to disconnect it . . .

But I didn't have to disconnect it, did I? I opened a toolbox and took out a hacksaw. This was an emergency, the vessel was in jeopardy, and actions had to be taken. In an instant, I had sawed through the rubber hose. I now had a free discharge line, but no effective bilge pump if I needed it.

I looked out the port. I had only a few more minutes before *Serenity* struck solid rock.

I connected the end of the bilge discharge to the intake of the engine seawater pump, pulled out the damaged impeller and replaced the cover. I now needed to supply water to my bilge pump. I needed to flood my bilge so the pump had something to send to the engine.

An unsettling moment passed in which I didn't think there was any way to do that other than chop a hole in the hull. What about the diesel seawater line, the one coming off the hull valve and leading to the strainer? I took a screwdriver and loosened the two clamps holding it in place and pulled the hose off. Seawater sprayed everywhere. I grabbed a plastic bucket and used it to control the spray and sent it to the bilge. I would take a moment for the automatic bilge pump to sense the water and turn on, sending water through the heat exchanger.

I couldn't wait. I went topside and stood behind the wheel. The rocks were now less than two hundred feet away, less than a football field. Seagulls were going crazy overhead. I stuck my head into the companionway hatch: *I could hear the bilge pump running.*

This was it. I had to trust that the pump was sending water through the heat exchanger. I mean, where else could it go? And what other choice did I have? I started the engine, waited ten seconds, put the clutch in forward, and throttled up to about seventy percent. The boat responded and moved forward, gradually picking up speed. The rocks receded, and *Serenity* headed out to open sea. The high temperature alarm remained silent.

The boat on autopilot, I went below and checked on the bilge. The pump, a high capacity model, was keeping up with the water flooding from the open seacock, but just barely. I found out later that the bilge pump had a rubber impeller not too different from the ones used in diesel seawater pumps, so the heat exchanger didn't know the difference.

I gathered up the six wrong impellers that cost me over two hundred dollars. When I got to San Diego, should I drive back out to Escondido and throw them in the face of the idiot who sold them to me? A few years ago, I once bought a new suit from The Men's Wearhouse, and after the adjustments were finished, I picked it up. I brought it with me on a cruise ship because most dinners aboard would require a suit and tie. Imagine my surprise and anger when I took the suit out of the plastic covering and found there were no pants. The clerk had simply left them in the back room. And I did not have another pair of long pants with me.

The following week, I returned to the store in a rage and demanded my money back. I thought it would feel good to throw the mistake in their faces, but it didn't feel good. The manager simply asked me, "If it was so important to you, why didn't you check before you left?

And he was right. And I felt like an idiot. They took the suit back, but there was no feeling of justice in it.

Here again, if it was so important, why didn't I check?

The following day I had less than thirty gallons of fuel remaining and more than three hundred miles to go. No question, I would stop at Bahia Tortugas.

I entered the bay at about three o'clock in the afternoon. The Bahia was a different place without a hundred and sixty yachts at anchor. Today there were six or seven. People waved politely as I motored past and took position to drop hook.

Setting anchor single-handed was not difficult. All I had to do was position the boat, put the engine in neutral, drop the anchor and make sure the chain was playing out freely, then motor straight back a hundred feet or so before cutting the engine and letting my momentum dig it in. Once the engine was silent I sat back and enjoyed the sweet silence and pristine scenery.

It did not take long before Hector came out with his fuel *panga*. This was the same *hombre* we had met and bought fuel from on the way down: a hard and dangerous-looking dude with scorpion and death's head tattoos up and down his muscular arms, chest and back. He pulled alongside, tied up, and we shook hands and negotiated a price. As he began filling through the deck plate, I went below and got us a couple of beers.

We sat ten feet apart and for a couple of minutes we listened to the churning of the fuel pump. Hector scrutinized the boat. Did he recognize *Serenity* from the trip up? Maybe he remembered the three women on board. After all, they had talked to him more than I did. Maybe he was wondering why they were not on deck *now*? What the hell had I done with them? Maybe he was a bit afraid of looking below.

Hector turned his gaze toward my rig, my lines, my winches and other sailing hardware. His eyes swept along the deck and then back to me, a man who probably struck him as small and soft in appearance.

"Just you on this boat, man?"

"*Sí.*"

Hector looked up and down the length of the deck again. Up and down the mast, again. Then he looked directly at me.

"You *mucho macho.*"

He said it like he meant it.

"*Sí.*" I nodded. "*Mucho macho.*"

He nodded back.

As I watched the fuel *panga* motor back to the village, one thought went through my mind over and over: that had to be the first time anyone had said *anything* like that to me—without intending to mock me. I mean, this was *me,* short little Glenn, the skinny kid, the fat adult, the stereotypically last person to be picked for any kind of team that required physical power, physical coordination, mastery of self and physical environment—exhibiting *manliness.*

I realized that Hector regarded me, with my boat, as being entirely different than I formerly saw myself. He looked at me and saw a man—maybe even a fearless man.

Being Is Becoming

The wind became less reliable as I headed closer to California waters. Two days from landfall, I was able to get on a beam reach for a few hours and used just the staysail because I was tired of turning that furling drum by hand, and playing Russian roulette with my fingers.

It grew cooler, too, as it was December. I exchanged T-shirts and shorts for sweats. An hour before sunset, I put on my last pair of clean, dry sweatpants and then dropped the main for the last time. Out of nowhere a freak wave smashed against the side of the boat and sent a huge tongue of seawater flying through the air, catching me right in the back. I was soaked from head to foot.

That night I scanned the horizon after midnight and saw a distinct orange glow on the northern horizon. At first I thought it was the dawn. No, too early and in the wrong direction. Moonrise? No. A huge forest fire ashore?

It was Southern California. I could now see, albeit indirectly, the United States.

Home.

My last day at sea, there was little wind but huge, almost flat-sided swells rolling in from due west. A monstrous storm far away, no doubt. The swells hit me broadside non-stop for over twelve hours. *Serenity* did forty-degree rolls all day long. I wanted to cook some spaghetti, but it was out of the question. It was exhausting work just to hold on, hour after hour, and keep from flying around the cabin.

On the bright side, I didn't feel even slightly sick.

By nightfall I could barely keep my eyes open. I adjusted course carefully by the GPS and calculated that if conditions stayed stable all night, I would be at the San Diego Harbor police dock between seven and eight in the morning. That was the check-in point for US Customs. I made sure my passport was handy and I felt a pleasant tingle of excitement run through my body, the same feeling I used to get in anticipation of a trip to the beach, when I was seven.

It would be a tricky night, because in the coming hours, shipping and boating traffic would increase exponentially. I already noticed a big increase in the number of lights, and on my right side, the lights on Baja itself were much closer together. It was vital to stay awake, because a crash now, hours before arrival home, would— for lack of a better term—really suck. If I were still alive.

By midnight I was surrounded by a lot of fast-moving ships, a lot of them Navy vessels coming in and out of San Diego, plus a number of pleasure craft, merchants, and cruise ships. Everyone had come out to play.

And yet, around two a.m., I fell asleep topside, and I did not wake up until just before dawn.

I looked around me and I could not believe what I saw: I was *there,* at San Diego, there was the skyline to my right and the Navy base further back. I was less than twenty minutes from the police dock, right where I should be, positioned to enter the channel in about ten minutes.

I checked out the GPS and grew more confused by the

minute. What just happened when I was fast asleep required several course corrections. I could see they had been made. But I was certain I had been fast asleep for hours. No question, I did not even remember first light. I was conscious around two, then awoke with a start to this gray, overcast day, with plenty of light to see.

Somehow, someway, the boat had threaded the needle on her own, her skipper snoring away on deck. Or did I pilot half-asleep and forget about it after waking? At the time, *Serenity* acting on her own seemed more realistic.

I brought out the dock lines and three fenders, all unused since the last time we were here, and readied them on deck. Then I took the wheel and guided her down the channel. The police dock was ahead. Tying up would be tricky. When I passed the dock I could see there was a gentle breeze from the south. My strategy then would be to approach from the north, cut the engine early, and let the breeze stop the boat right at the dock. Then grab a line and jump out and tie up.

As I approached, no one was around—it was just seven thirty, and there was plenty of open space to make a U-turn. My first attempt at docking failed. I cut the engine too late and had too much speed as *Serenity* neared the dock. I had no crew to stop the boat with the lines, so like a pilot, I had to do a missed approach procedure and "go around." On the second attempt, I cut out earlier and had little momentum as the hull kissed the dock. Nevertheless, *Serenity* bounced, then got blown back. I leaped off with a line and tied her up. Checked the time: 7:37 a.m.

The first order of business after cutting the engine was to go to one of the phones at the harbor police station and request a customs inspection. That done, I returned to the boat and called Paul on my cell.

"Yeah, bro, still alive after a few close calls I'll tell you all about later . . ."

Customs was prompt. In a few minutes, there were two inspectors with me below asking questions. I had not realized how messy the cabin had become. Thanks to the big rolls yesterday, everything was a total mess, and you couldn't even see the sole. They asked me four or five times if I had been the only person aboard and if I had been the only person aboard when the vessel left Mexico. I resisted the temptation to joke around about deep-sixing a first mate named Joyce. They examined my clear-out papers from Cabo and decided they believed me, and cleared me in.

Technically you couldn't leave your boat at the police dock. Official business only and all that. But it was a quiet morning and I could not put off any longer my urge for a nice, hot breakfast cooked by someone else and served on real dishes. There was a decent hotel right here at the tip of Shelter Island, and I found the restaurant and ordered coffee, fresh orange juice, blueberry pancakes, and a side of bacon. I probably smelled like a giant mass of seaweed, but the waitress would just have to suck it up. I picked up a *USA Today* and *The Wall Street Journal* and almost passed out with joy.

When breakfast came I closed my eyes and gave thanks. I am not a churchgoer, but I felt this was one of those occasions that warranted a silent prayer to express my appreciation for being home, and for a voyage that ended safely for everyone who had embarked aboard *Serenity*.

I began to eat and realized food really does taste better at home.

I had to find someplace to dock while I arranged for a broker to sell the boat. A broker may or may not provide dock space, but even if I found one who did, it would be at my expense.

The San Diego municipal docks were next door and there was already a line for space. The clerk announced there were only three large slips remaining for boats up to forty-five feet, at seventy-five dollars per day, for ten day maximum. I got the last one.

I re-docked *Serenity,* tied up, and began to throw some clothes into my knapsack. I wanted a shower, a real bed, a television, and Wi-Fi. All that and more could be found at the hotel next door. Curious cruisers approached the boat and introduced themselves. What attracted them, I found, was that the boat was obviously set up for voyaging and yet the word was I had just come *up* from Mexico. How could that be, since the fleet was migrating south right now? This was the season to leave the US, not come back.

I recounted my story in a highly condensed and sleep-deprived manner. People listened and nodded. I closed the companionway hatch but I had no lock for it, and I didn't care. I was sick of the boat, the sight of the boat, and the smell of the boat. It would still be here tomorrow.

I booked a room for a week and took a long, hot shower. Wi-Fi connected, I dropped a line to Joyce first to say I had arrived without a scratch in eight days, forty-five minutes, and eight hundred and seven miles by the GPS. I told her I'd had some close calls and that single-handing was rough, but at least I hadn't had to put up with any bullshit from crew.

Then I made up a general e-mail for everyone else. I briefly outlined what happened and why I made this decision to sail single-handedly home. By the time I woke up from my nap, everyone had responded. They were warm responses. Kevin said I was now the saltiest sailor he knew. No one expressed "sorrow" over my "disappointment."

They got it.

It felt like that scene at the end of *Cool Runnings,* when the Jamaican Olympic bobsled team crashed and they finished by carrying their broken bobsled on their shoulders. Everyone watched and understood, and began clapping their hands in unison. They didn't win any medals and they didn't finish their run, but they had *been there,* doing what had not come easily for them and what no one expected them to do.

I was no Olympian or Jamaican bobsledder, but I was certain that I had become something I was not since the moment I first stepped aboard *Serenity*. Plato philosophized over "being" versus "becoming." I believe that being *is* becoming. The process of becoming something you are not is the essence of life and existence and purpose, all rolled together. It's what we were meant to do.

You can have a billion dollars to your name, a wonderful family and terrific friends, but if you are not on the path of becoming, you are not on the path of life.

Epilogue

Rested, I went down to the docks to check on *Serenity*. As I approached I saw the companionway hatch wide open. Someone had entered my boat! I jumped on the deck and stuck my head down the hatch. The entire cabin had been cleaned top to bottom. Every item was neatly folded and stowed. The galley and the woodwork and the cabin sole sparkled.

I never found out who did it. No one around the docks would confess.

I was able to give away or sell a lot of the equipment to cruisers heading south. My thousand-dollar first aid kit would be donated to a Mexican village. I gave away my books. The pricey items such as the single sideband went for about twenty cents on the dollar. There was a family of five at the municipal docks heading to Tahiti in a thirty-two-foot sloop. They gladly bought my new life raft for thirteen hundred dollars. I asked them if they had a hand–bearing compass, and the father, a bearded man of about thirty five with optimistic eyes, told me no, but they probably should. I gave him my old blue Davis Instruments hand–bearing compass and watched him take it aboard his boat and saw his daughter try it out.

It took several days to locate a broker to represent *Serenity* but when I did find one, he was the best I could ever hope to meet. John was a live-aboard himself and found a reasonably priced slip fifty yards from his own. I explained the problem with the diesel cooling water impeller and the jury rig that had taken me the last several hundred miles. He said he would fix it. He did, with his own hands, for no charge.

Serenity sold the following April for $38,000, the exact price, less tax, I had paid myself.

Joyce became a US Coast Guard–licensed commercial captain. Doug purchased his own sailboat, a twenty-six-foot sloop, strictly for sailing on the Gulf.

Bob Porter, my colleague at InfoData, had some sort of problem with my coming back to work without completing a circumnavigation of the globe. When Peter released an e-mail welcoming me back, Bob responded by forwarding my original announcement of the voyage from my last day at work, with his own added anointment for all to see:

"You didn't do what you said you were going to do."

That needed a response, but I was at a loss for words. So I let Theodore Roosevelt do my speaking. I pasted the quote below and sent the reply message to everyone:

"It is not the critic who counts: not the man who points out how the strong man stumbles or where the doer of deeds could have done better. The credit belongs to the man who is actually in the arena, whose face is marred by dust and sweat and blood, who strives valiantly, who errs and comes up short again and again, because there is no effort without error or shortcoming, but who knows the great enthusiasms, the great devotions, who spends himself for a worthy cause; who, at the best, knows, in the end, the triumph of high achievement, and who, at the worst, if he fails, at least he fails while daring greatly, so that his place shall never be with those cold and timid souls who knew neither victory nor defeat."

Bob did not respond.

Today I'm in Marina del Rey, California, surrounded by one of the largest marinas in the world, but I do not own a boat. So far I have resisted. But I am breaking down. On September 22, 2012, I made an appointment with a broker, and let him show me two blue-water cruisers, a thirty-six-foot cutter and a forty-two-foot center cockpit sloop.

Would I commit to another boat and go again, after everything that happened? *Yes.* It doesn't add up in a logical sense, I admit. So why do it? Why even think about it? How can anyone make a case in favor of experience and adventure over safety and comfort? The answer, I think, lies in our true nature and what it means to be a *physical* being, which is the essence of being human. If our physical existence is to have any meaning at all, we should maximize experience every minute we are alive, for I believe we are not humans who occasionally have a brief spiritual experience. We are spiritual beings having a brief human experience.

Acknowledgments

I would like to thank the many friends who helped and encouraged me while writing *Breaking Seas:* Gene Gonzales, Scott Corrao, Bert Peters, Neil DiGiacomo, David Hannon, Nate Hall, John Lira, Michael Brown, Larry Urdahl, Mark Kirsnis, Nolen James, Dan Bohlke, John Stroud, Yvonne Bourgeois, Douglass Roberts, Randy Allen, Michael Moe, Steve Hansen, Joe Bayen, Terry Winters, Jan Brewer, Rob White, Karrie Ross, Barbara Griswold, and my editor Sarah Cypher.